T0116155

PRICE AND PRODUCTIVITY MEASUREMENT

Volume 2 - Seasonality

Volume Editors
W. Erwin Diewert, Bert M. Balk, Dennis Fixler
Kevin J. Fox, Alice O. Nakamura

Cover photo by Vancouver photo-artist Dan Heller.
https://www.danheller.com/

Cover design by Melissa and Denise Lee of www.owlgreetings.ca
http://owlgreetings.com/ViewPhoto.aspx?id=181

TRAFFORD
PUBLISHING

Order this book online at www.trafford.com
or email orders@trafford.com

Most Trafford titles are also available at major online book retailers.

© Copyright 2012 Alice O. Nakamura.
All rights reserved. No part of this publication may be reproduced, stored in a retrieval
system, or transmitted, in any form or by any means, electronic, mechanical, photocopying,
recording, or otherwise, without the written prior permission of the author.

Printed in the United States of America.

ISBN: 978-1-4120-7982-2 (sc)

Trafford rev. 02/05/2012

 www.trafford.com

North America & international
toll-free: 1 888 232 4444 (USA & Canada)
phone: 250 383 6864 ♦ fax: 812 355 4082

PRICE AND PRODUCTIVITY MEASUREMENT: Volume 2 -- Seasonality

W. Erwin Diewert, Bert M. Balk, Dennis Fixler, Kevin J. Fox and Alice O. Nakamura (editors)

Chapter 1

INTRODUCTION TO A VOLUME ON THE TREATMENT OF SEASONALITY IN MEASURES OF INFLATION

Bert M. Balk, W. Erwin Diewert and Alice O. Nakamura[1]

Though the problem was signaled already in the 1920s, seasonal products are largely ignored in the main stream of literature on the measurement of price level change. The usual, implicit or explicit, assumption governing the study of alternative index number formulas is that the periods considered are entire years. The application to subperiods, such as months or quarters, then runs into all the difficulties that come with seasonality. For a recent, concise treatment the reader is referred to Balk (2008; section 4.3).

Especially troublesome is the occurrence of missing data. The usual way out is either some form of imputation or the deletion of all or part of the seasonal products from the scope of an index. In any case, the resulting, monthly or quarterly, time series must be seasonally adjusted, using methods that are the culmination of a vast literature on the topic of the seasonal adjustment of economic time series. This literature in turn is an offshoot of an even larger literature on the general topic of the seasonal adjustment of time series of all sorts. The papers in this volume demonstrate that there is an important literature on how to more directly handle seasonal products in price indexes, without making the untenable assumption that prices can be measured for all products in all seasons.

In **chapter 2**, **W. Erwin Diewert** of the University of British Columbia, **Paul A. Armknecht** of the International Monetary Fund, and **Alice O. Nakamura** of the University of Alberta provide a selective survey of the treatment of seasonal products in economic time series. This paper serves three purposes. It provides an encapsulated overview of the material on seasonal adjustment in the international CPI and PPI Manuals. Secondly, it picks up a topic neglected in the CPI and PPI Manuals: the pervasively used X-11 family methods of seasonal adjustment methods. Third, it examines the current state of consensus on the treatment of seasonal products in official price index making, including briefly reviewing some of the literature on this topic since the publication of the 2004 CPI and PPI Manuals.

In **chapter 3**, **Diewert, William F. Alterman** of the Bureau of Labor Statistics and **Robert C. Feenstra** of the University of California at Davis revisit the fundamental issues of what is wanted from, and what it is feasible to accomplish with, seasonal adjustment methods.

---

[1] Bert Balk is with the Rotterdam School of Management, Erasmus University Rotterdam and Statistics Netherlands, and can be reached at email bbalk@rsm.nl. Erwin Diewert is with the Department of Economics at the University of British Columbia. He can be reached at diewert@econ.ubc.ca. Alice Nakamura is with the University of Alberta School of Business and can be reached at alice.nakamura@ualberta.ca.

Citation for this chapter:
Bert M. Balk, W. Erwin Diewert, and Alice O. Nakamura (2011), "Introduction to a Volume on the Treatment of Seasonality in Measures of Inflation," chapter 1, pp. 1-4 in
W.E. Diewert, B.M. Balk, D. Fixler, K.J. Fox and A.O. Nakamura (eds.),
PRICE AND PRODUCTIVITY MEASUREMENT: Volume 2 -- Seasonality, Trafford Press.

© Alice Nakamura, 2011. Permission to link to, or copy or reprint, these materials is granted without restriction, including for use in commercial textbooks, with due credit to the authors and editors.

In the CPI and PPI Manual treatments of seasonal adjustment, all the alternative methods considered are implemented and compared using the artificial Turvey data set (tabled in chapter 8 of this volume). Comparisons of different methods based on this artificial data are suggestive of the performance attributes of the different methods. Working through the numerical exercises in the CPI and PPI Manuals is helpful as well for readers interested in insuring they fully understand the various methods. However, the trial by fire for any empirical method is replicated application on real data. One such application is provided in **chapter 4**. In this chapter, **Diewert**, together with **Yoel Finkel** of the Israeli Central Bureau of Statistics and **Yevgeny Artsev** who was formerly with the Israeli Central Bureau of Statistics and is now with the Israeli National Roads Company, apply the methods introduced in the CPI and PPI Manuals to Israeli CPI program data. The objectives of this paper are to summarize the methods and findings on the treatment of seasonal products from the PPI and CPI manuals, to describe some of the methods used in the Israeli CPI to overcome seasonal fluctuations (and bias) in a month-to-month index, and to examine some of the conclusions from the manuals by simulating the methods with real Israeli CPI data. In two final appendices, the authors table the data used in this study, so it can be used by others interested in replicating and extending this research.

Andrew Baldwin of Statistics Canada in his **chapter 5** paper focuses on the Farm Product Price Index (FPPI) produced by Statistics Canada. It is a monthly series that measures the changes in prices that farmers receive for the agriculture commodities they produce and sell. Its primary purpose is to serve as a measure of Canadian agricultural commodity price movement and as a means to deflate agricultural commodity prices.

The FPPI is based on a five-year basket that is updated every year. This captures the continual shift in agricultural commodities produced and sold. The annual weight base is derived from the farm cash receipts series. The FPPI is not adjusted for seasonality, but seasonal baskets are used since the marketing of virtually all farm products is seasonal. The index reflects the mix of agriculture commodities sold in each given month. The FPPI allows the comparison, in percentage terms, of prices in any given time period to prices in the base period. The FPPI has a number of features inspired by the Prices Received by Farmers Index produced by the U.S. Department of Agriculture (USDA), including features that Baldwin views as an improvement on the U.S. methodology.

Some demographic groups are known to buy much higher proportions of their purchases at promotional sale prices than others. Unfortunately, scanner data information is not usually linked to the characteristics of the purchasers or their households. However, in **chapter 6 Rósmundur Guðnason** of Statistics Iceland describes another way of collecting expenditure (or quantity) information that does allow the purchases to be linked back to the characteristics of the buyers and their households, in Iceland at least.

In the **chapter 7** paper, **Peter Hein van Mulligen** and **May Hua Oei** of Statistics Netherlands, apply some of the proposed methods to Dutch scanner data. This paper also contains a fascinating account of how Statistics Netherlands is now introducing scanner data from a number of purchase channels in their official CPI program. At present, seasonal products are excluded from these scanner data. However, this paper reports on efforts to change this situation. A valuable additional contribution of this paper is to point out that promotional sales can produce fluctuations in product prices and quantities that raise some of the same problems as seasonal fluctuations. Whereas promotional sales prices have been ignored in traditional official price index practice, large proportions of total purchases for many sorts of products take place at promotional sales prices. Van Mulligen and Oei suggest that some of the same methods considered for dealing with seasonal products such as fruits and vegetables might also be used to incorporate promotional sales activity into official price statistics. A key advantage of scanner data, from this perspective, is that it includes purchase quantity information matched with the collected price information.

      Chapter 8 is an excerpt from a classic 1983 paper by **W. Erwin Diewert**. In particular, this excerpt includes the proposal in the original paper for a radically new way of dealing with seasonality in a CPI or PPI. This approach is studied in a number of papers in this volume. Also it has now been picked up and recommended in the international Consumer Price Index Manual (Hill, 2004) and Producer Price Index Manual (Armknecht). This except from Diewert's 1983 paper is included in this volume for the convenience of readers who do not have access to the Statistics Canada volume where the original paper appeared.

References

Armknecht, P. A. (ed.) (2004), *Producer Price Index Manual: Theory and Practice* (PPI Manual) (International Labour Office, International Monetary Fund, Organisation for Economic Co-operation and Development, Eurostat, United Nations, and The World Bank). Available free online, by chapter, at http://www.imf.org/external/np/sta/tegppi/index.htm.

Balk, B. M. (2008), *Price and Quantity Index Numbers: Models for Measuring Aggregate Change and Difference*, New York: Cambridge University Press.

Baldwin, A. (2011), "The Redesign of the Canadian Farm Product Price Index," chapter 5 in Diewert, W.E., B.M. Balk, D. Fixler, K.J. Fox and A.O. Nakamura (2011), *Price and Productivity Measurement: Volume 2 -- Seasonality*, Trafford Press, 79-104.

Diewert, W.E. (1983), "The Treatment of Seasonality in a Cost of Living Index", in W.E. Diewert and C. Montmarquette (eds.), *Price Level Measurement*, Statistics Canada, 1019-1045. http://www.econ.ubc.ca/diewert/living.pdf.

Diewert, W.E. (2011), "The Treatment of Seasonality in a Cost-Of-Living Index: An Introduction," chapter 8 in Diewert, W.E., B.M. Balk, D. Fixler, K.J. Fox and A.O. Nakamura (2011), *Price and Productivity Measurement: Volume 2 -- Seasonality*, Trafford Press, 121-126; excerpted from Diewert (1983).

Diewert, W.F., W.F. Alterman and R.C. Feenstra (2011), "Time Series Versus Index Number Methods of Seasonal Adjustment," chapter 3 in Diewert, W.E., B.M. Balk, D. Fixler, K.J. Fox and A.O. Nakamura (2011), *Price and Productivity Measurement: Volume 2 -- Seasonality*, Trafford Press, 29-52.

Diewert, W.E., P.A. Armknecht and A.O. Nakamura (2011), "Methods for Dealing With Seasonal Products In Price Indexes," chapter 2 in Diewert, W.E., B.M. Balk, D. Fixler, K.J. Fox and A.O. Nakamura (2011), *Price and Productivity Measurement: Volume 2 -- Seasonality*, Trafford Press, 5-28.

Diewert, W.E., Y. Finkel and Y. Artsev (2011), "Empirical Evidence on the Treatment of Seasonal Products: The Israeli CPI Experience," chapter 4 in Diewert, W.E., B.M. Balk, D. Fixler, K.J. Fox and A.O. Nakamura (2011), *Price and Productivity Measurement: Volume 2 -- Seasonality*, Trafford Press, 53-78.

Guðnason, R. (2011), "The Receipts Approach to the Collection of Household Expenditure Data," chapter 6 in Diewert, W.E., B.M. Balk, D. Fixler, K.J. Fox and A.O. Nakamura (2011), *Price and Productivity Measurement: Volume 2 -- Seasonality*, Trafford Press, 105-110.

Hill, T. P. (ed.) (2004), *Consumer Price Index Manual: Theory and Practice* (CPI Manual) (International Labour Office, International Monetary Fund, Organisation for Economic Co-operation and Development, Eurostat, United Nations, and The World Bank). Available free online, by chapter, at http://www.ilo.org/public/english/bureau/stat/guides/cpi/index.htm.

van Mulligen, P.H. and May Hua Oei (2011), "The Possible Use of Scanner Data in Dealing with Seasonality in the CPI," chapter 7 in Diewert, W.E., B.M. Balk, D. Fixler, K.J. Fox and A.O. Nakamura (2011), *Price and Productivity Measurement: Volume 2 -- Seasonality*, Trafford Press, 121-126.

Chapter 2
DEALING WITH SEASONAL PRODUCTS IN PRICE INDEXES

W. Erwin Diewert, Paul A. Armknecht and Alice O. Nakamura[1]

1.   The Problem of Seasonal Products

Product prices and sales quantities can change from one month to the next because of seasonal circumstances, such as lower production costs for strawberries in-season (usually from domestic sources) versus out-of-season (often imported). Inflationary pressure can also cause changes in prices and sales quantities from one month to the next. Inflationary pressure is what governments and central banks are interested in trying to control. Thus there is interest in how inflationary changes can best be measured, given that prices for many products also have fluctuations due to season-specific circumstances.

Strongly seasonal products are not available at all in the marketplace during certain seasons. Weakly seasonal products are available all year but have fluctuations in prices or quantities that are synchronized with the time of year.[2] For a country like the United States or Canada, seasonal purchases amount to one-fifth to one-third of all consumer purchases. Strongly seasonal products create the biggest problems for price statisticians. Often these products are simply omitted in price index making. In the case of weakly seasonal products, their calendar related fluctuations are widely viewed as noise.

As of now, neither the Consumer Price Index (CPI) nor the Producer Price Index (PPI) is seasonally adjusted by the national statistics agencies of most nations. This reflects, in part, a reluctance to revise these price series, with revisions being inevitable for the seasonally adjusted series produced using methods such as X11 and X12. Nevertheless, there is interest in finding conceptually acceptable and operationally tractable ways of including seasonal products in consumer and producer indexes without introducing a lot of seasonal fluctuation. These are some of the motivations for the treatment of seasonal products in chapter 22 of both the most recent international *CPI Manual* (ILO et al., 2004) and *PPI Manual* (IMF et al., 2004). This chapter is referred to hereafter simply as the *Manual chapter*. To aid readers in going on to read the Manual

---

[1] Diewert is with the Department of Economics of the University of British Columbia in Vancouver Canada and can be reached at diewert@econ.ubc.ca. Armknecht, who was previously with the International Monetary Fund in Washington DC, is now a private consultant and can be reached at paularmknecht@msn.com. Nakamura is with the University of Alberta School of Business and can be reached at alice.nakamura@ualberta.ca.

[2] This classification corresponds to Balk's (1980a, p. 7; 1980b, p. 110; 1980c, p. 68; 1981) narrow and wide sense seasonal products. Diewert (1998, p. 457) used the terms type 1 and type 2 seasonality. The definition of strongly seasonal products should not be confused with Granger's (1978) definition of strongly seasonal times series.

Citation for this chapter:
W. Erwin Diewert, Paul A. Armknecht and Alice O. Nakamura (2011), "Dealing with Seasonal Products in Price Indexes,"
chapter 2, pp. 5-28 in
W.E. Diewert, B.M. Balk, D. Fixler, K.J. Fox and A.O. Nakamura (eds.),
PRICE AND PRODUCTIVITY MEASUREMENT: Volume 2 -- Seasonality, Trafford Press.

© Alice Nakamura, 2011. Permission to link to, or copy or reprint, these materials is granted without restriction, including for use in commercial textbooks, with due credit to the authors and editors.

chapter, the present chapter has the same section headings as in the Manual chapter through section 10, and the Manual chapter equation numbers are shown as well [in square brackets].[3]

In the Manual chapter, the various methods discussed are applied using an artificial data set: the modified Turvey data set which is introduced in section 2. In section 3, year-over-year monthly price indexes are introduced. Strongly seasonal products cause serious problems in conventional month-to-month price indexes. However, these problems are largely resolved by using indexes that compare the prices for the same month in different years.

Year-over-year monthly indexes can be combined to form an annual index. Calendar year annual year-over-year indexes are introduced in section 4, and "rolling year" non-calendar year annual indexes are considered in section 5. Seasonal adjustment factors (SAF) are defined using rolling year indexes, and section 6 presents a rolling year index centered on the current month.

Sections 7-10 explore more conventional month-to-month price index methods that have been proposed for accommodating seasonal products. These methods use different ways of compensating for missing price information for products not available in some months. In section 7, the maximum overlap index is introduced. Approaches for filling in data for the months when products are unavailable are to carry forward the last price that was observed for a product, or to impute the missing price in some other way. The carry forward approach is explored in section 8, and the alternative imputation approach is the subject of section 9. In section 10, yet another method that can be used even with strongly seasonal products is introduced: the Bean and Stine Type C, sometimes also called the Rothwell, index.

In section 11, seasonal adjustment factors (SAF values) that incorporate the year-over-year approach (from section 6) are calculated for the various methods presented in section 7-11. In section 12, we discuss the alternative X-11 and X-12 family approaches for seasonally adjusting times series: approaches that are widely used by official statistics agencies but are only briefly mentioned in the Manual chapter. Section 13 concludes.

2.   A Seasonal Product Data Set

In the Manual chapter, the index number formulas considered are applied using an artificial data set developed by Ralph Turvey and then modified by Erwin Diewert to enhance its value for assessing alternative methods of dealing with seasonal products.[4] The full results are shown in the Manual chapter and the summary results are reported here.

Turvey constructed his original data set for five seasonal products (apples, peaches, grapes, strawberries, and oranges) over four years (1970-1973). Turvey sent this dataset to statistical agencies around the world, asking them to use their normal techniques to construct monthly and annual average price indexes. Turvey (1979, p. 13) summarizes the responses:

> "It will be seen that the monthly indexes display very large differences.... It will also be seen that the indexes vary as to the peak month or year."

---

[3] Readers are referred to the Manual chapter, listed in the references as Diewert and Armknecht (2004).

[4] The modified Turvey data set is tabled in the Manual chapter, and the original Turvey data set is tabled in Turvey's 1979 paper and in Diewert (1983, 2011).

W. Erwin Diewert, Paul A. Armknecht and Alice O. Nakamura

3.   Year-over-Year Monthly Indexes

One way of dealing with seasonal products is to change the focus from short-term month-to-month price indexes to year-over-year comparisons for given months. This approach can accommodate even seasonal products. The formulas for the chained Laspeyres, Paasche and Fisher year-over-year monthly indexes are given in box 1 below.

It has been recognized for over a century that making year-over-year price level comparisons[5] is the simplest method for removing the effects of seasonal fluctuations so that trends in the price level can be measured. For example, Jevons (1863; 1884, p. 3) wrote:

> "In the daily market reports, and other statistical publications, we continually find comparisons between numbers referring to the week, month, or other parts of the year, and those for the corresponding parts of a previous year. The comparison is given in this way in order to avoid any variation due to the time of the year. And it is obvious to everyone that this precaution is necessary. Every branch of industry and commerce must be affected more or less by the revolution of the seasons, and we must allow for what is due to this cause before we can learn what is due to other causes."

The economist Flux (1921, pp. 184-185) also endorsed the idea of making year-over-year comparisons to minimize the effects of seasonal fluctuations:

> "Each month the average price change compared with the corresponding month of the previous year is to be computed...."

More recently, Zarnowitz (1961, p. 266) endorsed the use of year-over-year monthly indexes:

> "There is of course no difficulty in measuring the average price change between the same months of successive years, if a month is our unit 'season,' and if a constant seasonal market basket can be used, for traditional methods of price index construction can be applied in such comparisons."

Suppose that data are available for the prices and quantities for all products available for purchase each month for two or more years. Then year-over-year monthly chained and fixed base Laspeyres (L), Paasche (P) and Fisher (F) price indexes, defined in box 1, can be used for comparing the prices in some given month for two different years.

The Manual chapter provides and compares tabular results for the year-over-year monthly chained and fixed base Laspeyres, Paasche, and Fisher indexes. All of the resulting monthly series show year-to-year trends that are free of the purely seasonal variation in the modified Turvey data. The chained indexes are found to reduce the spread between Paasche and Laspeyres indexes compared with their fixed base counterparts. Since the Laspeyres and Paasche perspectives both have merit, the Manual chapter recommends as the target measure of inflation the chained year-over-year Fisher index, which is the geometric average of the Laspeyres and Paasche indexes.

The year-over-year monthly indexes defined in box 1 use monthly data for years t and t+1. Many countries collect price information monthly. However, the expenditure data needed for deriving the quantity observations are only available for intermittent years when a household

---

[5] In the seasonal price index context, this type of index corresponds to Bean and Stine's (1924, p. 31) Type D index.

7

expenditure survey (HES) has been conducted. In the Manual chapter it is argued that monthly expenditure share vectors can be used instead of the current and comparison year monthly expenditure share vectors in an index formula such as one of those in the box 1. This is how the approximate indexes are defined in box 2. When evaluated using the modified Turvey data, the year-over-year chained approximate indexes track their true chained counterparts closely.[6]

Box 1. Definitions for Year-over-Year Monthly Indexes

For each month $m=1,2,\ldots,12$, let $S(m)$ denote the set of products available for purchase that month in all years $t=1,2,\ldots,T$. Let $p_n^{t,m}$ and $q_n^{t,m}$ denote the price and quantity of product n available in month m of year t, and let $p^{t,m}$ and $q^{t,m}$ denote the corresponding month m and year t price and quantity vectors. The year-over-year monthly chained Laspeyres (L), Paasche (P) and Fisher (F) price indexes going from month m of year t to month m of t+1 can now be defined, respectively, as:[7]

$$(1)[22.4] \qquad P_L = \sum_{n \in S(m)} s_n^{t,m}\left(p_n^{t+1,m}/p_n^{t,m}\right), \qquad\qquad m=1,2,\ldots,12;$$

$$(2)[22.5] \qquad P_P = \left[\sum_{n \in S(m)} s_n^{t+1,m}\left(p_n^{t+1,m}/p_n^{t,m}\right)^{-1}\right]^{-1}, \qquad m=1,2,\ldots,12, \text{ and}$$

$$(3)[22.6] \qquad P_F = \sqrt{P_L P_P} \,,$$

where the monthly expenditure share for product $n \in S(m)$ in month m of year t is defined as:

$$s_n^{t,m} = \frac{p_n^{t,m} q_n^{t,m}}{\sum_{i \in S(m)} p_i^{t,m} q_i^{t,m}} \,.$$

The corresponding fixed base indexes have similar formulas to the chained indexes; the year t observations are simply replaced by the observations for the fixed base year 0.

The approximate year-over-year monthly Laspeyres and Paasche indexes will always satisfy inequalities (7) and (8) of box 2. The first of these inequalities says that the approximate year-over-year monthly Laspeyres index fails the time reversal test with an upward formula bias. The second of these inequalities says that the approximate year-over-year monthly Paasche index fails the time reversal test with a downward formula bias. The approximate Fisher formula is recommended because the upward bias of the Laspeyres index part of the Fisher index will balance out the downward bias of the Paasche index part of the Fisher index.

In general, the approximate year-over-year monthly Fisher index defined by (6) in box 2 will closely approximate the true Fisher index defined by (3) in box 1 when the monthly expenditure shares for the base year 0 are close in value to the corresponding year t and year

---

[6] The approximate Laspeyres index actually equals the original fixed base Laspeyres index.

[7] The numbers in square brackets are the equation numbers in the Diewert and Armknecht (2004) Manual chapter.

$t+1$ values.[8] The approximate Fisher indexes are just as easy to compute as the approximate Laspeyres and Paasche indexes, so it is recommended that statistical agencies make approximate Fisher index values available along with the approximate Laspeyres and Paasche ones.

Box 2. Definitions for Approximate Year-over-Year Monthly Indexes

Suppose that expenditure share data are available for some base year 0. If the base year monthly expenditure share vectors, $s^{0,m}$, is substituted for the current year monthly expenditure share vectors, $s^{t,m}$, in equation (1), and for the year $t+1$ monthly expenditure share vectors, $s^{t+1,m}$, in equation (2), this yields the approximate year-over-year monthly Laspeyres and Paasche indexes:

$$(4)[22.8] \qquad P_{AL} = \sum_{n \in S(m)} s_n^{0,m} \left(p_n^{t+1,m} / p_n^{t,m} \right), \qquad\qquad m=1,2,\ldots,12, \text{ and}$$

$$(5)[22.9] \qquad P_{AP} = \left[\sum_{n \in S(m)} s_n^{0,m} \left(p_n^{t+1,m} / p_n^{t,m} \right)^{-1} \right]^{-1}, \qquad\qquad m=1,2,\ldots,12,$$

where $s_n^{0,m}$ is the base period month m expenditure share for product n. The approximate Fisher year-over-year monthly index is defined by

$$(6)[22.10] \qquad P_{AF} = \sqrt{P_{AL} P_{AP}} \,,$$

where P_{AL} and P_{AP} are defined in (4) and (5), respectively.

The approximate year-over-year monthly Laspeyres and Paasche indexes satisfy the following inequalities:

$$(7)[22.11] \qquad P_{AL}(p^{t,m},p^{t+1,m},s^{0,m}) \times P_{AL}(p^{t+1,m},p^{t,m},s^{0,m}) \geq 1, \qquad m=1,2,\ldots,12, \text{ and}$$

$$(8)[22.12] \qquad P_{AP}(p^{t,m},p^{t+1,m},s^{0,m}) \times P_{AP}(p^{t+1,m},p^{t,m},s^{0,m}) \leq 1, \qquad m=1,2,\ldots,12,$$

with strict inequalities holding if the monthly price vectors $p^{t,m}$ and $p^{t+1,m}$ are not proportional to each other.

4.   Year-over-Year Annual Indexes

For some policy purposes, it is useful to have a summary measure of annual price level change from year to year in addition to, or as an alternative to, the 12 month-specific measures of year-to-year price level change defined in the previous section. Treating each product in each month as a *separate annual product* is the simplest and theoretically most satisfactory method for dealing with seasonal products when annual price and quantity indexes can be used. Annual measures of price level change can then be defined, as in box 3, as (monthly) share weighted averages of the year-over-year monthly chain linked Laspeyres, Paasche and Fisher indexes. Thus once the year-over-year monthly indexes defined in the previous section have been numerically calculated, it is easy to calculate the corresponding annual indexes.

---

[8] If the monthly expenditure shares for the base year, $s_n^{0,m}$, are all equal, then the approximate Fisher index defined by equation (6) reduces to Fisher's (1922, p. 472) formula 101.

Box 3. Definitions for Annual Indexes

The Laspeyres and Paasche annual chain link indexes which compare the prices in every month of year t with the corresponding prices in year t + 1 can be defined as follows:

$$(9)[22.16] \qquad P_L = \sum_{m=1}^{12} \sum_{n \in S(m)} \sigma_m^t s_n^{t,m} \left(p_n^{t+1,m} / p_n^{t,m} \right) \text{ and}$$

$$(10)[22.17] \qquad P_P = \left[\sum_{m=1}^{12} \sum_{n \in S(m)} \sigma_m^{t+1} s_n^{t+1,m} \left(p_n^{t+1,m} / p_n^{t,m} \right)^{-1} \right]^{-1},$$

where the expenditure share for month m in year t is defined as

$$\sigma_n^t = \frac{\sum_{n \in S(m)} p_n^{t,m} q_n^{t,m}}{\sum_{i=1}^{12} \sum_{j \in S(i)} p_j^{t,i} q_j^{t,i}}, \ m = 1,2,\ldots,12, \qquad\qquad t = 0,1,\ldots,T.$$

The annual chain linked Fisher index P_F, which compares the prices in every month of year t with the corresponding prices in year t + 1, is the geometric mean of the Laspeyres and Paasche indexes, P_L and P_P, defined by equations (9) and (10); i.e.,

$$(11)[22.18] \qquad P_F = \sqrt{P_L P_P} .$$

Fixed base counterparts to the formulas defined by equations (9)-(11) can readily be defined: simply replace the data pertaining to period t with the corresponding data pertaining to the base period 0.

The annual chained Laspeyres, Paasche, and Fisher indexes can readily be calculated using the equations (9)-(11) in box 3 for the chain links. For the modified Turvey data, the use of chained indexes is found to substantially narrow the gap between the Paasche and Laspeyres indexes.

When monthly expenditure share data are only available for some base year, approximate annual Laspeyres, Paasche and Fisher indexes can be calculated. The fixed base Laspeyres price index uses only expenditure shares for a base year; consequently, the approximate fixed base Laspeyres index is equal to the true fixed base Laspeyres index. For the modified artificial Turvey data set, the approximate Paasche and approximate Fisher indexes are quite close to the corresponding true annual Paasche and Fisher indexes. Also, the true annual fixed base Fisher is closely tracked by the approximate Fisher index P_{AF} (or the geometric Laspeyres index P_{GL}).[9]

The annual fixed base Fisher index is close to the annual chained approximate Fisher counterpart. This approximate index can be computed using the information usually available to statistical agencies. However, the true annual chained Fisher index is still recommended as the

---

[9] The fixed base geometric Laspeyres annual index, P_{GL}, is the weighted geometric mean counterpart to the fixed base Laspeyres index, which is equal to a base period weighted arithmetic average of the long-term price relative. It can be shown that P_{GL} approximates the approximate fixed base Fisher index P_{AF} to the second order around a point where all of the long-term price relatives are equal to unity.

target index and should be computed when the necessary data are available, and used as a check on the quality of the approximate Fisher index.[10]

5. Rolling Year Annual Indexes

In the previous section, the price and quantity data pertaining to the 12 months of a current calendar year were compared to the 12 months of some base calendar year. However, there is no need to restrict attention to calendar years. Any two periods of 12 consecutive months can be compared, provided that the January data are compared to the January data, the February data are compared to the February data, and so on.[11] Alterman, Diewert, and Feenstra (1999, p. 70) and Diewert, Alterman and Feenstra (2011) define what they refer to as *rolling year indexes*.[12] The specifics of constructing rolling year indexes are spelled out in the Manual chapter for both the chained and fixed base cases. The rolling year index series constructed using the modified Turvey data are found to be free from erratic seasonal fluctuations. These rolling year indexes offer statistical agencies an objective and reproducible method of incorporating seasonal products into price indexes.

For the rolling year indexes, when evaluated using the modified Turvey data, it is found that chaining substantially narrows the gap between the Paasche and Laspeyres indexes. The chained Fisher rolling year index is thus deemed to be a suitable target seasonally adjusted annual index for cases in which seasonal products are in scope for a price index.[13]

When necessary owing to data availability limitations, the current year weights can be approximated by base year weights,[14] yielding the annual approximate chained and fixed base rolling year Laspeyres, Paasche, and Fisher indexes. When evaluated using the modified Turvey data, these approximate rolling year indexes are found to be close to their true rolling year counterparts. In particular, the approximate chained rolling year Fisher index (which can be computed using just base year expenditure share information along with base and current period information on prices) is close to the preferred target index: the rolling year chained Fisher index.

---

[10] The approach to computing annual indexes outlined in this section, which essentially involves taking monthly expenditure share-weighted averages of the 12 year-over-year monthly indexes, is contrasted in the Manual chapter with the approach that takes the unweighted arithmetic mean of the 12 monthly indexes. The key problem with the latter approach is that months where expenditures are below the average (for example, February) are given the same weight in the annual average as months with above average expenditures (e.g., December).

[11] Diewert (1983) suggested this type of comparison and termed the resulting index a *split year* comparison.

[12] Crump (1924, p. 185) and Mendershausen (1937, p. 245), respectively, used these terms in the context of various seasonal adjustment procedures. The term *rolling year* seems to be well established in the business literature in the United Kingdom. In order to theoretically justify the rolling year indexes from the viewpoint of the economic approach to index number theory, some restrictions on preferences are required. The details of these assumptions can be found in Diewert (1996, pp. 32-34; 1999, pp. 56-61).

[13] Diewert (2002) discusses measurement issues involved in choosing an index for inflation targeting purposes.

[14] These weights are $s_n^{t,m}$ and σ_m^t and $s_n^{t+1,m}$ and σ_m^{t+1} for the chain link equations (9)-(11). The corresponding fixed base formulas can be approximated using the corresponding base year weights, $s_n^{0,m}$ and σ_m^0.

6.   Predicting a Rolling Year Index

In a regime where the long-run trend in prices is smooth, changes in the year-over-year inflation rate for this month compared with last month theoretically could give valuable information about the long-run trend in price inflation. This conjecture is demonstrated for the modified Turvey data for the year-over-year monthly fixed base Laspeyres rolling year index. The Laspeyres case is used for showing how indexes of this sort can be used for prediction.

The fixed base rolling year Laspeyres index, P_{LRY}, for month m and current year t is a weighted average of year-over-year price relatives over the 12 months in the current and the base year period. Consider, for example, the December fixed base rolling year Laspeyres index. This index value is a weighted average of year-over-year monthly price relatives for years t and 0 that is centered between June and July of the years being compared. Thus, an approximation of this index value could be obtained by taking the arithmetic average of just the June and July year-over-year monthly indexes for years t and 0.[15] Similarly, this sort of approximation can be made for each month for the rolling year Laspeyres index, P_{LRY} This approximation to the rolling year P_{LRY} index, based on averaging the year-over-year monthly index values for the months at the center for the rolling year for the P_{LRY} index, is denoted by P_{ARY}.

Seasonal adjustment factors, SAF, are defined as the ratios of the P_{LRY} to the P_{ARY} values using the initial 12 months of values for these series. These estimated monthly adjustment factors are assumed to be the same for all subsequent years.[16] Once the seasonal adjustment factors have been defined, the approximate rolling year index, P_{ARY}, can be multiplied by the corresponding seasonal adjustment factor, SAF, to form a seasonally adjusted approximate rolling year index, P_{SAARY}.[17]

With this approach, users could obtain a reasonably accurate forecast of trend inflation. It is not *necessary* to use rolling year indexes in the seasonal adjustment process, but this is recommended as a way of increasing the objectivity and reproducibility of the seasonally adjusted indexes. The method of seasonal adjustment used in this section is crude in that no adjustments have been made for other known factors such as differences for the same month in the numbers of trading days and holiday effects. These refinements would be laborious but straightforward to add.

---

[15] Suppose the middle two months are June and July. Then if an average of the year-over-year monthly indexes for more months such as for May, June, July, and August were taken instead, a better approximation to the annual index could be obtained, and if an average of the year-over-year monthly indexes for April, May, June, July, August, and September were taken, an even better approximation could be obtained, and so on.

[16] If SAF is greater than 1, this means that the two months in the middle of the corresponding rolling year have year-over-year rates of price increase that average out to a number below the overall average of the year-over-year rates of price increase for the entire rolling year. The opposite is true if SAF is less than 1.

[17] The rolling year fixed base Laspeyres index P_{LRY} and the seasonally adjusted approximate rolling year index P_{SAARY} will be identical by construction for the first 12 observations. However, after that, the rolling year index P_{LRY} will differ from the corresponding seasonally adjusted approximate rolling year index.

In the previous sections, the suggested indexes are based on year-over-year monthly indexes and their averages. In sections 7-10, attention is turned to more conventional approaches.

7. Maximum Overlap Month-to-Month Price Indexes

One approach for dealing with strongly seasonal products in a month-to-month price index is the maximum overlap method. The first step for this index is to identify the maximum overlap of products: the products available in each of a pair of months. For this set of products, some index formula such as the Fisher is defined, as in box 4. Thus, the bilateral index number formula is applied only to the subset of products that are present in both months for which prices are being compared.[18] The question now arises: should the comparison and the base months be adjacent (thus leading to a chained index), or should the base month be fixed (leading to a fixed base index)? One reason for preferring chain indexes is that, from one month to the next, new products are introduced and old ones are withdrawn, so fixed base indexes inevitably become unrepresentative over time. Hence the Manual chapter recommends the use of chained indexes that can more closely follow market developments.

The expenditure shares that appear in the maximum overlap month-to-month Laspeyres index, defined by equation (14) in box 4, are given by (12). These are the shares that result from expenditures on seasonal products present in month m of year t *and also* present in the following month. Similarly, the expenditure shares that appear in the maximum overlap month-to-month Paasche index, defined by equation (15) in box 4, are given by (13). These are the shares that result from expenditures on seasonal products that are present in month m + 1 of year t *and* are also present in the following month. The maximum overlap month-to-month Fisher index, defined by equation (16) in box 4, is the geometric mean of the Laspeyres and Paasche indexes.

For the artificial modified Turvey data set, the maximum overlap index suffers from a significant downward bias. Part of the problem seems to involve the seasonal pattern of prices for peaches and strawberries (products 2 and 4 in the modified Turvey data). For the first month of the year when each of these fruits become available, they are relatively high priced; in subsequent months, their prices drop substantially. The effects of the initially high prices (compared with the relatively low prices in the last month of the previous year) are not captured by the maximum overlap month-to-month indexes, so the resulting indexes build up a tremendous downward bias. The downward bias is most pronounced for the Paasche index, which uses the quantities or volumes of the current month. These volumes are relatively large compared to those of the initial month when the products become available, reflecting the effects of falling prices as the quantity available in the market increases.

---

[18] Keynes (1930, p. 95) called this the highest common factor method for making bilateral index number comparisons. This target index drops those strongly seasonal products that are not present in the marketplace during one of the two months being compared. Thus, the index number comparison is not completely comprehensive. Mudgett (1951, p. 46) called the error in an index number comparison that is introduced by the highest common factor method (or maximum overlap method) the homogeneity error.

Box 4. Definitions for Maximum Overlap Month-to-Month Indexes

Let there be N products that are each available in one or more months of some year and let $p_n^{t,m}$ and $q_n^{t,m}$ denote the price and quantity of product n that is in the marketplace in month m of year t. (If the product is unavailable, $p_n^{t,m}$ and $q_n^{t,m}$ are set equal to 0.) Let $p^{t,m} \equiv [p_1^{t,m}, p_2^{t,m}, ..., p_N^{t,m}]$ and $q^{t,m} \equiv [q_1^{t,m}, q_2^{t,m}, ..., q_N^{t,m}]$ be the month m and year t price and quantity vectors, respectively. Let S(t,m) be defined as the set of products present in month m of year t *and the following month*.

The expenditure shares of product n in month m and m+1 of year t, using the set of products that are present in month m of year t and the subsequent month, are defined as follows:

(12)[22.23]
$$s_n^{t,m}(t,m) = \frac{p_n^{t,m} q_n^{t,m}}{\sum_{i \in S(t,m)} p_i^{t,m} q_i^{t,m}}, \qquad m=1,2,...,11;\ n \in S(t,m),$$

$$= 0 \text{ otherwise; and}$$

(13)[22.24]
$$s_n^{t,m+1}(t,m) = \frac{p_n^{t,m+1} q_n^{t,m+1}}{\sum_{i \in S(t,m)} p_i^{t,m+1} q_i^{t,m+1}}, \qquad m=1,2,...,11;\ n \in S(t,m),$$

$$= 0 \text{ otherwise,}$$

where $s_n^{t,m+1}(t,m)$ must be distinguished from $s_n^{t,m+1}(t,m+1)$. The expenditure share $s_n^{t,m+1}(t,m)$ is the share of product n in month m+1 of year t with n restricted to the set of products that are present in month m of year t *and* the subsequent month, whereas $s_n^{t,m+1}(t,m+1)$ is the share of product n in month m+1 of year t with n restricted to the set of products that are present in month m+1 of year t *and* the subsequent month.

Using these share definitions, the maximum overlap Laspeyres, Paasche, and Fisher indexes, going from month m of year t to the following month, can be defined as follows:[19]

(14)[22.25]
$$P_L = \sum_{n \in S(t,m)} s_n^{t,m}(t,m)\left(p_n^{t+1,m}/p_n^{t,m}\right), \qquad m=1,2,...,11;$$

(15)[22.26]
$$P_P = \left[\sum_{n \in S(t,m)} s_n^{t,m+1}(t,m)\left(p_n^{t+1,m}/p_n^{t,m}\right)^{-1}\right]^{-1}, \qquad m=1,2,...,11;\ \text{and}$$

(16)[22.27]
$$P_F = \sqrt{P_L P_P},$$

where P_L and P_P are now defined by (14) and (15). Note that P_L, P_P, and P_F depend on the (complete) price and quantity vectors for months m and m + 1 of year t, $p^{t,m}$, $p^{t,m+1}$, $q^{t,m}$, $q^{t,m+1}$, but they also depend on S(t,m), which is the set of products present in both months.

Results are also shown in the Manual chapter using the chained Laspeyres, Paasche, and Fisher indexes with the data for the modified Turvey dataset for just products 1, 3 and 5 (that is, using only the three year-round products). These series are still found to suffer from substantial seasonal variability. For the modified Turvey data, the quantity of grapes (product 3) available in

---

[19] It is important that the expenditure shares that are used in an index number formula add up to unity. The use of unadjusted expenditure shares would lead to a systematic bias in the index number formula. The equations are slightly different for the indexes that go from December to January of the following year. In order to simplify the exposition and convey the main concepts, these equations are left for the reader to work out.

the market varies tremendously over the course of a year, with substantial increases in price for the months when grapes are almost out of season. The price of grapes decreases as the quantity increases during the last half of each year, and then the annual increase in the price of grapes takes place in the first half of the year when the quantities are small. This pattern of seasonal price and quantity changes causes a downward bias.[20] Basically, the monthly varying high volumes are associated with low or declining prices and the low volumes are associated with high or rising prices. These weight effects magnify the seasonal price declines relative to the seasonal price increases using month-to-month index number formulas with monthly varying weights.[21]

All of the month-to-month chained indexes show substantial seasonal fluctuations in prices over the course of a year:[22] probably too much seasonal fluctuation if the purpose of a month-to-month price index is to indicate changes in general inflation.

8. Annual Basket Indexes with Carry Forward of Unavailable Prices

The various indexes introduced that use monthly expenditure share information can be approximated by indexes where the monthly expenditure shares are replaced by annual expenditure shares. When this substitution is made because monthly expenditure or quantity data are unavailable, this approach is similar in spirit to another common statistical agency practice. Official statistics agencies commonly have price data that are collected monthly, but expenditure data that are collected less frequently. Thus, statistical agencies commonly use some sort of a Lowe index: a type of index that allows for different base periods for the prices and the quantity or expenditure weights.[23] An annual basket Lowe index is defined by (17) in box 5. The annual basket Young index, defined in equation (18) in box 5, could also be used. Yet another annual basket monthly index is the geometric Laspeyres defined in equation (19) in box 5. The geometric Laspeyres index makes use of the same information as the Young index, but a geometric average of the price relatives is taken instead of an arithmetic one.

---

[20] Baldwin (1990) used the original Turvey data to illustrate various treatments of seasonal products. He provides a good discussion of what causes various month-to-month indexes to behave badly. "It is a sad fact that for some seasonal product groups, monthly price changes are not meaningful, whatever the choice of formula" (p. 264).

[21] Another problem with month-to-month chained indexes is that purchases and sales of individual products can become irregular as the time period becomes shorter and shorter and the problem of zero purchases and sales becomes more pronounced. Feenstra and Shapiro (2003, p. 125) find an *upward* bias for their chained *weekly* indexes for canned tuna compared to a fixed base index; their bias was caused by variable weight effects due to the timing of advertising expenditures. In general, these drift effects of chained indexes can be reduced by lengthening the unit time period, so that the *trends* in the data become more prominent than the *high-frequency fluctuations*.

[22] Irregular high-frequency fluctuations will tend to be smaller for quarters than for months. For this reason, chained quarterly indexes can be expected to perform better than chained monthly or weekly indexes. Statistical agencies should check that their month-to-month indexes are at least approximately consistent with the corresponding year-over-year indexes.

[23] See Hill (2011) and Balk and Diewert (2011). Often data for per unit prices come from surveys in retail outlets, and on expenditures come from household expenditure surveys. The quantity estimates are then obtained by dividing the expenditure figures by per unit prices.

Box 5. Lowe, Young and Geometric Laspeyres Annual Basket Indexes

The annual basket monthly Lowe (1823) index for month m is defined by:

$$(17)[22.28] \qquad P_{LO} = \frac{\sum_{n=1}^{N} p_n^m q_n}{\sum_{n=1}^{N} p_n^0 q_n},$$

where $p^0 \equiv [p_1^0, p_2^0, \ldots, p_N^0]$ is the price vector for the price reference period, $p^m \equiv [p_1^m, p_2^m, \ldots, p_N^m]$ is the price vector for the current month m, and $q \equiv [q_1, \ldots, q_N]$ is the quantity weight vector for the quantity (or expenditure) reference year. In the context of seasonal price indexes, this type corresponds to Bean and Stine's (1924, p. 31) Type A index.

The annual basket monthly Young (1812) index is also sometimes used:

$$(18)[22.30] \qquad P_Y = \sum_{n=1}^{N} s_n (p_n^m / p_n^0),$$

where $s \equiv [s_1, \ldots, s_N]$ is the reference year vector of expenditure share weights.

The annual basket monthly geometric Laspeyres index is defined as:

$$(19)[22.32] \qquad P_{GL} = \prod_{n=1}^{N} (p_n^m / p_n^0)^{s_n^0}.$$

In the Manual chapter, the above three annual basket indexes are compared with the fixed base Laspeyres rolling year indexes. However, the rolling year index that ends in the current month is centered five and a half months backwards. Hence the annual basket type indexes are compared with an arithmetic average of two rolling year indexes that have their last month 5 and 6 months forward, respectively. This centered rolling year index is labeled P_{CRY}.[24]

The Lowe, Young, and geometric Laspeyres annual basket indexes display considerable seasonality and do not seem to track their rolling year counterparts well.[25]

Andrew Baldwin's (1990, p. 258) comments on annual basket (AB) type indexes such as the three defined above are also relevant for those considering use of these indexes:

"For seasonal goods, the AB index is best considered an index partially adjusted for seasonal variation. It is based on annual quantities, which do not reflect the seasonal fluctuations in the volume of purchases, and on raw monthly prices, which do incorporate seasonal price fluctuations. Zarnowitz (1961, pp. 256–257) calls it an index of 'a hybrid sort.' Being neither of sea nor land, it does not provide an appropriate measure either of monthly or 12 month price change. The question that an AB index answers with respect to price change from January to February say, or January of one year to January of the next, is 'What would the change in consumer prices have been if there were no seasonality in purchases in the months in question, but prices nonetheless retained their own seasonal behaviour?' It is hard to believe that this is a question that anyone would be interested in asking. On the other hand, the 12 month ratio of an AB index based on

---

[24] The series was normalized to equal 1 in December 1970 for comparability with the other month-to-month indexes.

[25] The four series, P_{LO}, P_Y, P_{GL}, and P_{CRY}, are examined graphically in the Manual chapter.

seasonally adjusted prices would be conceptually valid, if one were interested in eliminating seasonal influences."

Annual basket indexes are of interest to us though because they are used by some statistical agencies.

9.   Annual Basket Indexes with Imputation of Unavailable Prices

The poor performance of the annual basket type of indexes considered in section 8 is likely due to the carry forward of prices of strongly seasonal products into months when the products were not available. This could augment the seasonal movements in the indexes. Hence in this section, the properties are examined of the Lowe, Young, and geometric Laspeyres indexes when a different way of imputing the missing prices is used.[26] In this section, prices in months when they are not observed are assumed to have increased at some given rate.[27] The resulting indexes are compared with the centered rolling year index, P_{CRY}, and are found to be a little less variable.[28] Nevertheless, the Lowe, Young, and geometric Laspeyres annual basket indexes that incorporate imputed prices still display tremendous seasonality when evaluated for the modified Turvey data, and they fail to closely track their rolling year counterparts.

10.   The Bean and Stine Type C or Rothwell Index

The Bean and Stine Type C (1924, p. 31), also called the Rothwell (1958, p. 72), index is defined in box 6. This index makes use of monthly baskets for a base year. The index also makes use of a vector of base year unit value prices. The quantity weights for this index change from month to month. Thus the monthly movements in this index are a mixture of price and quantity changes.[29] The conclusion reached in the Manual chapter based on comparisons using the modified Turvey data is that the Rothwell index has smaller seasonal movements than the Lowe index (defined in box 5) and is less volatile in general.[30] However, there still are large seasonal movements in the Rothwell index.

---

[26] Alternative imputation methods are discussed, for example, by Armknecht and Maitland-Smith (1999) and Feenstra and Diewert (2001).

[27] In the applications for the Manual chapter based on the modified Turvey data, a multiplicative rate of 1.008 is used, except for the last year when this rate is escalated by an additional 1.008.

[28] The imputed indexes are preferred to the carry forward indexes on general methodological grounds. In high inflation environments, the carry forward indexes will be subject to sudden jumps when previously unavailable products become available.

[29] Rothwell (1958, p. 72) showed that the month-to-month movements in the index have the form of an expenditure ratio divided by a quantity index.

[30] In the Manual chapter, the Rothwell index, P_R, is compared to the Lowe index with carry forward of missing prices, P_{LO}. To make the two types of series more comparable, the normalized Rothwell index, P_{NR}, is also presented; this index equals the original Rothwell index divided by its first observation.

Box 6. The Bean and Stine Type C, also Known as the Rothwell, Index

For the Bean and Stine Type C or Rothwell index, the seasonal baskets in the base year are denoted as the vectors $q^{0,m}$ for the months m = 1,2,...,12. The index also makes use of a vector of base year unit value prices, $p^0 \equiv [p_1^0,...,p_5^0]$, where the nth price in this vector is defined as:

$$(20)[22.33] \qquad p_n^0 \equiv \frac{\sum_{m=1}^{12} p_n^{0,m} q_n^{0,m}}{\sum_{m=1}^{12} q_n^{0,m}} \, .$$

The Rothwell price index for month m in year t can now be defined as follows:

$$(21)[22.34] \qquad P_R = \frac{\sum_{n=1}^{N} p_n^{t,m} q_n^{0,m}}{\sum_{n=1}^{N} p_n^0 q_n^{0,m}} , \qquad\qquad\qquad m=1,...,12 \, .$$

11.   Adjustment of Seasonal Data

The fact that the maximum overlap method [section 7], the annual basket indexes with carry forward of unavailable prices [section 8], and the annual basket indexes with imputation of unavailable prices [section 9] produce price index series that still display considerable seasonality when seasonal products are included has stimulated interest in adjustment of the data for seasonal products prior to incorporating these products into annual basket indexes such as the Lowe, Young, Geometric Laspeyres or Rothwell. The Manual chapter reports results for two alternative ways of carrying out this pre-adjustment. The first is that the modified Turvey data are seasonally adjusted using SAF terms computed as specified in section 6: an approach based on year-over-year month specific comparisons.[31] Second of all, the X-11 method is used to seasonally adjust the data before it is used to evaluate the alternative indexes. Since little is said in the Manual chapter about the X-11 method, this approach is now taken up in the next section.[32]

In the Manual chapter, the predicted values of the month-to-month indexes with pre-adjustment of the data for the seasonal products are fairly close to the corresponding target index

---

[31] More specifically, for each of the price index series -- the Lowe (LO), Young (Y), Geometric Laspeyres (GL), and Rothwell (ROTH) -- a seasonal adjustment factor (SAF) is defined, as in section 6, as the centered rolling year index P_{CRY} divided, respectively, by P_{LO}, P_Y, P_{GL} or P_{ROTH} to produce the first 12 observations, which are then replicated for the other years. The result is four SAF series: SAF_{LO}, SAF_Y, SAF_{GL}, and SAF_{ROTH}, respectively. Seasonally adjusted Lowe, Young, Geometric Laspeyres and Rothwell indexes are computed by multiplying each unadjusted index by the corresponding SAF vector.

[32] X-11 adjusted numerical results are included in the PPI Manual, but not in the CPI Manual, version of chapter 22. In the CPI Manual, X-11 type seasonal adjustment methods are mentioned only in the next to last footnote. In the PPI Manual, X-11 deflation is briefly mentioned, without specifics, and empirical results are presented for an X-11 type method in three columns added into table 22.27 and in the added figure 22.8b (the only figure not included in both the CPI and the PPI versions of the chapter, always with the same figure numbers).

values. It should also be noted that the seasonally adjusted geometric Laspeyres index is generally the best predictor of the corresponding rolling year index evaluated using the modified Turvey data, with the results for the Lowe index being quite similar and with the results for the seasonally adjusted Rothwell index being furthest away.

12. X-11 and X-12 Type Seasonal Adjustment

As already noted, the Manual chapter reports results that utilize the widely used X-11 approach to adjust the price indexes for seasonal patterns. Here, for completeness, we review the origins and essence of the X-11 approach, and how the X-11 approach relates to the X-12 family of methods.

All members of the X-11 family are conceptually based on univariate time series models. The idea that an observed time series could be usefully decomposed into components none of which can be directly observed -- a trend, cycle, seasonal variations and irregular fluctuations -- reportedly comes from astronomy and meteorology.[33] Trends and long cycles are difficult to distinguish with the sorts of data usually available for the macro economy, and hence are usually treated together and referred to collectively as "trends" in the literature on the seasonal adjustment of economic time series. That is, the four component model is collapsed to a three component model.

Research on seasonal adjustment for economic time series was stimulated during the 1920s and 1930s by the work of Persons (1919). He made simple transformations of the data to remove the trend, and then calculated seasonal estimates and used these in analyzing the original data. Persons called this the link-relative method. The method of Persons (1923) assumes the existence of fixed seasonal factors, though he acknowledged that the idea of strictly fixed seasonality is problematic. Indeed, the recognition that the seasonal factors in economic time series are mostly not rigidly tied to the calendar was one reason why Macauley and others chose instead to employ moving average methods in preference to using deterministic explicit functions of time. Moving averages are a type of filter that successively averages a shifting time span of data so as to produce a smoothed estimate of a time series. A filter removes or reduces the strength of certain cycles in the data.

12.1 X-11 development

Precursors of X-11 were developed in the 1950s. These include the U.S. Census Bureau's Census I and Census II methods. Julius Shiskin was a guiding force and key contributor in this development. With many intervening steps, the Census II method evolved into the X-11

---

[33] Nerlove, Grether, and Carvalho (1979) point out that the idea that an observed time series reflects several unobserved components came originally from astronomy and meteorology and became popular in economics in England during the period of 1825-1875. They discuss the work of the Dutch meteorologist Buys Ballot (1847) concerning the early development of seasonal adjustment methods. See also Yule (1921a) on this history.

method.[34] X-11 gave users the choice between additive and multiplicative adjustments.[35] In addition to moving average type filters, the X-11 package also enabled the operator to conveniently adjust for differing numbers of trading days: a feature that greatly contributed to its popularity.

The adjustment methods that were developed (including X-11) were basically modifications of previously used methods that attempted to incorporate automatically the professional judgment that had been required previously to envision and implement these types of adjustments. In addition to making it more feasible for statistical agencies around the world to produce the large volumes of seasonally adjusted data wanted by the policy community, Bell and Hillmer (1984) note that: "This helped lend an air of objectivity to the seasonal adjustment process, so that seasonal adjusters would not be accused of tampering with the data, a consideration that has become even more important in recent years." Dagum (1983) confirms that the design of the X-11 family was shaped by the objective that the method could be encoded in a packaged program that could be used by a statistical technician anywhere, who might have little specialized knowledge of the real world processes generating the series being seasonally adjusted.[36]

X-11-ARIMA was developed at Statistics Canada in the 1970s and entailed the addition of ARIMA (Auto Regressive Integrated Moving Average) features that augmented the capability for extrapolation of observations at the end points of the actual time series to be seasonally adjusted. This capability was also part of the original X-11 process, but in a more rudimentary, less convenient form.[37] The forecasted values are used in the X-11-ARIAMA adjustment process as though they were actual data. Using the extrapolated data *along with the real data* is what permits the use of filters in the seasonal adjustment process for the production of preliminary series that are more like the filters to be used in producing revisions of the seasonally adjusted series.

Shiskin, Young and Musgrave (1967) derived the original asymmetric weights for the Henderson moving average that are used in the X-11 family of adjustment packages. To obtain the weights, a compromise was struck between the two *assumed* objectives that the trend should be able to represent a wide range of curvatures and that it should be as smooth as possible.

The greater the amount of data that is available on each side of what is treated as the current period for a time series that is to be seasonally adjusted, the better the conformity will usually be between the preliminary seasonally adjusted time series released by the statistical agency and the final adjusted time series. *Symmetric moving average filters* are created making use of data both sides of what is taken to be the "current" period for the time series. Each symmetric filter is tailored by software algorithms to the specific time series being seasonally adjusted. In contrast, *asymmetric* filters are pre-made and generic in nature.

---

[34] This was primarily the work of Eisenpress (1956), Marris (1960) and Young (1965, 1968). See U.S. Bureau of the Census (1967) and also Shiskin (1978).

[35] The differences between the results for the additive and the multiplicative versions are sometimes substantial.

[36] For more background, see also Dagum (1975, 1988/1992). Budget limitations probably have also influenced the choices made. Nakamura and Diewert (1996) report on efforts in Canada to protect the reliability of the CPI while reducing the number of price quotes collected.

[37] This was recommended by Macauley (1931, pp. 95-96). Similar approaches were investigated by Geweke (1978) and by Kenny and Durbin (1982). See also Cleveland, W. P., and Tiao, G. C. (1976).

Research showed that use of X-11-ARIMA can drastically reduce the magnitude of subsequent revisions compared with the original X-11-ARIMA. Reports of this finding persuaded a number of statistical agencies to begin using X-11-ARIMA type methods. What statistical agency would not be happy to have smaller changes to report when issuing revisions to important data series! It is important to note, however, that the greater conformity between the original and revised seasonally corrected data probably primarily reflects the fact that the ARIMA based extrapolation that is part of X-11-ARIMA enables greater conformity *between the methods used to produce the original and the revised series*. This finding does not mean that the resulting series do a better job of tracking some agreed on "true" target index.

12.2 The X-11 family spawns the X-12 family

Events and circumstances that are foreseeable but have somewhat irregular calendar dates or represent seasonal irregularities in the calendar itself (e.g., leap year) were recognized early on as important factors to allow for in explaining the short-term movements of economic time series. Once computers were available, their power was used to implement automated ways of allowing for these sorts of foreseeable irregularities.[38] The Bureau of the Census developed an extension of X-11-ARIMA called X-12-ARIMA that had added tools to enable the estimation and diagnosis of a wide range of special effects.

X-12-ARIMA package features are used to make adjustments for the following sorts of calendar circumstances:

(1) Trading day effects. There are different numbers of working and shopping and stock market trading days from month to month, and often for the same month from year to year, due to factors including leap year and official holidays like Christmas and Easter.

(2) Major holidays and other events on fixed calendar dates that are associated with special buying and pricing patterns: e.g., Christmas.

(3) Major holidays and other events associated in known, but not fixed-date, ways with the calendar and that are associated with special buying behavior. The Chinese New Year is a festival of this sort. Some religious and ethnic groups, and some nations, have more holidays that are seasonal but not tied to specific calendar dates. For example, the moving Jewish festivals have always posed special problems for the Israeli CPI program.[39]

---

[38] See, for example, Joy and Thomas (1927), Homan (1933), Young (1965), and Hillmer, Bell and Tiao (1983). According to King (1924), the first to adjust data with varying seasonal factors were Sydenstricker and Britten of the U.S. Public Health Service, while investigating causes of influenza. Their graphical method is briefly described in Britten and Sydenstricker (1922). King (1924) modified Sydenstricker and Britten's method using moving medians, and emphasized the need to account for changing seasonality. Snow (1923) suggested fitting straight lines to each quarter (or month) separately, and checking for varying seasonality by examining the lines to see if they were parallel. Crum (1925) gave a general discussion of varying seasonality and modified Person's link relative method to handle this complication. Mendershausen (1937) reviews early efforts to deal with changing seasonality.

[39] As Burck and Gubman (2003) note, festival date movements in Israel are typical of festivals with dates fixed according to the lunar year, but vary according to the Georgian calendar. Jewish festivals usually move between two consecutive solar months. The date of the Passover festival moves between March and April. The dates of the Jewish New Year, the Day of Atonement (Yom Kippur) and the Feast of Tabernacles (Succoth) move between

X-12-ARIMA also includes packaged hypothesis testing features and special options for detecting and dealing with outliers.[40] The options that are available in the X-12-ARIMA package for making adjustments to reflect foreseeable monthly differences in the numbers of trading days and the timing of major holidays encouraged statistical agencies like the Israeli one to make the switch, at least partially, from using X-11-ARIMA to X-12-ARIMA.

Box 7. The Steps for an X-11-ARIMA Decomposition

The steps for an X-11-ARIMA decomposition (which are similar to the steps for an X-12-ARIMA one) are:

1. An ARIMA model is used to extend the series being adjusted. Extending the series provides forecast and backcast data that help minimize the use of asymmetric filters at the beginning and end of the series.

The next four steps involve three stages of iteration to produce estimates of the three time series components: trend (including cycle), seasonal and irregular.

2. An initial trend estimate is produced using a centered moving average. The estimated trend is removed from the original series to produce an estimate of the combined seasonal and irregular components. Initial seasonal factors are estimated using an iterative process. Stage 1 estimates of trend and seasonal factors are produced.

3. The stage 1 trend estimates are refined in the third step by using the stage 1 seasonal factors in combination with a Henderson filter.

Henderson (1916) derived moving average filters for use in actuarial applications. The Henderson filters are used with all of the X-11 family methods: X-11, X-11-ARIMA, X-11-ARIMA/88 and X-12-ARIMA. They smooth seasonally adjusted estimates and generate an estimated trend. Henderson filters are used in preference to simpler moving averages because they can reproduce polynomials of up to degree 3, thereby capturing trend turning points. Henderson filters can be either symmetric or asymmetric. *As already noted, symmetric moving averages can only be applied at points that are sufficiently far away from the ends of a time series.*

4. The refined trend is used to create refined seasonal factors following essentially the same process used to produce the stage 1 estimates. Stage 2 final estimates of the seasonal component (i.e., the seasonal factors) are obtained.

5. The third stage uses the stage 2 final seasonal factors combined with a Henderson filter to estimate a stage 3 final trend component. Lastly, using the stage 2 and 3 final seasonal and trend estimates, an estimate of the irregular component is produced.

The step 1 insertion into the data set of ARIMA created observations is what enables the greater use of symmetric Henderson filters in both the third and the fifth steps. Symmetric filters are what are also used in an X-11 type revision process as more real data become available.

13. Concluding Thoughts

A large proportion of products are seasonal. Strongly seasonal products that are not available at all in some months pose the most severe challenges for conventional price index methods. However, weakly seasonal products that are available in all months but have prices and quantities that have seasonal fluctuations can introduce considerable seasonal fluctuation into a consumer or producer price index. The conventional solution to these problems is to omit seasonal products in price index making. However, there are obvious drawbacks to a CPI or PPI

September and October. The Feast of Weeks (Shavuoth) and Independence Day are two other lunar holidays with dates moving between April and May, and between May and June, respectively.

[40] See Findley et al. (1998).

that fails to cover a large share of the products that households consume. These considerations have led to interest in alternative methods for dealing with both strongly and weakly seasonal products in price indexes.

Seasonal and other types of patterned variation can definitely be a source of spurious correlations, and can lead to causally wrong findings.[41] Thus, Granger (1978) argues that, "By using adjusted series, one possible source of spurious relationship is removed." Similarly, Bryan and Cecchetti (1994) argue for the use of trimmed means in the core inflation literature[42] on the grounds that these provide a more robust measure of central tendency than the standard CPI inflation rate, by reducing the influence of transitory price movements that distort the underlying inflationary impulse.

However, others including Bell and Hilmer (1984) and Ghysels (1988, 1990), have raised concerns that seasonal adjustment might lead to mistaken inferences. Orcutt and James (1948), 40 years earlier, noted the nub of concern: the choice of the relevant analogy for use in hypothesis testing:

> "The testing of the significance of a correlation involves a comparison with what would have been obtained between non-related series thought to be analogous to the observed series. And, of course, the significance found for the correlation will depend upon the analogy deemed to be appropriate.... "

Diewert, Alterman and Feenstra (2011) argue that time series methods for the seasonal adjustment of economic price or quantity series are not well suited for helping analysts uncover insights into inflationary developments. Moreover, they argue that, in general, these methods are not suited for producing month-to-month price series that are free of seasonal influences. Diewert, Alterman and Feenstra argue that this criticism of time series seasonal adjustment methods can be better understood by imagining a situation in which each seasonal product in an aggregate is present for only one season of each year. The price for each product would be affected by circumstances in that product market that would not necessarily affect any of the other product markets, and hence the price series for each of the products could have a different evolution over time. Diewert, Alterman and Feenstra argue that, in situations with elements of this nature, no amount of smoothing of the month-to-month price realizations will necessarily be of any use for predicting the future change in the price level going from one month to the next.

However, year-over-year monthly indexes can always be constructed, even for strongly seasonal products. Many users directly need these indexes, and these indexes are also the building blocks as well for annual indexes and for rolling year indexes. Statistical agencies

---

[41] Orcutt (1948) and Cochrane and Orcutt (1949) were early proponents of autoregressive filtering or differencing of the dependent and independent variables prior to testing the significance of regression coefficients in models with autocorrelated errors. On the need and also problems and results for autoregressive filters, see also Orcutt and Winokur (1969), Nakamura and Nakamura (1978), and Nakamura, Nakamura and Orcutt (1976). All tests of significance for apparent relationships among time series are seriously affected when the series themselves, or the error terms for the equations being estimated, contain substantial autoregressive or other non-white noise components. The coefficient estimates of the equation parameters may not be biased, but the estimates of the standard errors will be, thereby seriously distorting the significance test results. See also Durbin (1959, 1960), Jorgenson (1967), and Wallis (1974, 1978).

[42] The best known core inflation indicator is perhaps the CPI with food and energy excluded that Blinder (1982) proposed. See Bloem, Amknecht and Zieschang (2002) on the use of the CPI, PPI and other price indexes for inflation targeting in the conduct of monetary policies.

should compute these indexes. In addition, the Manual chapter argues for the importance of replicability, and year-over-year monthly indexes produce results that can readily be replicated by others given access to the same data.

Thus, we find that insights dating back more than 100 years are still valid today. The statistician Yule (1921b, p. 199) stated:

> "My own inclination would be to form the index number for any month by taking ratios to the corresponding month of the year being used for reference, the year before presumably, as this would avoid any difficulties with seasonal commodities. I should then form the annual average by the geometric mean of the monthly figures."

This approach was also promoted by Mudgett (1955) in the consumer price context and Stone in the producer price context. For example, Stone (1956, pp. 74-75) wrote:

> "The existence of a regular seasonal pattern in prices which more or less repeats itself year after year suggests very strongly that the varieties of a commodity available at different seasons cannot be transformed into one another without cost and that, accordingly, in all cases where seasonal variations in price are significant, the varieties available at different times of the year should be treated, in principle, as separate commodities."

More research needs to be done on the problems associated with the index number treatment of seasonal products. A consensus on what is best practice in this area has not yet formed. However, it appears that 12-month change indexes may offer the best approach for inflation monitoring.

References

Alterman, W.F., W.E. Diewert and R.C. Feenstra (1999), *International Trade Price Indexes and Seasonal Commodities*, Bureau of Labor Statistics, Washington D.C.

Armknecht, P.A. and F. Maitland-Smith (1999), "Price Imputation and Other Techniques for Dealing with Missing Observations, Seasonality and Quality Change in Price Indices," IMF Working Paper No. 99/78, Washington, D.C., June.

Baldwin, A. (1990), "Seasonal Baskets in Consumer Price Indexes," *Journal of Official Statistics* 6 (3), 251-273.

Balk, B.M. (1980a), "Seasonal Products in Agriculture and Horticulture and Methods for Computing Price Indices," *Statistical Studies*, Netherlands Central Bureau of Statistics.

Balk, B.M. (1980b), "Seasonal Commodities and the Construction of Annual and Monthly Price Indexes," *Statistische Hefte* 21, 110-116.

Balk, B.M. (1980c), "A Method for Constructing Price Indices for Seasonal Commodities," *Journal of the Royal Statistical Society Series A* 143, 68-75.

Balk, B.M. (1981), "A Simple Method for Constructing Price Indices for Seasonal Commodities," *Statistische Hefte* 22, 72-78.

Balk, B.M. and W.E. Diewert (2011), "The Lowe Consumer Price Index and Its Substitution Bias," in W.E. Diewert, B.M. Balk, D. Fixler, K.J. Fox, and A.O. Nakamura (eds.), *Price and Productivity Measurement: Volume 6 -- Index Number Theory*, Trafford Press.

Ballot, B.C. H. D. (1847), *Les Changements Criodiques de Tempbrature*, Utrecht: Kemink et Fils.

Bean, L.H. and O.C. Stine (1924), "Four Types of Index Numbers of Farm Prices," *Journal of the American Statistical Association* 19, 30-35.

Bell, W.R. and S.C. Hillmer (1984), "Issues Involved with the Seasonal Adjustment of Economic Time Series," *Journal of Business and Economic Statistics,* 2, 291-320.

Blinder, A. (1982), "Double-Digit Inflation in the 1970s", in R.E. Hall (ed.), *Inflation: Causes and Effects*, University of Chicago Press, 261-282.

Bloem, A. M., P.A. Armknecht and K.D. Zieschang (2002), "Price Indices for Inflation Targeting," International Monetary Fund.

Box, G.E.P. and Jenkins, G.M. (1970): *Time Series Analysis Forecasting and Control*, Holden Day.

Britten, R.H. and E. Sydenstricker (1922), "Mortality from Pulmonary Tuberculosis in Recent Years," Public Health Reports 37, U.S. Public Health Service, 2843-2858.

Bryan, M.F. and S.G. Cecchetti (1994), "Measuring Core Inflation," in N.G. Mankiw (ed), *Monetary Policy*, University of Chicago Press, 195-215.

Burck, L. and Y. Gubman (2003), "Pre-adjustment in X12-ARIMA," working paper of the Israel Central Bureau of Statistics. http://www.fcsm.gov/03papers/Burck.pdf

Cleveland, W. P., and Tiao, G. C. (1976), "Decomposition of Seasonal Time Series: A Model for the X-11 Program," *Journal of the American Statistical Association* 71, 581-587.

Cochrane, D., and G.H. Orcutt (1949), "Application of Least Squares Regression to Relationships Containing Autocorrelated Error Terms," *Journal of the American Statistical Association* 44, 32-61.

Crum, W.L. (1925), "Progressive Variation in Seasonality," *Journal of the American Statistical Association* 20, 48-64.

Crump, N. (1924), "The Interrelation and Distribution of Prices and their Incidence Upon Price Stabilization," *Journal of the Royal Statistical Society* 87, 167-206.

Dagum, E.B. (1975), "Seasonal Factor Forecasts from ARIMA Models," *Proceedings of the 40th Session of the International Statistical Institute*, Warsaw, 206-219.

Dagum, E.B. (1983), "The X-11 ARIMA Seasonal Adjustment Method," Statistics Canada Catalogue No. 12-564E.

Dagum, E.B. (1988, revised 1992), "Annex D: The X11ARIMA Seasonal Adjustment Program," *The X11ARIMA/88 Seasonal Adjustment Method - Foundations and User's Manual*, Statistics Canada.

Diewert, W.E. (1983), "The Treatment of Seasonality in a Cost of Living Index," in W.E. Diewert and C. Montmarquette (eds.), *Price Level Measurement*, Statistics Canada, 1019-1045. http://www.econ.ubc.ca/diewert/living.pdf. An excerpt is reprinted as chapter 8 in Diewert, W.E., Balk, B.M., Fixler, D., Fox, K.J. and Nakamura, A.O. (eds.) (2011), *Price and Productivity Measurement, Volume 2: Seasonality*, Trafford Press.

Diewert, W.E. (1995a), "Axiomatic and Economic Approaches to Elementary Price Indexes," Discussion Paper No. 95-01, Department of Economics, University of British Columbia. http://www.econ.ubc.ca/diewert/dp9501p1.pdf and http://www.econ.ubc.ca/diewert/dp9501p2.pdf.

Diewert, W.E. (1995b), "On the Stochastic Approach to Index Numbers," Discussion Paper No. 95-31. http://www.econ.ubc.ca/diewert/9531.pdf. Forthcoming also in Diewert, W.E., Balk, B.M., Fixler, D., Fox, K.J. and Nakamura, A.O. (eds.) (2011), *Price and Productivity Measurement: Volume 4 -- International Comparisons and Trade*, Trafford Press.

Diewert, W.E. (1996), "Seasonal Commodities, High Inflation and Index Number Theory," Discussion Paper 96-06, Department of Economics, University of British Columbia. http://www.econ.ubc.ca/dp9606.pdf

Diewert, W.E. (1998), "High Inflation, Seasonal Commodities and Annual Index Numbers," *Macroeconomic Dynamics* 2, 456-471. http://www.econ.ubc.ca/diewert/highinfl.pdf

Diewert, W.E. (1999), "Index Number Approaches to Seasonal Adjustment," *Macroeconomic Dynamics* 3, 48-68. http://www.econ.ubc.ca/diewert/seasonal.pdf

Diewert, W.E. (2002), "Harmonized Indexes of Consumer Prices: Their Conceptual Foundations," *Swiss Journal of Economics and Statistics* 138 (4), 547-637. http://www.econ.ubc.ca/diewert/harindex.pdf

Diewert, W.E., W.F. Alterman and R.C. Feenstra (2011), "Time Series versus Index Number Methods of Seasonal Adjustment," chapter 3 in W.E. Diewert, B.M. Balk, D. Fixler, K.J. Fox, and A.O. Nakamura (eds.) (2008), *Price and Productivity Measurement: Volume 2 -- Seasonality*, Trafford Press.

Diewert, W.E. and P.A. Armknecht (2004), "The Treatment of Seasonal Products," chapter 22 in ILO et al. (2004) and in IMF et al. (2004). Available for free download at http://www.imf.org/external/np/sta/tegppi/ch22.pdf

Diewert, W.E., Y. Finkel and Y. Artsev (2011), "Empirical Evidence on the Treatment of Seasonal Products: The Israeli CPI Experience," chapter 4 in W.E. Diewert, B.M. Balk, D. Fixler, K.J. Fox, and A.O. Nakamura (eds.), *Price and Productivity Measurement: Volume 2 -- Seasonality*, Trafford Press.

Durbin, J. (1959), "Efficient Estimation of Parameters in Moving Average Models," Biometrika, 46, 306-316. - (1960a), "Estimation of Parameters in Time Series Regression Models," Journal of the Royal Statistical Society Ser. B, 22, 139-153.

Durbin, J. (1960), "The Fitting of Time-Series Models," *Review of the International Statistical Institute*, 28, 233-243.

Eisenpress, H. (1956), "Regression Techniques Applied to Seasonal Corrections and Adjustments for Calendar Shifts," *Journal of the American Statistical Association* 51, 615-20

Feenstra, R.C. and W.E. Diewert (2001), "Imputation and Price Indexes: Theory and Evidence from the International Price Program," U.S. Bureau of Labor Statistics Working paper 335. http://www.bls.gov/ore/pdf/ec010030.pdf

Feenstra, R.C. and M.D. Shapiro (2003), "High Frequency Substitution and the Measurement of Price Indexes," in R.C. Feenstra and M.D. Shapiro (eds.), *Scanner Data and Price Indexes*, NBER Studies in Income and Wealth, University of Chicago Press, 123–146.

Findley, D.F., B.C. Monsell, W.R. Bell, M.C. Otto and B.-C. Chen (1998), "New Capabilities and Methods of the X-12-ARIMA Seasonal Adjustment Program," *Journal of Business and Economic Statistics* 16, 127-177.

Fisher, I. (1922), *The Making of Index Numbers*, Boston, MA: Houghton-Mifflin.

Fisher, A. (1937), "A Brief Note on Seasonal Variation," *Journal of Accountancy* 64, 174-199.

Flux, A.W. (1921), "The Measurement of Price Change," *Journal of the Royal Statistical Society* 84, 167-199.

Geweke, J. (1978), "Revision of Seasonally Adjusted Time Series," SSRI Report No. 7822, Department of Economics, University of Wisconsin.

Ghysels, E. (1988), "A Study towards a Dynamic Theory of Seasonality for Economic Time Series," *Journal of the American Statistical Association* 83, 168-172

Ghysels, E. (1990), "Unit Root Tests and the Statistical Pitfalls of Seasonal Adjustment: the Case of U.S. Post War Real GNP," *Journal of Business and Economics Statistics* 8, 145-152

Granger, C.W.J. (1978), "Seasonality: Causation, Interpretation, and Implications," in Arnold Zellner (ed.), *Seasonal Analysis of Economic Time Series*, U.S. Bureau of the Census, 33-46.

Hardy, G.H., J.E. Littlewood and G. Pólya (1934), *Inequalities*, Cambridge University Press.

Hill, T.P. (2011), "Lowe Indices," in Diewert, W.E., Balk, B.M., Fixler, D., Fox, K.J. and Nakamura, A.O. (eds.), *Price and Productivity Measurement: Volume 6 -- Index Number Theory*, Trafford Press.

Hillmer, S.C., W.R. Bell, and G.C. Tiao (1983), "Modeling Considerations in the Seasonal Adjustment of Economic Time Series," to appear in the Proceedings of the Conference on Applied Time Series Analysis of Economic Data, A. Zellner (ed.), U.S. Department of Commerce, Bureau of the Census.

Homan, J. (1933), "Adjusting for the Changing Date of Easter in Economic Series," *Journal of the American Statistical Association* 28, 328-332.

Henderson, R. (1916): "Note on Graduation by Adjusted Average", *Transactions of the Actuarial Society of America* 17, 43-48.

International Labour Office (ILO), International Monetary Fund, Organisation for Economic Co-operation and Development, Eurostat, United Nations, and The World Bank (2004), *Consumer Price Index Manual: Theory and Practice*. Available for free download in whole or by chapter at http://www.ilo.org/public/english/bureau/stat/guides/cpi/index.htm

International Monetary Fund (IMF), International Labour Office, Organisation for Economic Co-operation and Development, Eurostat, United Nations, and The World Bank (2004), *Producer Price Index Manual: Theory and Practice* (*PPI Manual*). Chapters and whole can be downloaded for free at http://www.imf.org/external/np/sta/tegppi/index.htm.

Jevons, W.S. (1863), "A Serious Fall in the Price of Gold Ascertained and its Social Effects Set Forth," reprinted in *Investigations in Currency and Finance*, Macmillan, 1884, 13-118.

Jorgenson, D.W. (1967), "Seasonal Adjustment of Data for Econometric Analysis," *Journal of the American Statistical Association* 62, 137-140.

Joy A., and W. Thomas (1927), "Adjustments for the Influence of Easter in Department Stores Sales," *Journal of the American Statistical Association* 22, 493-496.

Kenny, P.B. and J. Durbin (1982), "Local Trend Estimation and Seasonal Adjustment of Economic and Social Time Series," *Journal of the Royal Statistical Society*, Series A, 145, 1-41.

Keynes, J.M. (1930), *A Treatise on Money in Two Volumes*, Macmillan.

King, W.W.I. (1924), "An Improved Method for Measuring the Seasonal Factor," *Journal of the American Statistical Association* 19, 301-313.

Lowe, J. (1823), *The Present State of England in Regard to Agriculture, Trade and Finance, Second Edition*, Longman, Hurst, Rees, Orme and Brown.

Macauley, F.R. (1931), *The Smoothing of Time Series*, National Bureau of Economic Research.

Marris, S.N. (1960), "The Measurement of Calendar Variation," *Seasonal Adjustment in Electronic Computers*, OECD, 345-60

Mendershausen, H. (1937), "Annual Survey of Statistical Technique: Methods of Computing and Eliminating Changing Seasonal Fluctuations," *Econometrica* 5, 234-262.

Mudgett, B.D. (1951), *Index Numbers*, John Wiley and Sons.

Mudgett, B.D. (1955), "The Measurement of Seasonal Movements in Price and Quantity Indexes," *Journal of the American Statistical Association* 50, 93-98.

Nakamura, A.O. and W.E. Diewert (1996), "Can Canada Afford to Spend Less on National Statistics?" *Canadian Business of Economics* 4 (3), 33-34.

Nakamura, A.O. and M. Nakamura (1978), "On the Impact of the Tests for Serial Correlation Upon the Test of Significance for the Regression Coefficient," *Journal of Econometrics* 7, 199-210.

Nakamura, A.O., M. Nakamura and G.H. Orcutt (1976), "Testing for Relationships between Time Series," *Journal of the American Statistical Association, Theory and Methods Section* 71 (March), 214-222.

Nakamura, E. (2005), "Inflation Forecasting using a Neural Network," *Economic Letters* 86(3), pp. 373-378.

Nerlove, M., Grether, D. M., and Carvalho, J. L. (1979), *Analysis of Economic Time Series: A Synthesis*, Academic Press.

Orcutt, G.H., 1948, "A Study of the Autoregressive Nature of the Time Series Used for Tinbergen's Model of the Economic System of the United States, 1919-1932," *Journal of the Royal Statistical Society*, Series B, 1-45.

Orcutt, G.H., and S.F. James (1948), "Testing the Significance of Correlation between Time Series," *Biometrika* 35, 397-413.

Orcutt, G.H. and H.S. Winokur, Jr. (1969), "First Order Autoregression: Inference, Estimation, and Prediction," *Econometrica* 37 (1) Jan., 1-14.

Persons, W.M. (1919), "Indices of Business Conditions," *Review of Economics and Statistics* 1, 5-107.

Persons, W.M. (1923), "'Correlation of Time Series," *Journal of the American Statistical Association* 18, 713-726.

Rothwell, D.P. (1958), "Use of Varying Seasonal Weights in Price Index Construction," *Journal of the American Statistical Association*, Vol. 53, 66-77.

Shiskin, J. (1957), "Electronic Computers and Business Indicators," *Journal of Business* 30 (October).

Shiskin, J. (1978), "Seasonal Adjustment of Sensitive Indicators," in A. Zellner (ed.), *Seasonal Analysis of Economic Time Series*, U.S. Department of Commerce, Bureau of the Census, 97-103.

Shiskin, J., Young, A.H., and Musgrave, J.C. (1967), "The X-11 Variant of the Census Method II Seasonal Adjustment Program," Technical Paper 15, U.S. Bureau of the Census.

Silver, M. (2007), "Core Inflation: Measurement and Statistical Issues in Choosing Among Alternative Measures," IMF Staff Papers.

Slutzky, E. (1937), "The summation of random causes as the source of cyclical processes," *Econometrica* 5, 105-146.

Snow, E.C. (1923), "Trade Forecasting and Prices," *Journal of the Royal Statistical Society* 86, 332-376.

Stone, R. (1956), *Quantity and Price Indexes in the National Accounts*, OECD.

Turvey, R. (1979), "The Treatment of Seasonal Items in Consumer Price Indices," *Bulletin of Labour Statistics*, *Fourth Quarter*, ILO, 13-33.

U.S. Bureau of the Census (1967), *The X-11 Variant of the Census Method II Seasonal Adjustment Program*. Technical Paper No. 15.

Wallis, K.F. (1974), "Seasonal Adjustment and Relations between Variables," *Journal of the American Statistical Association* 69, 18-32.

Young, A. (1812), *An Inquiry into the Progressive Value of Money in England as Marked by the Price of Agricultural Products*, Hatchard.

Young, A.H. (1965), "Estimating Trading-day Variation in Monthly Economic Time Series," Technical Paper No. 12, U.S. Bureau of the Census.

Young, A.H. (1968), "Linear Approximations of the Census and BLS Seasonal Adjustment Methods," *Journal of the American Statistical Association* 63, 445-471.

Yule, G.U. (1921a), "On the Time Correlation Problem, with Especial Reference to the Variable Difference Correlation Method", *Journal of the Royal Statistical Society* 84, 497-526.

Yule, G.U. (1921b), "Discussion of Mr. Flux's Paper," *Journal of the Royal Statistical Society* 84, 199-202.

Zarnowitz, V. (1961), "Index Numbers and the Seasonality of Quantities and Prices," G.J. Stigler (ed.), *The Price Statistics of the Federal Government*, National Bureau of Economic Research, 233-304.

Chapter 3

TIME SERIES VERSUS INDEX NUMBER METHODS FOR SEASONAL ADJUSTMENT

W. Erwin Diewert, William F. Alterman and Robert C. Feenstra[1]

1. Introduction

This chapter argues that time series methods for the seasonal adjustment of economic price or quantity series cannot in general lead to measures of short term month-to-month measures of price or quantity change that are free of seasonal influences. This impossibility result can be seen most clearly if each seasonal commodity in an aggregate is present for only one season of each year. However, time series methods of seasonal adjustment can lead to measures of the underlying trend in an economic series and to forecasts of the underlying trend. In this context, it is important to have a well defined definition of the trend and the chapter suggests that index number techniques based on the moving or rolling year concept can provide a good target measure of the trend. The almost forgotten work of Oskar Anderson (1927) on the difficulties involved in using time series methods to identify the trend and seasonal component in a series is reviewed.

Economists and statisticians have struggled for a long time with the time series approach to seasonal adjustment. In fact, the entire topic is somewhat controversial as the following quotation indicates:

> "We favor modeling series in terms of the original data, accounting for seasonality in the model, rather than using adjusted data. … In the light of these remarks and the previous discussion, it is relevant to ask whether seasonal adjustment can be justified, and if so, how? It is important to remember that the primary consumers of seasonally adjusted data are not necessarily statisticians and economists, who could most likely use the unadjusted data, but people such as government officials, business managers, and journalists, who often have little or no statistical training. … In general, there will be some information loss from seasonal adjustment, even when an adjustment method appropriate for the data being adjusted can be found. The situation will be worse when the seasonal adjustment is based on incorrect assumptions. If people will often be misled by using seasonally adjusted data, then their use cannot be justified."
>
> William R. Bell and Steven C. Hillmer (1984; 291).

---

[1] Diewert is with the Department of Economics at the University of British Columbia, and can be reached at diewert@econ.ubc.ca. Alterman is with the U.S. Bureau of Labor Statistics (BLS), and can be reached at alterman_w@bls.gov. Feenstra is with the Department of Economics at the University of California at Davis, and can be reached at rcfeenstra@ucdavis.edu. The first author is indebted to the Social Sciences and Humanities Research Council of Canada for financial support. This chapter draws heavily on Chapter 5 of Alterman, Diewert and Feenstra (1999).

Citation for this chapter:
W. Erwin Diewert, William F. Alterman and Robert C. Feenstra (2011),
"Time Series versus Index Number Methods of Seasonal Adjustment," chapter 3, pp. 29-52 in
W.E. Diewert, B.M. Balk, D. Fixler, K.J. Fox and A.O. Nakamura,
PRICE AND PRODUCTIVITY MEASUREMENT: Volume 2 -- Seasonality, Trafford Press.

© Alice Nakamura, 2011. Permission to link to, or copy or reprint, these materials is granted without restriction, including for use in commercial textbooks, with due credit to the authors and editors.

If the seasonal component in a price series is removed, then it could be argued that the resulting seasonally adjusted price series could be used as a valid indicator of short term month-to-month price change. [2] However, in this chapter, we will argue that there are some methodological difficulties with traditional time series methods for seasonally adjusting prices, particularly when some seasonal commodities are not present in the marketplace in all seasons. Under these circumstances, seasonally adjusted data can only represent *trends* in the movement of prices rather than an accurate measure of the change in prices going from one season to the next. Before we can adjust a price for seasonal movements, it is first necessary to measure the seasonal component. Thus as the following quotations indicate, it is first necessary to have a proper definition of the seasonal component before it can be eliminated:

> "The problem of measuring—rather than eliminating—seasonal fluctuations has not been discussed. However, the problem of measurement must not be assumed necessarily divorced from that of elimination."
>
> Frederick R. Macaulay (1931; 121).

> "This discussion points out the arbitrariness inherent in seasonal adjustment. Different methods produce different adjustments because they make different assumptions about the components and hence estimate different things. This arbitrariness applies equally to methods (such as X-11) that do not make their assumptions explicit, since they must implicitly make the same sort of assumptions as we have discussed here. ... Unfortunately, there is not enough information in the data to define the components, so these types of arbitrary choices must be made. We have tried to justify our assumptions but do not expect everyone to agree with them. If, however, anyone wants to do seasonal adjustment but does not want to make these assumptions, we urge them to make clear what assumptions they wish to make. Then the appropriateness of the various assumptions can be debated.
>
> This debate would be more productive than the current one regarding the choice of seasonal adjustment procedures, in which no one bothers to specify what is being estimated. Thus if debate can be centered on what it is we want to estimate in doing seasonal adjustment, then there may be no dispute about how to estimate it."
>
> William R. Bell and Steven C. Hillmer (1984; 305).

As the above quotations indicate, it is necessary to specify very precisely what the definition of the seasonal is. The second quotation also indicates that there is no commonly accepted definition for the seasonal. In the subsequent sections of this chapter, we will spell out some of the alternative definitions of the seasonal that have appeared in the literature. Thus in sections 2 and 3 below, we spell out the very simple additive and multiplicative models of the seasonal for calendar years. In section 4, we show that these calendar year models of the seasonal are not helpful in solving the problem of determining measures of month-to-month price change free of seasonal influences. Thus in section 5, we consider moving year or rolling year models of the seasonal that are counterparts to the simple calendar year models of sections 2 and 3. These rolling year models of the seasonal are more helpful in determining month-to-month movements in prices that are free from seasonal movements. However, we argue that these seasonally adjusted measures of monthly price change are movements in an annual trend rather than true short term month-to-month movements.

---

[2] For example, consider the following quotation: "In the second place, if comparisons are required between seasons rather than between years then the estimation of the normal seasonal variation of prices appropriate to the base year forms an integral part of the calculations." Richard Stone (1956; 77).

In section 6, we consider a few of the early time series models of the seasonal. In section 7, we consider more general time series models of the seasonal and present Anderson's (1927) critique of these unobserved components models. The time series models discussed in sections 6 and 7 differ from the earlier sections in that they add random errors, erratic components, irregular components or white noise into the earlier decomposition of a price series into trend and seasonal components. Unfortunately, this addition of error components to the earlier simpler models of the seasonal greatly complicates the study of seasonal adjustment procedures since it is now necessary to consider the tradeoff between fit and smoothness. There are also complications due to the nature of the irregular or random components. In particular, if we are dealing with micro data from a particular establishment, the irregular component of the series provided to the statistical agency can be very large due to the sporadic nature of production, orders or sales. A business economist with the Johns-Manville Corporation made the following comments on the nature of irregular fluctuations in micro data:

> "Irregular fluctuations are of two general types: random and non-random. Random irregulars include all the variation in a series that cannot be otherwise identified as cyclical or seasonal or as a nonrandom irregular. Random irregulars are of short duration and of relatively small amplitude. Usually if a random irregular movement is upward one month, it will be downward the next month. This type of irregular can logically be eliminated by such a smoothing process as a fairly short term rolling average. Non-random irregulars cannot logically be identified as either cyclical of seasonal but are associated with a known cause. They are particularly apt to occur in dealing with company data. An exceptionally large order will be received in one month. A large contract may be awarded in one month but the work on it may take several months to complete. Sales in a particular month may be very large as a result of an intensive campaign or an advance announcement of a forthcoming price increase, and be followed by a month or two of unusually low sales. It takes a much longer rolling average to smooth out irregularities of this sort than random fluctuations. Even after fluctuations are smoothed out, a peak or trough may result which is not truly cyclical, or it may occur at the wrong time. Existing programs for seasonal adjustment do not, I believe, give sufficient attention to eliminating the effects of non-random irregulars."
>
> Harrison W. Cole (1963; 135).

Finally, in section 8, we return to the main question asked in this chapter: can price data that are seasonally adjusted by time series methods provide accurate information on the short term month-to-month movement in prices? Our answer to this question is: basically, no! Seasonally adjusted prices can only provide information on the longer term trend in prices. In view of the general lack of objectivity, reproducibility and comprehensibility of time series methods of seasonal adjustment, we suggest that a better alternative to the use of traditionally seasonally adjusted data to represent trends in prices would be the use of the centered rolling year annual indexes explained in Diewert (1983) (1996) (1999).

2. Calendar Year Seasonal Concepts: Additive Models

In this chapter, we will restrict ourselves to considering the problems involved in seasonally adjusting a single price (and or quantity) series. Let $p_{y,m}$ and $q_{y,m}$ denote the observed price and quantity for a commodity in year y and "month" m where there are M "months" in the year. As usual, it will sometimes be convenient to switch to consecutive periods or seasons t where

(1) $\qquad t = (y-1)M + m$, $\qquad\qquad y = 1,2,\ldots,Y$ and $m = 1,2,\ldots,M$.

Thus when it is convenient, we will sometimes relabel the price for year y and month m, $p_{y,m}$, as p_t where t is defined by (1).

We first consider the problem of defining seasonal factors for the quantity series, $q_{y,m}$.

Our reason for considering the quantity case before the price case is that a natural annual measure of quantity is simply the annual amount produced or the annual amount demanded, $\sum_{m=1}^{M} q_{y,m}$. Then it is natural to compare the quantity pertaining to any month, $q_{y,m}$, with the annual calendar year average quantity, Q_y, , defined as:

(2) $\qquad\qquad Q_y \equiv (1/M)\sum_{m=1}^{M} q_{y,m}$, $\qquad\qquad y = 1,2,\ldots,Y$.

Note that Q_y, is the arithmetic average of the "monthly" quantities $q_{y,m}$ in year y. The *additive seasonal factor* $S_{y,m}$ for month m of year y can now be defined as the difference between the actual quantity for month m of year y, $q_{y,m}$, and the calendar year annual average quantity Q_y, :

(3) $\qquad\qquad S_{y,m} \equiv q_{y,m} - Q_y$, $\qquad\qquad y = 1,2,\ldots,Y$ and $m = 1,2,\ldots,M$.

Using definitions (2) and (3), it can be verified the additive seasonal factors, $S_{y,m}$, sum to zero over the seasons in any given year; i.e., we have the following restrictions on the seasonals:

(4) $\qquad\qquad \sum_{m=1}^{M} S_{y,m} = 0$ $\qquad\qquad$ for $y = 1,2,\ldots,Y$.

Note that the seasonal factors defined by (3) cannot be defined until the end of the calendar year y when information on the quantity for the last season in the year becomes available. The above algebra explains how additive seasonal factors can be defined. The next step is to explain how the seasonal factors may be used in a seasonal adjustment procedure. The basic hypothesis in a seasonal adjustment procedure is that seasonal factors estimated using past data will persist into the future. Thus let $S_{y,m}^{*}$ be an estimator for the month m seasonal factor in year y that is based on past seasonal factors, $S_{y-1,m}, S_{y-2,m}, \ldots$ for month m for years prior to year y. Now rewrite equation (3) as follows:

(5) $\qquad\qquad Q_y = q_{y,m} - S_{y,m}$.

If we now replace the actual seasonal factor $S_{y,m}$ in (5) by the estimated or forecasted seasonal factor $S_{y,m}^{*}$, then the right hand side of (5) becomes a forecast for the average annual quantity for year y; i.e., we have

(6) $\qquad\qquad Q_y^{*} \equiv q_{y,m} - S_{y,m}^{*}$.

Once an estimate for average annual output $Q_{y,m}^*$ or input is known, then annual output or input can be *forecasted* as M times $Q_{y,m}^*$. This illustrates one possible use for a seasonal adjustment procedure.

The above algebra can be repeated for prices in place of quantities. Thus define the *average level of prices* for calendar year y as:

$$(7) \qquad P_y = (1/M)\sum_{m=1}^{M} p_{y,m}, \qquad\qquad y=1,2,\ldots,Y \text{ and } m=1,2,\ldots,M.$$

Define the *additive seasonal price factor* $S_{y,m}$ for month m of year y as the difference between the observed month m, year y price $p_{y,m}$ and the corresponding calendar year y annual average level of prices P_y :[3]

$$(8) \qquad S_{y,m} \equiv p_{y,m} - P_y, \qquad\qquad y=1,2,\ldots,Y \text{ and } m=1,2,\ldots,M.$$

Again, it can be verified using definitions (7) and (8) that the seasonal price factors, $S_{y,m}$ defined by (8), satisfy the restrictions (4), $\sum_{m=1}^{M} S_{y,m} = 0$, for each calendar year y.

As in the quantity case, if we have an estimator $S_{y,m}^*$ for the month m seasonal factor for year y that is based on prior year seasonals of the form defined by (8), then we can forecast the average level of prices in year y, $P_{y,m}^*$, by using the following counterpart to (6):

$$(9) \qquad P_y^* \equiv p_{y,m} - S_{y,m}^*.$$

The only difference between the price and quantity cases is that usually, we are interested in forecasts of *annual total output* (or input) in the quantity case, while in the price case, we are generally interested in the *average annual level of prices*. We will now focus our attention on the price case for the remainder of this chapter. In this case, it is no longer so clear that we will always want to define the average annual level of prices for year y, P_y, by the arithmetic mean, (7); why should we not use a geometric mean or some other form of symmetric mean? Furthermore, why should the seasonal $S_{y,m}$ be additive to the annual average level of prices P_y as in (8)? Perhaps a multiplicative seasonal factors model would lead to more "stable" estimates of the seasonal factors. Thus in the following section, we consider these alternative models for the seasonal.

---

[3] To economise on notation, we have used the same symbol for the seasonal factors in both the price and quantity contexts. However, in the remainder of this chapter, we will concentrate on the price case.

3. Calendar Year Seasonal Concepts: Multiplicative Models

We now define the calendar year y average price level p_y as the geometric mean of the "monthly" prices in that year:[4]

$$(10) \qquad p_y \equiv [\textstyle\prod_{m=1}^{M} p_{y,m}]^{1/M}, \qquad\qquad y = 1,2,\dots,Y.$$

Define the *multiplicative seasonal price factors* $s_{y,m}$ for month m of year y as the ratio of the observed month m, year y price $p_{y,m}$ to the corresponding annual average p_y defined by (10):

$$(11) \qquad s_{y,m} \equiv p_{y,m}/p_y, \qquad\qquad y = 1,2,\dots,Y \text{ and } m = 1,2,\dots,M.$$

Using definitions (10) and (11), it can be verified that the multiplicative seasonal factors satisfy the following restrictions:

$$(12) \qquad [\textstyle\prod_{m=1}^{M} s_{y,m}]^{1/M} = 1, \qquad\qquad y = 1,2,\dots,Y.$$

If we raise both sides of (12) to the power M, then the multiplicative seasonal factors $s_{y,m}$ also satisfy the following equivalent restrictions:

$$(13) \qquad \textstyle\prod_{m-1}^{M} s_{y,m} = 1, \qquad\qquad y = 1,2,\dots,Y.$$

As in the previous section, if the multiplicative seasonal factors defined by (11) are "stable" over years, then an estimator for the year y, month m seasonal factor based on prior year seasonal factors, $s_{y,m}^{*}$, can be obtained and a prediction or forecast for the annual average level of prices in year y can be obtained as follows:

$$(14) \qquad p_y^{*} \equiv p_{y,m}/s_{y,m}^{*}, \qquad\qquad y = 1,2,\dots,Y \text{ and } m = 1,2,\dots,M.$$

The multiplicative model presented in this section made two changes from the additive model considered in the previous section:

- The annual average level of prices was changed from the arithmetic mean of the monthly prices, P_y defined by (7), to the geometric mean p_y defined by (10).

- The additive model of the seasonal defined by (8) was replaced by the multiplicative model (11).

Obviously, we do not have to make both of these changes at the same time. Thus we could combine the arithmetic mean definition for the average level of prices, P_y, with a

---

[4] Obviously, this model breaks down unless *all* prices in the year are positive. We make this assumption whenever we consider multiplicative seasonal models.

multiplicative model for the seasonal factors. In this alternative model, the seasonal factors would be defined as follows:

$$(15) \qquad \sigma_{y,m} \equiv p_{y,m}/p_y, \qquad\qquad y = 1,2,\ldots,Y \text{ and } m = 1,2,\ldots,M.$$

The "mixed" seasonal factors $\sigma_{y,m}$ defined by (15) and (7) satisfy the following restrictions:

$$(16) \qquad (1/M)\sum_{m=1}^{M} \sigma_{y,m} = 1, \qquad\qquad y = 1,2,\ldots,Y.$$

There is another model that would combine the geometric mean of the monthly prices pertaining to a year , p_y defined by (10), as the "right" measure of the average level of prices for a year with the following "additive" model of the seasonal factors:

$$(17) \qquad \alpha_{y,m} \equiv p_{y,m} - p_y, \qquad\qquad y = 1,2,\ldots,Y \text{ and } m = 1,2,\ldots,M.$$

The seasonal factors $\alpha_{y,m}$ defined by (17) and (10) satisfy the following somewhat messy restrictions:

$$(18) \qquad \prod_{m=1}^{M}\{(\alpha_{y,m}/p_y)+1\} = 1, \qquad y = 1,2,\ldots,Y.$$

Which of the above four models of the seasonal is the "right" one? The answer to this question depends on the purpose one has in mind. If the purpose is to *forecast* or *predict* an annual level of prices based on observing a price for one season of the year, then the determination of the "right" seasonal model becomes an empirical matter; i.e., the alternative models would have to be evaluated empirically based on how well they predicted on a case by case basis. Thus with the forecasting purpose in mind, there can be no unambiguously correct model for the seasonal factors. Of course, the actual *model evaluation problem*, if our focus is prediction, is vastly more complicated than we have indicated for at least two reasons:

- The arithmetic and geometric mean definitions for the annual average level of prices could be replaced by more general definitions of an average such as a mean of order r,[5] $[\sum_{m=1}^{M}(1/M)(p_{y,m})^r]^{1/r}$, or by a homogeneous symmetric mean[6] of the prices pertaining to year y, say $\mu(p_{y,1},p_{y,2},\ldots,p_{y,M})$.

- . Once the "right" mean is found, then the most "stable" seasonal factors need not be of the simple additive or multiplicative type that we have considered thus far. Hence if $\mu_y \equiv \mu(p_{y,1},p_{y,2},\ldots,p_{y,M})$ is the "right" annual mean for year y, the most stable seasonals might be defined as the following sequence of factors: $f(p_{y,1},\mu_y), f(p_{y,2},\mu_y),\ldots,f(p_{y,M},\mu_y)$, where f is a suitable function of two variables.

Thus corresponding to different choices for the functions μ and f, there are countless infinities of possible seasonal models that could be evaluated on the basis of their predictive powers for seasonally adjusting a specific series.   However, suppose that our purpose in considering

---

[5] See Hardy, Littlewood and Polyá (1934) for material on means of order r.
[6] See Diewert (1993; 361-364) for material on homogeneous symmetric means.

seasonal adjustment procedures is to determine whether seasonally adjusted price series can provide useful information on the month-to-month movement of prices, free from seasonal influences. In the following section, we show that concepts of the seasonal that are based on calendar year concepts are useless for this purpose.

4.   Calendar Year Seasonal Adjustment and Month-to-month Price Change

Suppose we use the additive calendar year method for defining seasonal factors; i.e., we use (7) and (8) in section 2 above to define the seasonal factors $S_{y,m}$ for month m of year y. Obviously, at the end of year y, we can use the additive seasonal factors $S_{y,m}$ defined by (8) to form the seasonally adjusted data for year y, $p_{y,m}^a$:

$$(19) \qquad p_{y,m}^a \equiv p_{y,m} - S_{y,m}$$

$$= p_{y,m} - [p_{y,m} - P_y] \qquad \text{using definition (8) for } S_{y,m}$$

$$= P_y \qquad y = 1,2,\dots,Y \text{ and } m = 1,2,\dots,M.$$

Similarly, if we use the multiplicative model of the seasonal defined by (10) and (11) in section 3 above, at the end of the year, we can use the multiplicative seasonal factors $s_{y,m}$ defined by (11) to form the seasonally adjusted data for year y:

$$(20) \qquad p_{y,m}^a \equiv p_{y,m} / s_{y,m}$$

$$= p_{y,m} / [p_{y,m} / p_y]$$

$$= p_y \qquad y = 1,2,\dots,Y \text{ and } m = 1,2,\dots,M.$$

Thus for both the additive model and the multiplicative model, if we compare the level of the seasonally adjusted prices in months i and j in the same year y, using (19) or (20), we find that:

$$(21) \qquad p_{y,i}^a / p_{y,j}^a = 1, \qquad\qquad y = 1,2,\dots,Y \text{ and } m = 1,2,\dots,M.$$

Thus seasonally adjusted data based on calendar year models can provide absolutely no information about the month-to-month change in seasonally adjusted prices for months in the same year.

Faced with the above negative result for methods of seasonal adjustment based on calendar years, we turn to noncalendar year methods of seasonal adjustment.

5. Rolling Year Concepts for the Seasonal

The calendar year is an artificial construct that is determined by tradition. Hence instead of comparing the price of a commodity in a given season of a calendar year to an average of the calendar year prices, why not compare this price to an average of the prices in the rolling year centered around the given season?

Thus if the number of seasons M in the year is odd,[7] then the centered rolling average of the prices in the rolling year centered around a given period $t \equiv (y-1)M + m$ is defined as

$$(22) \quad P_t \equiv (1/M)\{[\textstyle\sum_{m-1}^{(M-1)/2} p_{t-m}] + p_t + \sum_{m=1}^{(M-1)/2} p_{t+m}]\}.$$

If M is even,[8] then the centered rolling average of the prices in the "year" surrounding period t is conventionally defined as[9]

$$(23) \quad P_t \equiv (1/M)\{(1/2)p_{t-M/2} + [\textstyle\sum_{m=1}^{(M/2)-1} p_{t-m}] + p_t + [\sum_{m=1}^{(M/2)-1} p_{t+m}] + (1/2)p_{t+M/2}\}.$$

Note that when M is even, the centered rolling average extends over M+1 seasons with the two seasons furthest away from the center period t receiving only one half of the weight that the other prices receive. In words, the P_t defined by (22) or (23) are (arithmetic) average levels of prices for a year centered around the given period t. Given the centered annual average levels of prices defined by (22) or (23), we can now define the corresponding period t additive rolling year seasonal factors S_t:

$$(24) \quad S_t \equiv p_t - P_t.$$

We can also use P_t in order to define the period t multiplicative rolling year seasonal factor s_t:

$$(25) \quad s_t \equiv p_t/P_t.$$

The multiplicative model defined by (22) or (23) and (25) is known as a ratio to moving average model[10] of the seasonal and it dates back to Macaulay[11] at least:

"A few years ago the writer was approached by the statistical department of a government bureau and asked to propose a good but simple method of discovering any seasonal fluctuations which might exist in economic time series of moderate length. He replied that, as he did not know of any simple and yet really ideal method, he would suggest graduating [smoothing] the data roughly by means of a 2 months rolling average

[7] This will be the case for days and semesters.
[8] This will be the case for weeks, months and quarters.
[9] Macaulay (1931; 122) was an early pioneer in the use of this convention.
[10] Joy and Thomas (1928; 241) use this terminology. Joy and Thomas (1928; 242) attributed the method to Dr. Fred R. Macaulay of the National Bureau of Economic Research.
[11] The Federal Reserve Board (1922; 1416) used this method as a building block into its method of seasonal adjustment but the method was attributed to Mr. F. R. Macaulay of the National Bureau of Economic Research. The Board continued to use Macaulay's method as a building block for many years; see Barton (1941; 519-520).

of a 12 months rolling average, taking the deviations of the data from this rolling average (centered), and arriving at seasonal fluctuations from these deviations. Rough as is the method, it has been widely used and favorably noticed year after year. Moreover, though the method is extremely simple, in most cases the results are quite good."

Frederick R. Macaulay (1931; 121-122).

Macaulay's method is known as the *ratio to moving average method*.

Obviously, we could replace the centered arithmetic average of prices defined by (22) (if the number of seasons M is odd) or by (23) (if the number of seasons in the year is even) by corresponding geometric averages (provided that all prices are positive)[12]. This substitution would generate additional models for the seasonal factors. However, note that the new seasonal factors generated by these rolling year models will no longer necessarily satisfy counterparts to our calendar year consistency constraints (4), (13), (16) or (18).

As was done for our calendar year models for the seasonal factors, after half a year has passed, we can generate seasonally adjusted data for each period t. Thus after M/2 seasons have passed (in the case where M is even), the measure of the average level of prices centered around period t, P_t defined by (23), can be calculated and using the additive seasonal model (24), the seasonally adjusted level of price p_t^a for period t can be defined as:

$$(26) \qquad p_t^a \equiv p_t - S_t$$
$$= p_t - [p_t - P_t] \qquad \text{using (24)}$$
$$= P_t.$$

In the case of the rolling year multiplicative seasonal model (25), the seasonally adjusted level of price p_t^a can be defined as:

$$(27) \qquad p_t^a \equiv p_t / s_t$$
$$= p_t / [p_t / P_t] \qquad \text{using definition (25)}$$
$$= P_t.$$

For both the additive and multiplicative models of the seasonal, it now makes sense to compare the seasonally adjusted level of prices in period t to the seasonally adjusted level of prices in period r, even if both periods are in the same year. Thus using (26) or (27), we have:

$$(28) \qquad p_t^a / p_r^a = P_t / P_r \qquad \text{for all periods t and r.}$$

However, using (28), the structure of the comparison of the seasonally adjusted prices for period t relative to period r, p_t^a / p_r^a, becomes clear: we are comparing two measures of the average

---

[12] Suppose there are missing prices in our data set. If we set these missing prices equal to zero, then the centered moving (arithmetic) averages of prices can still be defined and the ratio to moving average seasonal factors can still be defined. However, if any price in the rolling year is zero, then the centered moving geometric average of the prices in the rolling year is zero, which is not informative!

annual level of prices centered around the two comparison periods, P_t/P_r . Thus using seasonally adjusted data for making price comparisons between two periods leads to comparisons of two annual measures of average prices centered around the two periods being compared. Note that it is immaterial whether we use the additive or multiplicative model of the seasonal; both models lead to the same seasonally adjusted comparison given by (28). However, note that the form of the centered annual average still matters; if we replace the arithmetic means in (22) or (23) by say geometric means, then we would in general obtain different numbers on the right hand side of (28). Thus the theory of seasonal adjustment based on the rolling year concept (instead of the calendar year concept) is still not completely unambiguous. We still have to decide on what is the most appropriate functional form for the mean function, $\mu(p_{t-(m-1)/2}, \ldots, p_{t-1},$ $p_t, p_{t+1}, \ldots, p_{t+(m+1)/2})$, that aggregates the M prices (if M is odd) that are centered around period t into an annual average.

However, for our purposes, the important lesson that has been learned in this section thus far is that *seasonally adjusted data based on the calendar year or rolling year models that we have considered thus far cannot provide any information whatsoever on the short run movement of prices going from one season to the next*. In the case of rolling year models of seasonal adjustment, the seasonally adjusted number for a given period is actually an estimate of an annual average level of prices centered around the period in question; i.e., it is a measure of longer run trend rather than a true short run period to period measure of price.[13]

In the following section, we ask whether more general time series models of the seasonal can generate valid estimates of the underlying short run period to period movement in prices.

6.   Early Time Series Models for the Seasonal

The rolling year model of the seasonal that was defined by (24) in the previous section can be rewritten as the following additive model of the seasonal:

$$(29) \qquad p_t = P_t + S_t, \qquad\qquad t = 1, 2, \ldots, T$$

where p_t is the observed price in period t, P_t is a seasonal free measure of the price in period t and S_t is the period t additive seasonal factor. Similarly, the rolling year model of the seasonal defined by (25) can be rewritten as the following multiplicative model of the seasonal:

$$(30) \qquad p_t = P_t s_t, \qquad\qquad t = 1, 2, \ldots, T$$

where p_t and P_t are still the actual and seasonally adjusted price for period t and s_t is a multiplicative seasonal factor.[14] Time series models (or statistical models) of the seasonal can be obtained by appending random errors or irregular components to the right hand sides of (29) or

---

[13] However, for inflation targeting purposes, central banks are very much interested in up to date measures of the trend in prices such as a rolling year average of prices.

[14] Note that by taking logarithms, the multiplicative model (30) can essentially be transformed into the additive model (29).

(30). Thus let us append an unobserved additive error term to the right hand side of (29) in order to obtain the following time series model for additive seasonal factors:

$$(31) \qquad p_t = P_t + S_t + E_t, \qquad\qquad t = 1,2,\ldots,T.$$

Obviously, the unobserved components on the right hand side of (31) cannot be estimated without further identifying restrictions. In the remainder of this section, we shall consider a few of the early approaches to identification that have appeared in the literature.

Early approaches to identifying the components on the right hand side of (31) were made by Hart (1922) and Stone (1956; 81). Stone assumed that the trend P_t was linear and the seasonal effects S_t were constant over years; i.e., Stone assumed that the following linear regression model parameterised (31):

$$(32) \qquad p_t = \alpha + \beta[t-1] + \gamma_m + E_t, \qquad t = (y-1)M + m = 1,2,\ldots,T$$

where the trend P_t is defined to be the linear in time function $\alpha + \beta[t-1]$ and the seasonal factor for season m is the fixed parameter γ_m for $m = 1,2,\ldots,M$. The fixed additive seasonal effects γ_m were assumed to satisfy the following linear restriction:

$$(33) \qquad \sum_{m=1}^{M} \gamma_m = 0.$$

In Hart's (1922) approach to the seasonal, he first fitted a linear trend to the p_t observations. He then took the arithmetic means of the deviations from the trend to represent the seasonal factors γ_m. Stone (1956; 81) showed that his formal regression model was equivalent to Hart's two stage procedure.[15]

Another early approach to identifying the unobserved components on the right hand side of (31) is due to Leser (1963; 1034) who added seasonal dummies to the Whittaker (1923) Henderson (1924) penalised least squares method of smoothing.[16] In this method, the trend parameters P_t and the M fixed seasonal parameters γ_m are determined by minimising the following objective function with respect to $P_1, P_2, \ldots, P_T$ and $\gamma_1, \gamma_2, \ldots, \gamma_M$:

$$(34) \qquad \sum_{t=1}^{T}(p_t - P_t - \gamma_m)^2 + \lambda \sum_{t=2}^{T-1}(\Delta^2 P_t)^2,$$

where $t = (y-1)M + m$ as usual and the M seasonal fixed effects γ_m satisfy the linear constraint (33) above. $\Delta^2 P_t$ is the centered second difference of the trend time series P_t; i.e.,

$$(35) \qquad \Delta^2 P_t \equiv [P_{t+1} - P_t] - [P_t - P_{t+1}] = P_{t+1} - 2P_t + P_{t-1}.$$

The positive parameter λ, which appears in the objective function (34), is a *smoothing parameter* which trades off how well the estimated $P_t + \gamma_m$ will fit the actual data p_t (the smaller λ is, the better will be the fit) versus how smooth the trend series P_t will be (the larger

---

[15] Stone (1956; 77) required that the number of observations be a multiple of the number of seasons in the year.

[16] Macaulay (1931; 89-99 and 151-156) devotes an entire chapter and appendix to this method of smoothing but he does not simultaneously estimate the P_t and the γ_m; instead, just the P_t are estimated.

λ is, the closer P_t will be to a linear trend). In the macroeconomic literature, it is conventional to a priori choose λ to equal 1600[17] but it is possible to devise more "objective" ways of choosing λ. The basic idea for trading off fit and smoothness in order to smooth a series can be traced back to the early actuarial literature[18] where it was necessary to "graduate" or smooth mortality tables:

> "Where, however, we have a series of observations at consecutive ages it is necessary to substitute a smooth series for the irregular one representing the ungraduated observations. The substituted series must, from the nature of things, be the result of a compromise between the two factors of smoothness and closeness to the observed facts. It is theoretically possible to assign a basis for the numerical measurement of the irregularity of a series as well as for its departure from the observed facts, and by assigning the proportion in which an increase in the one is to be taken as counterbalancing a decrease in the other, to arrive by a mathematical process at the series which best harmonizes the two factors. On any basis suggested, however, the resulting equations are numerous and unwieldy to such an extent as to render the process practically prohibitive."[19]
>
> Robert Henderson and H. N. Sheppard (1919).

Thus Henderson and Sheppard had a clear conception of the basic idea that smoothing involves a tradeoff between goodness of fit and the "smoothness" of the resulting measure of central tendency, P_t. We will return to this point later.

A problem with both the Stone (1956; 81) and Leser (1963; 1034) methods for estimating the trends P_t is that their methods seasonally adjust the entire data set of $T = YM$ observations on p_t in one step. This has the disadvantage that when another year's data become available, the entire seasonal adjustment procedure has to be done all over again; i.e., in principle, their estimates of the seasonally adjusted data are never "final".[20] Thus these procedures are not very well adapted to the needs of statistical agencies. Macaulay noted this disadvantage of the Whittaker-Henderson method for the determination of the trend:

> "Professor Whittaker stresses the fact that in obtaining the graduation all observations are used. The position of each datum point affects the position of every point on the smooth curve. ... It would be highly undesirable that a change in the position of a datum point should seriously affect the position of distant parts of the smooth curve. For example, one of the great disadvantages of harmonic analysis is that the configuration of the data in one section may seriously affect the shape of the fitted curve in a far distant section."

---

[17] See Hodrick and Prescott (1980; 5) or Kydland and Prescott (1990; 9).

[18] The early actuarial literature is responsible for other modern smoothing techniques as well. De Forest (1873; 290-292) showed how least squares rolling average smoothing functions of varying window length could be derived that were exact for cubic functions. De Forest (1873; 322-324) also showed how the weights for his exact rolling average estimators could be chosen to resemble kernel smoother weights. The concept of a spline curve (a curve made up of polynomial segments which are joined up in a continuously differentiable manner) is due to the actuary Sprague (1891; 277).

[19] Both Whittaker (1923) and Henderson (1924) used the sum of squared residuals as their formal measures of fit; Whittaker used the sum of squares of third differences in place of the second differences $\Delta_2 P_t$ which appear in (34) while Henderson considered using the sum of squares of first, second and third differences as formal measures of smoothness. The general solution to the quadratic Whittaker-Henderson smoothing problem, which involves minimising (34), requires the inversion of a large matrix, which was not technologically possible in 1919 when Henderson and Sheppard wrote their study. However, Henderson (1924) showed how by strategically choosing the smoothness parameter λ and applying the theory of difference equations, one could obtain solutions.

[20] Balk (1981; 77) noted that his method of seasonal adjustment suffered from this practical disadvantage.

Frederick R. Macaulay (1931; 96-97).

Thus Macaulay also noted some of the practical problems associated with using strictly periodic functions such as sines and cosines to represent trends: the resulting "smooth" curves tend to have too many wiggles that show up in the "wrong" places.[21] Finally, Macaulay noted that all smoothing methods have difficulties in approximating the trend near the beginning and the end of the sample period:

> "A Whittaker-Henderson graduation needs no extrapolation; it covers the entire range of the data. This is a distinct element of mathematical elegance and sometimes an important practical consideration. However, graduation of the ends of almost any series is necessarily extremely hypothetical unless facts outside the range covered by the graduation are used in obtaining the graduation. This is as true of the Whittaker-Henderson graduation as of any other type."
>
> Frederick R. Macaulay (1931; 94-95).

In view of the above difficulties with the Stone and Leser methods, we turn to a third class of methods that might be used to identify the components on the right hand side of (31), namely *moving average models*. These models have their origins in the ancient actuarial literature where the process of smoothing a mortality table was known as graduating the data.[22] However, the most comprehensive study of moving average models in the context of seasonal adjustment is the monograph written by Macaulay (1931) and we now turn to his work.[23] Macaulay noted the following problem with representing the trend of an economic time series by a simple centered rolling average of the type defined by (22) or (23) in section 5 above:

> "It has, however, serious drawbacks. The resulting curve is seldom very smooth and it will not give a perfect fit to data except in ranges which can be adequately described by a straight line. For example, a simple moving average, if applied to data whose underlying trend is of a second-degree parabolic type, falls always within instead of on the parabola. If applied to data whose underlying trend is of a sinusoidal type, it falls too low at maximum points and too high at minimum points."
>
> Frederick R. Macaulay (1931; 23).

Thus a simple, equally weighted moving average, when applied to a quadratic curve, will not exactly reproduce it; it will reproduce exactly only linear trends. Macaulay identified another potential problem with the use of an annual centered moving average to represent the trend:

> "In general, if a type of smoothing be desired which shall, when applied to monthly data, eliminate seasonal and erratic fluctuations and at the same time give a smooth curve adequately describing the remaining cyclical and trend factors, something much more than a simple 12 months moving average must be used."
>
> Frederick R. Macaulay (1931; 23-24).

Thus Macaulay identified two problems with the use of an annual centered moving average with equal weights to represent the trend:

---

[21] Higher order polynomial approximations to the trend also suffer from this defect. Cole (1963; 135) observed that the Census II program also had a tendency to put too many wiggles in the smoothed data. The Census II seasonal adjustment procedure is described in Shiskin and Eisenpress (1957). The X-11 procedure was a further refinement of Census II; see Shiskin, Young and Musgrave (1967).

[22] One of the earliest moving average models was due to the actuary Woolhouse (1870). This moving average actuarial literature was reviewed by Henderson and Sheppard (1919; 23-42) except that the early work of De Forest (1873) was not discussed. Wolfenden (1925) reviewed the work of De Forest.

[23] Macaulay's work was used as a basic building block for the seasonal adjustment methods that were pioneered by the U.S. Bureau of the Census; e.g., see Shiskin and Eisenpress (1957) and Shiskin, Young and Musgrave (1967).

- If the erratic or random fluctuations E_t in the additive model (31) are very large, then the annual centered moving averages of the form defined by (22) or (23) may also have large fluctuations and hence may not be very smooth.

- The equally weighted centered rolling averages of the type defined by (22) or (23) above are exact only for linear trends; i.e., these simple moving averages will not reproduce nonlinear "smooth" trends.

Let us address the second problem first. It is possible to set up a simple linear regression model of the following type for n consecutive data points:

$$(36) \qquad p_t = \alpha + \beta t + \lambda t^2 + E_t, \qquad\qquad t = 1, 2, \ldots, n.$$

Now assume n is odd and derive a formula for the predicted value for the p_t in the middle of the sample period. If $n = 5$, De Forest (1873; 327) showed that the resulting least squares estimator of the trend for P_3, the middle season in the run of 5 seasons, is:

$$(37) \qquad P_3 = (1/35)[-3p_1 + 12p_2 + 17p_3 + 12p_4 - 3p_5].$$

Obviously, a moving average formula of the type will exactly reproduce both linear and quadratic trends. De Forest (1873; 327) also listed the corresponding least squares moving average formulae that are exact for quadratic trends for $n = 7$ and 9 observations as well while Macaulay (1931; 46) listed the corresponding least squares based moving average formulae for $n = 13$ observations that is exact for linear and quadratic trends. Macaulay (1931; 49) called this method of generating moving average estimators for the trend, the *method of moving parabolas*. Obviously, this idea can be extended to models where the trend is a polynomial of higher order.[24] Recall Macaulay's first objection to the use of an annual centered rolling average as an estimator of the trend; i.e., that this estimator will not be sufficiently smooth if the random component E_t on the right hand side of (31) is large relative to the size of the trend. In theory, this problem can be resolved by increasing the window length n; i.e., by increasing the length of the rolling average that is exact for a least squares polynomial regression model with n observations. This will result in a smoother trend but this improvement in smoothness is achieved at a cost in terms of how closely the estimated $P_t + S_t$ will fit the actual p_t.[25] This is the classic conflict between fit and smoothness that we have already alluded to. As usual, Macaulay had a pretty clear understanding of the problem:

> "Unless the erratic fluctuations of the data are very small as compared with the amplitude of the cyclical movements, a large number of terms will have to be used in the parabolic set of weights or the data will not be adequately 'smoothed'. However, unless the cycles of the original data have very long periods, it will not be possible to use a large number of terms without departing too far from the underlying fundamental curve."
>
> Frederick R. Macaulay (1931; 49-50).

---

[24] See Sheppard (1914; 175) and Whittaker and Robinson (1926; 291-297) for models of this type.

[25] Once the appropriate estimate of the trend P_t has been obtained, the seasonal factors S_t can be estimated by averaging the detrended data $p_t - P_t$ over periods t that correspond to the same season of the year. However, for our purposes the exact method for the determination of the seasonal effects does not matter very much since our focus is on obtaining estimates for the trend P_t.

There is no completely unambiguous "best" way to resolve this conflict between smoothness and fit although various model selection techniques like cross validation have been developed to help solve this problem.[26] It is interesting to note that De Forest also had a pretty clear idea of some of the difficulties involved in estimating an unknown trend function in the face of noisy data:

> "Not only is absolute accuracy unattainable, but we cannot even decide, by the method of least squares, that a certain result is the most probable of any; for the true form of the function being unknown, any particular residual error, or difference between the observed and computed values of a term, will in general be the aggregate of two errors, one of them due to the difference of form between the assumed function and the true one, and the other due to the error of observation or difference between the observed value and the true value."
>
> Erastus L. De Forest (1873; 301).

Macaulay had another very important objection to the use of least squares based moving average estimates for the trend when there is seasonality in the data:

> "A first reason is that such a graduation [smoothing by a centered least squares moving average formula] will entirely eliminate seasonal fluctuations by only the most improbable accident. If, neglecting for the moment erratic fluctuations, the original monthly data be thought of as made up of two parts, (1) a smooth curve and (2) a seasonal fluctuation superposed on the smooth curve, the results of fitting a parabola to the smooth curve and another parabola to the seasonal fluctuations and added together, each month, the pairs of resulting ordinates. Now, if the seasonal fluctuations were constant from year to year, the smooth curve fitted to them should by the definition of seasonal fluctuations, be simply y=0 . In general, a curve fitted to seasonals will give continuous zero values only if its weight diagram is such that equal weights to each nominal month. A simple 12 months moving average gives such equal weights to each nominal month."
>
> Frederick R. Macaulay (1931; 47-48).

What Macaulay seems to be saying is this: suppose that we have an additive model of the form (31) where both the trend terms P_t and error terms E_t are known to be zero. Further suppose that the seasonal terms St are constant in each season; i.e., $S_t = S_{(y-1)M+m} = \gamma_m$ and the γ_m satisfy (33). Now fit a polynomial trend using least squares to the $p_t = S_t$ for some window length n. In general, the resulting estimate of the trend will not be zero as it should be.[27] However, part of the problem is that Macaulay is following in the traditions of the literature of his day when the trend was measured first and then the detrended data were used in order to estimate seasonal factors. Macaulay's observation shows that that this two stage procedure runs into identification problems: some of the seasonal will generally be imputed to the trend! The same problem can occur even if the trend and seasonal parameters are estimated simultaneously in a single stage procedure. In more general models of the seasonal where the seasonal factors are allowed to change over time, it becomes impossible to disentangle the effects of changing seasonal factors from the trend.[28] For additional material on the early history of seasonal

---

[26] See for example Craven and Wahba (1979) and Akaike (1980).

[27] Macaulay seemed to think that the method would work provided only that we fit a linear trend but this is not always the case. Think of a trimester model where we have data for 3 periods and the seasonal is −1 in period 1, 0 in period 2 and +1 in period 3. If we fit a linear trend using only n=3 observations, the linear trend will completely absorb the seasonal and hence the correct seasonal for trimesters 1 and 3 will not be recovered. The problem diminishes as n increases but it never completely disappears.

[28] Wisniewski (1934; 180) emphasised this point.

adjustment methods plus a comprehensive review of more recent methods for seasonal adjustment, see Bell and Hilmer (1984; 293-299).

The discussion in this section should alert the reader to the fact that seasonal adjustment is not as simple as it appears at first glance. Several problems have been encountered:

- In the face of noisy data, it is impossible to know what the true functional form for the "smooth" part of the price series is.[29]

- Once the "noise" term E_t has been introduced to the right hand side of the basic equation $p_t = P_t + S_t + E_t$, we encounter the problem of trading off fit against "smoothness" and there is no unique answer to this tradeoff.[30]

- Once the seasonal factors S_t are allowed to change over time, it becomes very difficult to disentangle the trend P_t from these changing seasonals.

In the following section, we will consider the problems associated with time series methods for seasonal adjustment more generally.

7.   Anderson's Critique of Time Series Models

The basic problem with all of the above time series methods for seasonal adjustment is that each method is more or less arbitrary. For example, let us start with Person's (1919; 8) decomposition of a time series into unobserved components. Using his classification, our representative price series p_t is assumed to have the following decomposition:

$$(38) \qquad p_t = T_t + C_t + S_t + E_t, \qquad\qquad t = 1, 2, \ldots, T,$$

where T_t is the long term trend portion of p_t at period t, C_t is the business cycle component of the series at time t, S_t is the seasonal component and E_t is an "error" or "erratic" component for period t. Thus comparing (38) with our earlier additive decomposition (31), it can be seen that our earlier trend term P_t is now decomposed into a longer term trend T_t plus a shorter term trend C_t that represents trends over the course of a normal business cycle.[31] Recall our earlier discussion in section 3 above where we noted that there were other alternatives to the additive model of the seasonal. The same discussion is relevant to our present more complex additive model of the seasonal defined by (38) above. Thus, after further refection on the adequacy of the

---

[29] Note that it is also not a trivial matter to define exactly what "smooth" means.

[30] In every nonparametric method for smoothing, a *smoothing parameter* determines the tradeoff between fit and smoothness. See Buja, Hastie and Tibshirani (1989) for a catalogue of these smoothing parameters.

[31] This type of decomposition can be traced back to Cournot. Cournot (1838; 25) initially distinguished "secular variations" and "periodic variations" (which correspond to the T_t and C_t parts of Person's decomposition) and later, Cournot (1863; 149) added "transitory" or "accidental" perturbations (which correspond to the E_t part of Person's decomposition).

additive model, we may decide that the following multiplicative model of the seasonal is more plausible:

$$(39) \qquad p_t = T_t\, C_t\, S_t\, E_t, \qquad\qquad t = 1,2,\ldots,T.$$

Upon even more reflection, we might decide that both the additive and the multiplicative models of the seasonal, (38) and (39) respectively, are too restrictive and so we postulate the existence of a function F such that

$$(40) \qquad p_t = F(T_t, C_t, S_t, E_t), \qquad\qquad t = 1,2,\ldots,T.$$

It is very obvious that it will be necessary to:

- Make some arbitrary assumptions in order to determine the functional form for F.

- . Even if F is determined as in (38) or (39), it will be necessary to make further arbitrary assumptions in order to identify the components, T_t, C_t, S_t and E_t.

The above *fundamental functional form determination and unobserved component identification problem* has been noticed in the literature but the most complete statement of it by Anderson has been largely forgotten:

> "We must either obtain the missing $(mN-N)$ equations from other sources, which can happen only in very exceptional cases, or introduce some preliminary assumptions, some hypotheses concerning the construction of the aggregates V, which would replace the missing equations. Thus, in most cases with which the social investigator has to deal in practice, in the decomposition of series into components, neither the definition of the function F nor the finding of the numerical meanings of the effects caused by the aggregates of cases V', V'', V''', V'''' [T_t, C_t, S_t, E_t] is possible without the introduction of different hypotheses which are more or less arbitrary."
>
> Oskar Anderson (1927; 552-553).

Assuming that we have solved the functional form problem and say have chosen the additive model (38), Anderson went on to explain how the various components on the right hand side of (38) might be identified:

> "Further, the investigator again limits arbitrarily the circle of his possibilities. For example:
>
> (a) assuming that the secular component [T_t] represents a polynomial function of the argument t (time or ordinal number) …
>
> (b) assuming that the cyclical component [C_t] can be represented as a more or less complex trigonometrical function;
>
> (c) assuming that the residual component e [E_t] is a random series."
>
> Oskar Anderson (1927; 554).

From the above quotations, it can be seen that Anderson had a very clear conception of the difficulties involved in finding the "right" functional form for a time series seasonal model and in determining the unobserved components in such a model. Similar criticisms of time series models of the seasonal have been expressed in more recent times:

> "It is necessary, in these situations, to restrict the class (20) of models so that the seasonal component of a series can be determined, theoretically and empirically. Often, restrictions are provided by the nature of the problem or by specific information … The problem here, as elsewhere, is that a consensus on this theory is lacking. One person prefers to define trend or cyclic effects in one way, another differently. In multivariate approaches, there are probably as

many varieties of plausible specifications of relationships among and between their components, all essentially compatible with the data, as there are social scientists (economists, statisticians, etc.) to specify these variables and relationships. This situation is evidently a general one in econometric modelling, where a variety of specifications, including a purely autoregressive equation, are all compatible with the data and all have comparable predictive power."

David A. Pierce (1978; 245-246).

The above Anderson critique of time series models indicates that these models generate a huge range of plausible seasonal adjustment factors. How could this range be reduced? One possible solution would be to take an *axiomatic* or *test approach* to the determination of the unknown function F and the unobserved components in (40).

In this approach, alternative seasonal adjustment procedures would be judged by their axiomatic properties. This test approach to seasonal adjustment procedures has in fact been formally and informally pursued by Hart (1922; 342-347), Macaulay (1931; 100-104), Lovell (1963) (1966), Grether and Nerlove (1970), Fase, Koning and Volgenant (1973) and Pierce (1978; 246-247) among others[32] but no consensus has been reached on what the appropriate set of axioms should be. Perhaps part of the problem has been that it is too difficult to work with the very general seasonal model defined by (40). Perhaps, it would be better to start with the very simple seasonal model defined by

(41) $$p_t = f(P_t, S_t)$$

where p_t is the series to be seasonally adjusted, P_t is the trend and S_t is the seasonal component; i.e., we have combined the trend and cycle terms T_t and C_t in (41) into a single trend term P_t and we have dropped the irregular term E_t in the simplified model defined by (41). P_t and S_t would be functions of the price data surrounding p_t for some window length n; i.e., we would also have:

(42) $$P_t = g(p_{t-n}, \dots, p_{t-1}, p_t, p_{t+1}, \dots, p_{t+n}); \quad S_t = h(p_{t-n}, \dots, p_{t-1}, p_t, p_{t+1}, \dots, p_{t+n})$$

for some functions g and h and for some window length n. Thus the functions f, g and h would have to be determined (perhaps along with the window length n)[33] by this simplified axiomatic approach. The axiomatic framework generated by (41) and (42) would appear to be a closer counterpart to the test or axiomatic approach to index number theory, which also abstracts from stochastic elements. If a consensus set of axioms for the model (41)-(42) were to lead to a definite seasonal adjustment procedure, then perhaps, stochastic considerations could be introduced at a later stage, as is the case with index number theory based on the test approach. However, until economists and statisticians can agree on a "reasonable" axiomatic framework for the test approach to seasonal adjustment procedures, this approach will not be of much help to statistical agencies.

---

[32] Cole (1963; 136) informally introduced a "test" in the following quotation: "Theoretically, a twelve month rolling average of a seasonally adjusted series should be the same as the twelve month rolling average of the original series. In the exhibit I have given you, you can see that in certain cases differences were almost as much as 10%. When differences as great as these occur, we have reason to wonder if the other results obtained are reliable."

[33] As we have seen earlier, choosing the "right" window length is not a trivial problem.

8.   The Interpretation of Seasonally Adjusted Data

What are we to make of the above catalogue of problems associated with time series methods for seasonally adjusting a price series? A number of tentative conclusions can be drawn from the above discussion:

- For each of the methods of time series seasonal adjustment that we have considered above, in every case, the seasonally adjusted period t price P_t has the interpretation as a measure of longer term trend in the unadjusted series p_t. Thus month-to-month comparisons of the seasonally adjusted prices are best interpreted as month-to-month comparisons in the *trend* of the price series rather than a true short run month-to-month comparison of prices.

- In all of the time series methods for seasonal adjustment that we have considered, either: (a) a final estimate for the trend P_t for a given period t is not available until at least an additional half year of data on p_t have been collected[34] or (b) as new data become available, new estimates for the trend factors P_t have to be *recomputed*, and thus in principle, estimates are never final. Moving average methods of seasonal adjustment like the Census II method[35] or the X-11 method[36] fall into category (a) while the Stone and Leser methods fall into category (b). This point indicates that seasonally adjusted price series that use time series methods cannot provide timely and accurate information on the short term movement of prices.

Information provided by a statistical agency should be *objective* and *reproducible*. Objective means that the methods used to generate data should be based on definite criteria that can be explained to the informed public. Moreover, there should be some consensus among

---

[34] Again recall Macaulay's (1931; 26) point that smoothing methods are inherently inaccurate at the endpoints of the data set in their domain of definition: "The tail end of any curve has necessarily a large probable error, and thoroughly inadequate results which would be likely to check with later data, when received are generally quite improbable. This is just as true of graduations such as the Whittaker-Henderson, which need no extrapolation, as of graduations which require extrapolation. Moreover, mathematical extrapolation does not solve this difficulty."

[35] The length of time it takes to determine final estimates depends on the length of the rolling average formula selected to represent the trend. Shiskin and Eisenpress (1957; 419-420), while discussing the Census II method, made the following observations on how the length of the moving average should be determined: "Graduation formulas are available which provide smooth and flexible curves and also eliminate seasonal fluctuations; for example, Macaulay's 43 term formula. But such formulas involve the loss of a relatively large number of points at the beginnings and ends of series. Graduation formulas which provide similarly smooth and flexible curves and involve the loss of relatively few points do not also eliminate seasonal variations. The computation for a preliminary seasonally adjusted series is now easy mechanically; on the other hand, the replacement of missing points is difficult conceptually. We, therefore, choose one of the formulas that requires a preliminary seasonally adjusted series, but also minimizes the loss of points, the Spencer fifteen-month weighted rolling average." Thus using the Census II method for seasonal adjustment, it would be necessary to wait seven months after the collection of the unadjusted p_t in order to obtain a final estimate for the corresponding seasonally adjusted P_t. Spencer's (1904) 15 term formula is described in Macaulay (1931; 55).

[36] Bell and Hillmer (1984; 308) make the following observation: "For X-11 with standard options, the final adjustment is effectively obtained three years after the initial adjustment..." Bell and Hilmer (1984; 296) also note that: "Eventually (typically after three years) the X-11 ARIMA adjustments converge to the X-11 adjustments..." Thus for these methods, one has to wait approximately three years to obtain final estimates.

experts that the criteria used are the "best" that are currently available. Reproducible means that if a competent statistician or economist were brought into the statistical agency and given the relevant criteria and methodology and told that he or she should produce a series, then these different statisticians and economists when given these instructions and the same data set would in fact produce roughly the same series. Given Anderson's (1927) fundamental critique of the general impossibility of unambiguous identification of the components in a time series model of the seasonal, *it seems doubtful that seasonally adjusted data can be completely objective since different analysts will generally make different functional form assumptions and place different identifying restrictions on the model in order to identify the unobserved components.* It also seems doubtful that seasonal adjustment procedures like X-11 and its successors are reproducible since different operators of these adjustment procedures will generally make different choices as they go through the menu of options that are available.

One could also argue that current times series methods for seasonal adjustment are not *comprehensible*; i.e., they are so complex that they cannot be readily explained to the informed public:

> "Even though the public appears for the most part to be comfortable with seasonally adjusted data, we doubt that many users understand the methods by which the data are produced. It may be too much to expect the statistically unsophisticated person to understand the procedures underlying seasonal adjustment, but even statistical experts are often mystified by these procedures, including the most widely used method, Census X-11. This method uses a set of moving averages to produce seasonally adjusted data; and although the basic idea of moving averages is simple enough, the method in which they are applied in the X-11 program is extremely complex. Moreover, the theoretical statistical underpinnings of X-11 and many other seasonal adjustment methods are not understood by many users. Thus many users of adjusted data merely trust that the adjustment procedure is providing useful data, and critics have advocated the abolishment of seasonal adjustment."
>
> William R. Bell and Steven C. Hillmer (1984; 291)

Finally, we have not stressed the difficult problems involved in seasonally adjusting sporadic or intermittently available data; i.e., for many micro international price series, the corresponding commodity is simply not available for one or more seasons of the year. This problem has received very little attention in the time series seasonal adjustment literature (and in the index number literature as well, although Zarnowitz[37] (1961; 243-246), Turvey (1979) and Balk (1980) (1981) are notable exceptions), even though, in many data sets, the problem is pervasive. If we attempt to seasonally adjust price series of this type (which can be done using additive models for the seasonal), then *it is clear that comparisons of the resulting seasonally adjusted prices from one season to the next cannot give any information about the actual short run changes in price for comparison periods when the commodity is not available.* This point just reinforces our earlier conclusion that seasonally adjusted data cannot adequately represent the short term season to season change in prices; they can only represent movements in the longer term trend in prices. In principle, seasonally adjusted data could provide valuable information on the longer run trend in prices. However, major problem with existing time series methods for seasonal adjustment is that these methods decompose a price or quantity series into trend, seasonal and irregular components but the method of decomposition is far from being

---

[37] "There is simply no escape from the truism that any comparison of two magnitudes such as p_i and p_j requires that both of them be actually given." Zarnowitz (1961; 244).

unique, as Anderson's critique shows. Thus it may be helpful to use some ideas from the index number literature to unambiguously determine the trend.

This can be done using the rolling or rolling year indexes suggested by Diewert (1983) (1996) (1999). Once the trend component has been determined in a unique fashion using index numbers, econometric methods could be utilized in order to use current information to forecast this unambiguous trend component.[38] The major advantage of the rolling year index number method for finding the trend in a price or quantity series is that it is perfectly *reproducible* once a consensus has been reached on the choice of the index number formula to be used. On the other hand, when using econometric methods for finding the trend that are based on moving average methods, one has to decide on the structure of the seasonal (Anderson's identification problem), the length of the moving average window and the tradeoff between fit and smoothness. The rolling year index number method is much more "objective".[39]

However, it should be noted that the rolling year index for say February of this year is a measure of annual price change that is centered around a rolling year that lags the current rolling year ending in February by six months. Thus to obtain the rolling year measure of the seasonally adjusted trend in prices that is centered around this February, we would have to wait seven months. Hence although the production of rolling year indexes might lead to unemployment for the seasonal adjusters in a statistical agency, they could readily find new employment in the *forecasting* branch of the agency, since there would still be a demand on the part of users for forecasts of the annual rolling year estimate of price change that is centered around the current month.

References

Akaike, H. (1980), "Seasonal Adjustment by a Bayesian Modeling", *Journal of Time Series Analysis* 1, 1-13.

Alterman, W.F., W.E. Diewert and R.C. Feenstra (1999), *International Trade Price Indexes and Seasonal Commodities*, Washington DC: Bureau of Labor Statistics.

Anderson, O. (1927), "On the Logic of the Decomposition of Statistical Series into Separate Components," *Journal of the Royal Statistical Society* 90, 548-569.

Balk, B.M. (1980), *Seasonal Products in Agriculture and Horticulture and Methods for Computing Price Indices*, Statistical Studies no. 24, The Hague: Netherlands Central Bureau of Statistics.

Balk, B.M. (1981), "A Simple Method for Constructing Price Indices for Seasonal Commodities," *Statistische Hefte* 22:1, 72-78.

Barton, H.C. (1941), "Adjustment for Seasonal Variation," *Federal Reserve Bulletin*, June, 518-528.

Bell, W.R. and S.C. Hillmer (1984), "Issues Involved With the Seasonal Adjustment of Economic Time Series," *Journal of Business and Economic Statistics* 2, 291-320.

Buja, A., T. Hastie and R. Tibshirani (1989), "Linear Smoothers and Additive Models (with discussion)," *The Annals of Statistics* 17, 453-555.

---

[38] Diewert (1983) (1996; 52-54) (1999), building on the pioneering ideas of Mudgett (1955) and Stone(1956), argued for the use of rolling year indexes as a substitute for seasonally adjusted data.
[39] Moreover the index number method for finding price and quantity trends in expenditure aggregates can easily deal with strongly seasonal commodities whereas econometric methods will either fail or be highly complex.

Cole, H.W. (1963), "Special Problems of Seasonally Adjusting Company Data," *American Statistical Association Proceedings of the Business and Economic Statistics Section*, 134-143.

Cournot, A. (1838), *Researches into the Mathematical Principles of the Theory of Wealth*, 1929 translation by N.T. Bacon, New York: The MacMillan Co.

Cournot, A. (1863), *Principles de la théorie des richesses*, Paris: Librarie Hachette.

Craven, P. and G. Wahba (1979), "Smoothing Noisy Data with Spline Functions: Estimating the Correct Degree of Smoothing by the Method of Generalized Cross-Validation," *Numerische Mathematik* 31, 377-403.

De Forest, E.L. (1873), "On Some Methods of Interpolation Applicable to the Graduation of Irregular Series, such as Tables of Mortality," *Annual Report of the Board of Regents of the Smithsonian Institution for the Year 1871*, pp. 275-339, Washington D.C.: Government Printing Office.

Diewert, W.E. (1983), "The Treatment of Seasonality in a Cost of Living Index," pp. 1019-1045 in *Price Level Measurement*, W.E. Diewert and C. Montmarquette (eds.), Ottawa: Statistics Canada. An excerpt of this original chapter is published as chapter 8 in Diewert, W.E., Balk, B.M., Fixler, D., Fox, K.J. and Nakamura, A.O. (eds.) (2011), *Price and Productivity Measurement, Volume 2: Seasonality*, Trafford Press.

Diewert, W.E. (1993), "Symmetric Means and Choice under Uncertainty," pp. 355-433 in *Essays in Index Number Theory*, W.E. Diewert and A.O. Nakamura (eds.), Amsterdam: North-Holland.

Diewert, W.E. (1996), "Seasonal Commodities, High Inflation and Index Number Theory," Discussion Chapter 96-06, Department of Economics, University of British Columbia, Vancouver, Canada, V6T 1Z1.

Diewert, W.E. (1999), "Index Number Approaches to Seasonal Adjustment," *Macroeconomic Dynamics* 3, 1-21.

Engle, R.F., C.W.J. Granger, J. Rice and A. Weiss (1986), "Semiparametric Estimates of the Relation Between Weather and Electricity Sales," *Journal of the American Statistical Association* 81, 310-320.

Fase, M.M.G., J. Koning and A.F. Volgenant (1973), "An Experimental Look at Seasonal Adjustment: A Comparative Analysis of Nine Adjustment Methods," *De Economist* 121, 177-180.

Federal Reserve Board (1922), "Index of Production in Selected Basic Industries," *Federal Reserve Bulletin*, January, 1414-1421.

Grether, D.M. and M. Nerlove (1970), "Some Properties of 'Optimal' Seasonal Adjustment," *Econometrica* 38, 682-703.

Hardy, G.H., J.E. Littlewood and G. Polyá (1934), *Inequalities*, London: Cambridge University Press.

Hart, W.L. (1922), "The Method of Monthly Means for Determination of a Seasonal Variation," *Journal of the American Statistical Association* 18, 341-349.

Henderson, R. (1924), "A New Method of Graduation," *Transactions of the Actuarial Society of America* 25, 29-40.

Henderson, R. and H.N. Sheppard (1919), *Graduation of Mortality and Other Tables*, New York: The Actuarial Society of America.

Hodrick, R.J. and E.D. Prescott (1980), "Post-War U.S. Business Cycles: An Empirical Investigation," Discussion Chapter 451, Department of Economics, Carnegie-Mellon University.

Joy, A. and W. Thomas (1928), "The Use of Rolling Averages in the Measurement of Seasonal Variations," *Journal of the American Statistical Association* 23, 241-252.

Kydland, F.E. and E.C. Prescott (1990), Business Cycles: Real Facts and a Monetary Myth," *Federal Reserve Bank of Minneapolis Quarterly Review*, Spring, 3-18.

Leser, C.E.V. (1963), "Estimation of Quasi-Linear Trend and Seasonal Variation," *Journal of the American Statistical Association* 58, 1033-1043.

Lovell, M.C. (1963), "Seasonal Adjustment of Economic Time Series and Multiple Regression Analysis," *Journal of the American Statistical Association* 58, 993-1010.

Lovell, M.C. (1966), "Alternative Axiomatizations of Seasonal Adjustment," *Journal of the American Statistical Association* 61, 800-802.

Macaulay, F.R. (1931), *The Smoothing of Time Series*, New York: The National Bureau of Economic Research.

Mudgett, B.D. (1955), "The Measurement of Seasonal Movements in Price and Quantity Indexes," *Journal of the American Statistical Association* 50, 93-98.

Persons, W.M. (1919), "Indices of Business Conditions," *Review of Economic Statistics* 1, 5-107.

Pierce, D.A. (1978), "Seasonal Adjustment when both Deterministic and Stochastic Seasonality are Present," pp. 242-269 in *Seasonal Analysis of Economic Time Series*, A. Zellner, (ed.), Washington D.C.: Bureau of the Census.

Schlicht, E. (1981), "A Seasonal Adjustment Principle and a Seasonal Adjustment Method Derived from this Principle," *Journal of the American Statistical Association* 76, 374-378.

Sheppard, W.F. (1914), "Graduation by Reduction of Mean Square Error," *Journal of the Institute of Actuaries* 48, 171-185.

Shiskin, J. and H. Eisenpress (1957), "Seasonal Adjustments by Electronic Computer Methods," *Journal of the American Statistical Association* 52, 415-449.

Shiskin, J., A.H. Young and J.C. Musgrave (1967), *The X-11 Variant of the Census Method II Seasonal Adjustment Program*, Revised: February 1967, Washington D.C.: Bureau of the Census.

Spencer, J. (1904), "On the Graduation of the Rates of Sickness and Mortality Presented by the Experience of the Manchester Unity of Oddfellows during the Period 1893-97," *Journal of the Institute of Actuaries* 38, 334-343.

Spoerl, C.A. (1937), "The Whittaker-Henderson Graduation Formula A," *Actuarial Society of America Transactions* 38, 403-462.

Sprague, T.B. (1891), "Explanation of a New Formula for Interpolation," *Journal of the Institute of Actuaries* 22, 270-285.

Stone, R. (1956), *Quantity and Price Indexes in National Accounts*, Paris: The Organization for European Cooperation.

Turvey, R. (1979), The Treatment of Seasonal Items in Consumer Price Indices," *Bulletin of Labour Statistics*, 4th Quarter, International Labour Office, Geneva, 13-33.

Wahba, G. and S. Wold (1975), "A Completely Automatic French Curve: Fitting Spline Functions by Cross Validation," *Communications in Statistics* 4, 1-17.

Wisniewski, J. (1934), "Interdependence of Cyclical and Seasonal Variation," *Econometrica* 2, 176-181.

Whittaker, E.T. (1923), "On a New Method of Graduation," *Proceedings of the Edinburgh Mathematical Society* 41, 63-75.

Whittaker, E.T. and G. Robinson (1926), *The Calculus of Observations: A Treatise on Numerical Mathematics*, Second Edition, London: Blackie and Son Ltd.

Wolfenden, H.H. (1925), "On the Development of Formulae for Graduation by Linear Compounding, with Special Reference to the Work of Erastus L. De Forest," *Actuarial Society of America Transactions* 26, 81-121.

Woolhouse, W.S.B. (1870), "Explanation of a New Method of Adjusting Mortality Tables," Journal of the Institute of Actuaries 12, 136-176.

Zarnowitz, V. (1961), "Index Numbers and the Seasonality of Quantities and Prices," pp. 233-304 in *The Price Statistics of the Federal Government*, G.J. Stigler (Chairman), New York: National Bureau of Economic Research.

Chapter 4

EMPIRICAL EVIDENCE ON THE TREATMENT OF SEASONAL PRODUCTS: THE ISRAELI CPI EXPERIENCE

W. Erwin Diewert, Yoel Finkel and Yevgeny Artsev[1]

1.   Introduction

The treatment of seasonal products in a Consumer Price Index (CPI) or Producer Price Index (PPI) is dealt with in chapter 22 of the new international manuals on the CPI and PPI.[2] Several methods are explored. In chapter 22 of the manuals (referred to hereafter simply as the Manual chapter), numerical demonstrations of performance for the alternative methods were carried out using a single artificial dataset: the modified Turvey data.[3] In this article we report on the results of implementing many of the methods proposed in the Manual chapter using real data from the Israeli CPI program.[4]

This new study has three main objectives. As background for our empirical research, we selectively summarize the material in the Manual chapter. Second, we briefly describe some of the special methods used in the Israeli CPI program for dealing with seasonal fluctuations in a month-to-month index. Third, we summarize our empirical results. Israeli CPI data are used to implement the methods considered in the Manual chapter. Results are obtained first using real Israeli CPI data and then using the Israeli CPI data with artificial modifications to check the sensitivity of key findings to data characteristics. We comment on how these results compare with the Manual chapter results. Formulas for the various methods used for dealing with seasonal products are given in appendix A.[5]

---

[1] Diewert is with the Department of Economics at the University of British Columbia and can be reached at diewert@econ.ubc.ca. Finkel is with the Israeli Central Bureau of Statistics and can be reached at yoel@cbs.gov.il. Artsev was formerly with the Israeli Central Bureau of Statistics and is now with the Israeli National Roads Company. He can be reached at YevgenyA@iroads.co.il.

[2] Web addresses for the *CPI Manual* (Hill 2004) and the *PPI Manual* (Armknecht 2004) are given in the references. The original chapter 22 was authored by Erwin Diewert, the first author of this paper, together with Paul Armknecht (2004) of the International Monetary Fund who is also the editor for the new 2004 *PPI Manual*.

[3] Diewert modified Turvey's (1979) artificial dataset to facilitate the complex computations in chapter 22.

[4] For more on the Israeli CPI program, see Karshai (1992), Sabag and Finkel (1994), Burck and Salama (2003), and Artsev, Roshal and Finkel (2006).

[5] In appendix A we indicate where full explanations of the formulas and methods used can be found in the Manual chapter and in the extended overview of the Manual chapter provided by Diewert, Armknecht and Nakamura (2011).

Citation for this chapter:
W. Erwin Diewert, Yoel Finkel and Yevgeny Artsev (2011),
"Empirical Evidence on the Treatment of Seasonal Products: The Israeli CPI Experience," chapter 4, pp. 53-78 in
W.E. Diewert, B.M. Balk, D. Fixler, K.J. Fox and A.O. Nakamura (eds.),
PRICE AND PRODUCTIVITY MEASUREMENT: Volume 2 -- Seasonality. Trafford Press.

© Alice Nakamura, 2011. Permission to link to, or copy or reprint, these materials is granted without restriction, including for use in commercial textbooks, with due credit to the authors and editors.

2.   The Treatment of Seasonal Products in the Manual Chapter

The Manual chapter 22 is organized into 12 sections. Here we indicate where the results can be found that relate to the findings of this study.

The first section in the Manual chapter (par. 22.1-22.13)[6] explains the problem of seasonal products. Products are defined as being (a) *strongly seasonal* when they are not available at all in the marketplace during certain seasons of the year and (b) *weakly seasonal* when they are available throughout the year but have regular fluctuations in prices or quantities that are synchronized with the season or the time of the year.[7] Strongly seasonal products are most challenging for compilers of price indexes since having different bundles of products in the index basket in the time periods being compared leads to a breakdown of traditional bilateral index number methodology. Two categories of approaches are presented in the Manual chapter for dealing with strong seasonality: month-to-month and year-over-year index approaches.

In the second section (par. 22.14-22.15), the modified Turvey data is introduced.

The third section (par. 22.16-22.34) presents the concept of year-over-year monthly comparisons. Even strongly seasonal products typically reappear in the same months each year. The overlap of products -- that is, the extent to which the same products appear in both the periods for which prices are being compared -- is maximized in the year-over-year monthly indexes. The remainder of the third section introduces and compares different types of year-over-year monthly indexes, including true versus approximate, and chained versus fixed base. Both true and approximate Laspeyres, Paasche and Fisher formulas are presented, and both the fixed base and the chained variants are defined.[8] It was found in the Manual chapter that use of chained indexes tends to reduce the spread between the Paasche and Laspeyres indexes compared to their fixed base counterparts. Since an approximate Fisher is just as easy to compute as an approximate Paasche or Laspeyres, and is more appropriate on other grounds, it is recommended that statistical agencies make the approximate Fisher indexes available to the public.[9]

The fourth section in the Manual chapter (par. 22.35-22.44) moves on from year-over-year monthly indexes to year-over-year annual ones.[10] The approach to computing annual indexes, which essentially involves taking monthly expenditure share-weighted averages of the 12 year-over-year monthly indexes, should be distinguished from taking a simple arithmetic mean of the 12 monthly indexes. The key problem with the latter approach is that months when

---

[6] The paragraph numbers for the sections are the same for chapter 22 in both the CPI Manual and the PPI Manual except for a one-paragraph difference in the last two sections. The paragraph numbers shown in parentheses in this paper thus apply to both manuals, except for the final two sections where these are the numbers for the CPI Manual.

[7] This classification of seasonal products corresponds to Balk's narrow and wide sense seasonal products; see Balk (1980a, p. 7; 1980b, p. 110; 1980c, p. 68). See also Balk (1981). Diewert (1998, p. 457) used the terms type 1 and type 2 seasonality. For other related references, see also Baldwin (1990) and Diewert (2002).

[8] See appendix section A.1 in this paper for the relevant formulas.

[9] Both the year-over-year and month-to-month Laspeyres and Paasche indexes fail the time reversal test: the Laspeyres with an upward bias and the Paasche with a downward bias.

[10] See appendix section A.2 in this paper for the formulas.

expenditures are below average (for example, February) are given the same weight as months when expenditures are above the average (for example, December).

Rolling year-over-year indexes are the subject of the fifth section of the Manual chapter (par. 22.45-22.54).[11] In the previous section, the indexes are defined over a calendar year. However, there is no need to confine comparisons to calendar year time periods. Prices can be compared for any specified 12 consecutive month period in different years, provided that January data is compared to January data, February data is compared to February data, and so on.[12] Rolling year indexes are computed using Laspeyres, Paasche and Fisher formulas, and the approximate Laspeyres, Paasche and Fisher formulas. Alterman, Diewert, and Feenstra (1999, p. 70) termed the resulting indexes rolling year indexes.[13] The specifics of constructing rolling year indexes for the modified Turvey data set are spelled out in the Manual chapter for both fixed base and chained rolling year indexes.

The sixth Manual chapter section (par. 22.55-22.62) shows how a year-over-year monthly index may be used to predict a rolling year index that is centered at the current month. It is shown that under a regime where the long run trend in prices is smooth, the current month year-over-year monthly index along with last month's year-over-year monthly index can be used to forecast a rolling year index that is centered on the last two months.

The seventh through tenth sections examine the treatment of seasonality using the traditional month-to-month approach. Section seven (par. 22.63-22.77) considers the maximum overlap month-to-month price index method which uses the set of products that are present in the marketplace in both months for which the price comparison is being made.[14] When strongly seasonal products are included, the maximum overlap index suffers from a serious downward bias for the artificial modified Turvey dataset. In the eighth section (par. 22.78-22.84), annual basket indexes with carry forward of unavailable prices are evaluated using the Lowe (1823), Young (1812) and geometric Laspeyres formulas,[15] and the movements of these are compared to the fixed base Laspeyres centered rolling year index. The ninth section (par. 22.85-22.86) replicates the section eight exercise, except that now imputed prices are computed rather than using the "carry forward" method. The indexes are still found to suffer from seasonality and do not closely approximate their rolling year counterparts.

---

[11] For more on rolling year indexes, see appendix section A.2, and also Diewert (1983), and Diewert, Armknecht and Nakamura (2007).

[12] Diewert (1983) suggested this type of comparison and termed the resulting index a split year comparison.

[13] Crump (1924, p. 185) and Mendershausen (1937, p. 245), respectively, used these terms in the context of various seasonal adjustment procedures. The term "rolling year" seems to be well established in the business literature in the United Kingdom. In order to theoretically justify the rolling year indexes from the viewpoint of the economic approach to index number theory, some restrictions on preferences are required. The details of these assumptions can be found in Diewert (1996, pp. 32-34; 1999, pp. 56-61).

[14] See appendix section A.3 for a brief introduction to maximum overlap indexes.

[15] The fixed base geometric Laspeyres annual index, P_{GL}, is the weighted geometric mean counterpart to the fixed base Laspeyres index, which is equal to a base period weighted arithmetic average of the long-term price relative. It can be shown that P_{GL} approximates the approximate fixed base Fisher index P_{AF} to the second order around a point where all of the long-term price relatives are equal to unity.

In the tenth section (par. 22.87-22.90), a final month-to-month index is considered: the Bean and Stine (1924) Type C, also known as the Rothwell (1958) type index.[16]

The eleventh section (par. 22.91-22.96) presents an attempt to forecast current month rolling year indexes using month-to-month annual basket indexes.[17] Seasonal adjustment factors are computed for the Lowe, Young, geometric Laspeyres and Rothwell indexes based on a centered rolling year index that is used as the target index.

The final section restates some of the main conclusions of the Manual chapter

(1) Year-over-year monthly indexes and rolling year indexes should be computed by the statistical agencies, at least as analytical series, along side the month-to-month ones;

(2) Annual basket indexes can be successfully used in the context of seasonal products;

(3) The spread between Laspeyres and Paasche indexes will usually be reduced by chaining, but the results should be checked against the year-over-year counterparts periodically to guard against chain drift that can be expected when a Laspeyres or Paasche index is used;

(4) Laspeyres and Paasche indexes can typically be viewed as of equal importance, so a Fisher (1922) type index is preferable when the data are available to compute this;

(5) The approximate year-over-year Fisher index accurately tracks the true year-over-year Fisher index for the modified Turvey data, and this result should hold for other datasets so long as the current period expenditure shares are similar to the past period shares used in the approximate indexes;

(6) The approximate Fisher and also the geometric Laspeyres indexes can be computed with the data that statistical agencies normally have at hand on a current basis; and

(7) The maximum overlap month-to-month indexes suffer from substantial bias when they include seasonal products.

3. The Main Treatment of Seasonal Products in the Israeli Index

Taken together, seasonal products make up nearly one fifth of the total expenditures covered by the Israeli CPI. We describe the methods used in the CPI program for dealing with seasonal products, focusing on clothing and boots, and on fresh fruits and vegetables.

3.1 Clothing and footwear

Clothing and footwear represent 2.9 percent of total expenditures covered by the Israeli CPI. The weights for this consumption group and specific products in it reflect the average monthly expenditures on the specified products over the base year as a percentage of the average monthly expenditure on the total basket covered by the CPI basket. The data source is the

---

[16] See appendix section A.5 for the formulas.

[17] See appendix section A.6.

Household Expenditure Survey (HES) conducted annually by the Israeli Central Bureau of Statistics. The price indexes are computed using the Lowe (1923) formula, defined in appendix equation (A-17).[18] The price changes for products that have disappeared due to seasonality are imputed using the average weighted percentage change in the price indexes of all clothing (or footwear) products present in the market. When the seasonal products reappear, "true" price indexes are computed for them.

There are many end-of-season sales that take place twice yearly: at the end of the summer season (usually in August-September) and at the end of the winter season (usually in February-March). Products are then sold at large discounts. These sales will tend to cause a downward bias problem. In order to overcome this problem, the price indexes of affected products are corrected in June and December.[19] These months were chosen because they are mid-season. The correction process is done using a three-stage computation method introduced into the CPI in 1989.

In stage one, the price indexes of seasonal products are computed using biannual year-over-year comparisons (December-over-December and June-over-June) and those for the other products (those found throughout the year like underwear) are computed using a 6-months prior comparison month (December versus June in December, and June versus December in June).

For clothing and footwear, the frequent changes in fashion cause many changes in the products, whether they are seasonal or not. Thus, in stage two, the prices for the potentially large number of products that have been replaced during the 12-month or 6-month period are imputed; more specifically, their last observed prices are increased by the average percentage change of the other products that could be compared over the annual or 6 month period.

Stage three involves averaging indexes for all clothing or footwear products.

The price indexes for clothing and footwear products are computed like the price indexes of other products, by the method of chaining: comparing current period prices with the previous period rather than base period prices.

3.2   Fruits and vegetables

Fruits and vegetables represent 3.5 percent of total expenditure in the Israeli CPI. The weights of the consumption groups and specific products in the categories are determined using the percentages of the average monthly expenditure in the base year versus the average monthly expenditure on the total basket. The data source is the Household Expenditure Survey (HES).

Until 1987, the fruit and vegetable price indexes were computed using the Rothwell formula, defined in appendix equations (A-20) and (A-21). From January 1988 on, these indexes have been computed according to the annual basket month-to-month Lowe formula (appendix equation (A-17)). Missing prices were imputed (in contrast to being filled in using the carry forward method). Research, conducted by the Israeli Central Bureau of Statistics over the past decade has not been conclusive about whether this transition led to an "improved" index. This

---

[18] For this formula, the base period for the weights is price updated to the base period of the CPI. See Balk and Diewert (2011) and T.P. Hill (2011) for more on the properties of the Lowe index.

[19] Hedonic methods may be used to solve this problem.

motivated our experimentation with the year-over-year methods described in the Manual chapter. Our findings for these methods are noted in section 4.

3.3   Seasonal adjustment methods in the Israeli CPI

Various approaches to seasonal adjustment were used in the Israeli CPI program in the mid-eighties and early nineties. Seasonal adjustment was conducted, at first, by Arima X-11, which was then replaced by Arima X-12.[20] The Israeli Bureau of Statistics publishes every month seasonally adjusted indexes for the nine following series: the total CPI, the CPI excluding housing, the CPI excluding housing and fruits and vegetables, fresh fruit, fresh vegetables, clothing, footwear, recreation and vacation, and travel abroad.[21]

4.   Implementation of Methods from the Manual Chapter

4.1   Israeli CPI program data

The Central Bureau of Statistics of Israel (CBS) conducts a monthly CPI and an annual HES. The sample for the Israeli HES consists of 6,200 households (with 500 households or more interviewed each month).[22]

For this study, we used actual CPI and HES data for the five-year period of 1997-2002 (72 monthly observations) for (1) fresh fruits[23] (lemons, apricots, avocado, watermelon, persimmon, grapefruits and bananas), and for (2) fresh vegetables[24] (cabbage, cauliflower, cucumbers, potatoes, carrots, lettuce and eggplants). For each of the selected fresh fruits, there are some months with no price observations, so these are strongly seasonal products. The fresh vegetables exhibit weak(er) seasonality; i.e., each of the selected vegetables is present throughout the year but there are large price fluctuations in the vegetable prices and quantities. We applied all the methods in the Manual chapter for both the fresh fruits and fresh vegetables.

Here we present only the findings that are connected to tentative conclusions reached in the Manual chapter where our results seem to differ in important ways. To focus the discussion, we examine only our results for fresh fruits.[25]

---

[20] See Diewert and Armknecht (2006, section) for a brief introduction to these methods and references. See also Burck and Salama (2003) and Burck and Gabman (2003) for specifics of the seasonal adjustment problems in Israel and the efforts that have been made over time to deal with these.

[21] In addition, trend indexes are published monthly for three series: Total CPI, CPI excluding housing, and the CPI excluding housing and fruits and vegetables. The estimation of the trend is conducted by Symmetric Henderson Moving Averages. See Diewert, Armknecht and Nakamura (2011) for more on the Arima X-11 and Arima X-12 software packages and Henderson filters.

[22] The Israeli HES has been annual since 1997. Over 500 households are sampled each month.

[23] See appendix B for the price and expenditure weight data.

[24] See appendix C for the price and expenditure weight data.

[25] Due to weaker seasonality for vegetables, the seasonal adjustment methods were always more successful for the vegetables than the fruits.

W. Erwin Diewert, Yoel Finkel and Yevgeny Artsev

4.2 Year-over-year monthly indexes

Can the approximate Laspeyres, Paasche and Fisher indexes introduced in section three of the Manual chapter -- formulas (A-4)-(A-6) in appendix A of this paper -- be used in place of the true Laspeyres, Paasche and Fisher -- formulas (A-1)-(A-3)? The key advantage of the approximate over the true current indexes is that they use only the data that statistical agencies normally have at hand.[26] Thus, in table 1 below we compare the year-over-year current month fixed base Fisher index with the approximate monthly fixed base Fisher index.[27] In 1997, by construction, the same data are used for both methods. In table 1 and the following five tables, entries where the relevant difference is 5 percentage points or more are shown in bold and larger sized type.

The relevant comparison in table 1 is for 1998-2002. In 11 out of the 60 months being compared, the differential is 5 percent or more. However, only six of these months have differentials of 10 percent or more (including four of the five Septembers).

Table 1. Ratio between Year-over-Year True and Approximate Fixed Base Monthly Fisher Indexes for Israeli CPI Data

Month/Year	1997	1998	1999	2000	2001	2002
1	1.00	1.01	0.99	0.99	1.02	0.98
2	1.00	1.00	1.01	1.00	1.00	1.00
3	1.00	1.00	1.00	1.01	1.01	1.01
4	1.00	1.00	0.98	1.01	1.00	1.02
5	1.00	0.99	1.04	**1.05**	**1.27**	0.97
6	1.00	1.01	1.00	1.01	1.01	1.03
7	1.00	1.01	**1.16**	1.01	**1.06**	1.02
8	1.00	0.99	1.02	1.00	1.04	**1.05**
9	1.00	**1.77**	**1.83**	1.04	**1.82**	**1.58**
10	1.00	1.01	1.00	1.01	1.01	0.96
11	1.00	0.99	0.98	0.99	0.98	**0.94**
12	1.00	1.01	0.99	1.00	1.00	**0.93**

In table 2 below, the same results are shown for year-over-year monthly chained Fisher indexes. The chained indexes are not approximated as well as the fixed base ones. The differences between the table 1 and 2 results show up beginning in 1999. In table 2, 16 observations (those shown in bold in table 2), the differences are 5 percent or more, and for 9 of those 16 the differences are 10 percent or more.

In the Manual chapter it is consistently found that the spread between the Laspeyres and Paasche type indexes is less for the chained than for the fixed base variants. In table 3 below we compare the spread between the Laspeyres and Paasche indexes for the fixed base and then for

[26] It is generally agreed that the Fisher index is to be preferred to the Laspeyres and Paasche indexes when the data are available that are needed to compute that Fisher index.

[27] The formulas for the true and approximate Fisher indexes are given in appendix equations (A-3) and (A-6).

59

the chained variants. The total period average Laspeyres/Paasche spread for the chained indexes seems to be slightly more, rather than less, on average, compared with the results for the fixed base indexes. These findings do not support the conclusion in the Manual chapter.

Table 2. Ratio between Year-over-Year True and Approximate Monthly Chained Fisher Indexes for Israeli CPI Data

MONTH/YEAR	1997	1998	1999	2000	2001	2002
1	1.00	1.01	0.98	0.99	**1.05**	1.01
2	1.00	1.00	1.03	0.99	1.00	1.00
3	1.00	1.00	1.00	1.02	1.03	1.04
4	1.00	1.00	0.98	1.03	1.01	**1.07**
5	1.00	0.99	**1.09**	**1.12**	**1.58**	**1.32**
6	1.00	1.01	1.00	1.00	1.00	**1.06**
7	1.00	1.01	**1.14**	1.01	**1.06**	1.02
8	1.00	0.99	1.01	1.00	**1.05**	1.04
9	1.00	**1.77**	**1.82**	**1.23**	**1.75**	**1.77**
10	1.00	1.01	1.02	1.01	1.02	**1.07**
11	1.00	0.99	0.99	1.02	1.01	0.99
12	1.00	1.01	1.01	1.01	1.01	0.99

Table 3: Mean Annual Ratio between Year-over-Year True Monthly Laspeyres and Paasche Indexes for Israeli CPI Data

	1997	1998	1999	2000	2001	2002
Fixed Base	1.00	0.97	0.974	1.03	0.94	0.93
Chained	1.00	0.97	0.972	0.98	0.93	0.94

4.3 Month-to-month indexes

The Manual chapter reports that the traditional month-to-month indexes all have large seasonal fluctuations and the maximum overlap method[28] is downward biased. Our findings are consistent with these Manual chapter conclusions. In figure 1 below, extreme (though regular) seasonal fluctuations are found for the annual basket Lowe (denoted by PLOI in figure 1; equation (A-27) in the appendix of this paper), Young (denoted by PYI; equation (A-30)) and geometric Laspeyres (PGLI; equation (A-19)) annual basket month-to-month indexes[29] with the target centered year rolling index[30] using imputed prices[31] (denoted in figure 1 by PCRY; see section A.6 in the appendix).

---

[28] See appendix section A.3 in this paper.

[29] See appendix section A.3 in this paper for the formulas for the maximum overlap method.

[30] This series was normalized to equal 1 in December 1997 so that it would be comparable to the other month-to-month indexes. Also, the centered rolling year indexes cannot be calculated for the last 6 months, since the data set does not extend 6 months into 2003.

**Figure 1. Lowe, Young, Geometric Laspeyres,
and Centered Rolling Year Indexes with Imputed Prices**

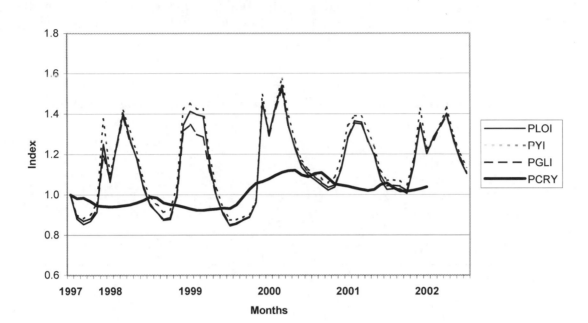

The year-over-year indexes defined in section 3, and their annual averages studied in sections 4 and 5, offer a theoretically satisfactory method for dealing with strongly seasonal products. However, because these methods rely on year-over-year comparisons of prices, they cannot be directly used to produce month-to-month or quarter-to-quarter indexes: typically the main focus of a CPI or PPI price index program. Thus, in sections 7-11, more traditional month-to-month price index methods are explored. If strongly seasonal products are to be included in the basket for traditional month-to-month price indexes, ways must be found to fill in the missing price information for products not available in one or the other of each pair of months compared.

It is of interest to compare the above three indexes that use annual baskets to the fixed base Laspeyres rolling year indexes. However, the rolling year index that ends in the current month is centered five and a half months backwards. Hence the above annual basket type indexes may be compared with an arithmetic average of two rolling year indexes that have their last month 5 and 6 months forward. This latter *centered rolling year index* is labeled P_{CRY}. It can be seen from figure 1 that the Lowe, Young and geometric Laspeyres indexes do not closely track their rolling year counterpart (PCRY).[32]

---

[31] The idea of the imputation method is to take the last available price and impute prices for the missing periods that trend with the category of fresh fruits. For each month m, the imputed price equals the price of the previous month (m-1) multiplied by the average of the fresh fruit category index for three adjacent months (m-1, m and m+1).

[32] The sample means of the indexes are 1.1220 (Lowe), 1.1586 (Young), 1.1190 (geometric Laspeyres) and 1.0072 (rolling year). Of course, the geometric Laspeyres index will always be equal to or less than the Young counterpart since a weighted geometric mean is always equal to or less than the corresponding weighted arithmetic mean.

Another finding from the Manual chapter was that the Rothwell index (PNR in figure 2)[33] has smaller seasonal movements than the Lowe index (PLO in figure 2) and is less volatile in general. The corresponding findings using the Israeli CPI program data are quite different, as can be seen in figure 2. The normalized Rothwell index is seen to be more volatile than the annual basket month-to-month Lowe index[34]. This finding supports the decision made in the Israeli CPI program to move to the Lowe index. However, both indexes exhibit large seasonal fluctuations.

Figure 2. Lowe and Normalized Rothwell Indexes for Israeli CPI Data[35]

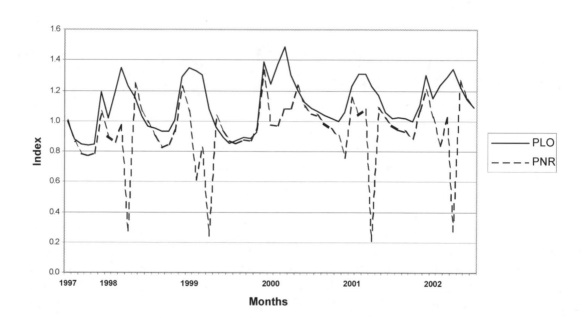

Section 11 of the Manual chapter documents an attempt to forecast rolling year indexes using month-to-month annual basket indexes. A seasonal adjustment factor was computed for the Lowe, Young and geometric Laspeyres indexes with imputed prices and the Rothwell index based on the centered rolling year index. Here, we introduce the actual Israeli CPI "fresh fruits" price index that has been seasonally adjusted using an Arima X-11 multiplicative model. This series enables us to compare whether the pattern of price change for the chosen set repeats the trend of the general category of the product or higher-level component of the CPI. The series has been normalized by dividing the original indexes by the first observation to make the series more comparable with the others. Our finding is that the predicted values of these "seasonally adjusted" indexes using the Israeli CPI data are fairly close to the corresponding target index

---

[33] See appendix section A.5.

[34] The Lowe index has a mean of 1.1087 and a standard deviation of .1677 while the normalized Rothwell has a mean of .9368 and a standard deviation of .2282.

[35] The Rothwell index is compared to the Lowe index with carry forward of missing prices (i.e., for the prices that are not available in the current month, the last available price is carried forward).

values.[36] The centered rolling year index for the chosen data does not seem to reliably represent the overall price index of fresh fruits with X-11 seasonal adjustment.[37] However, only the Seasonally-Adjusted Rothwell had outliers compared to the target indexes. This result perhaps weakens the argument for using this index in the Israeli CPI.

5.   Sensitivity Results Using on a Modified Israeli CPI Program Dataset

Comparison of the real Israeli CPI dataset used in this study with the artificial Turvey one on which the examples in the Manual chapter are based reveals structural differences that may account for some of the differences in findings. These data differences are summarized in table 4.

Table 4. Artificial Modified Turvey Versus Israeli CPI Program Data Differences

Presumption Built into the Artificial Turvey Data	Observed Reality
Annual price change of a product is always in one direction. An increase (decrease) in price in one year, compared to the previous one, cannot be followed by a decrease (increase) in price in the next year.	The trend of price change can change direction from year to year.
There is one seasonal cycle a year for each product.	Two seasonal cycles are possible.
A product is available (unavailable) in the same months each year.	Seasonal fluctuations are not completely synchronized with the calendar months for the products with strong seasonality. Thus, a product may appear/disappear a month before/later than in the previous year.
There is constant consumption behavior, in comparison with the same month in the previous year, independent of price behavior.	Consumption patterns are often erratic.

In the actual Israeli CPI program data, there is some variation over years regarding the months when strongly seasonal products appear/disappear. This seasonal irregularity might explain some of the difference between our findings and some of those in the Manual chapter, since strongly seasonal products are assumed to always be available only in the same months year after year in the artificial Turvey data used for used to explore the performance of the different methods in the Manual chapter. We explored this possibility by producing a modified Israeli data set. Starting with the Israeli CPI program dataset for fresh fruit used in the previous section,[38] some observations were altered so as to align the availability of products with strong

[36] For observations 13 through 66, we regressed the seasonally adjusted series on the centered rolling year series. For the seasonally adjusted Lowe index, an R^2 of .1916 is obtained; for the seasonally adjusted Young index, an R^2 of .1707 is obtained. For the seasonally adjusted geometric Laspeyres index, an R^2 of .3050 is obtained. And for the seasonally adjusted Rothwell index, an R^2 of .1298 is obtained, which is lower than for the other three indexes.

[37] For the X-11 seasonally adjusted series regressed on the centered rolling year series, the R^2 value is .0410.

[38] We modified the dataset of fruits only. There are no products with strong seasonality in the dataset of vegetables.

seasonality over the years. More specifically, 16 observations out of 504 were modified (3.2 percent). Eight of these observations were omitted for products that appeared in months when they were not usually available, and eight other observations were imputed by carrying forward/back[39] the price of the adjacent month for products that were unavailable in months when they usually were available.

The data modification led to substantial changes in some of the findings reported in section 4 above. We report these results to draw attention to the fact that some of the Manual conclusions seem quite sensitive to the properties of the data at hand.

In table 5, we again compare the year-over-year "current month" fixed base Fisher index with the approximate Fisher and find that the approximate Fisher index provides adequate approximations. The number of cases in which the difference between the indexes is 5 percentage points or more (shown in bold and larger sized type) is now just 5 (in contrast to 11 in table 1). Also, now there are no longer any differences of 10 percentage points or more.

Table 5. Ratio Between the Approximate and True Year-over-Year Monthly Fixed Base Fisher Indexes for the Modified Israeli CPI Data

Month/Year	1997	1998	1999	2000	2001	2002
1	1.00	1.01	0.99	0.99	1.02	0.98
2	1.00	1.00	0.99	1.00	1.00	1.00
3	1.00	1.00	0.99	1.00	1.00	1.01
4	1.00	1.00	0.98	1.01	1.00	1.02
5	1.00	0.99	1.04	**1.05**	**1.05**	1.02
6	1.00	1.01	1.00	1.01	1.01	1.03
7	1.00	1.01	1.02	1.01	1.04	1.00
8	1.00	1.01	1.02	1.01	1.04	1.03
9	1.00	1.00	1.03	1.01	1.00	**0.89**
10	1.00	1.01	1.00	1.01	0.99	0.96
11	1.00	0.99	0.98	0.99	0.98	**0.94**
12	1.00	1.01	0.99	1.00	1.00	**0.93**

In table 6 we return to the comparison of year-over-year monthly chained Fisher indexes. There is a decrease of about 50 percent in the number of cases in which the difference between indexes is 5 percent or more (seven in contrast to 16 cases), and only two observations are 10 percent or over.

---

[39] Imputation by carrying back the price of the following month was preferred only in cases when there was no price in the previous months of the same year.

Table 6. Ratio Between the Approximate and True Year-over-Year Monthly Chained Fisher Indexes for the Modified Israeli CPI Data

Month/Year	1997	1998	1999	2000	2001	2002
1	1.00	1.01	0.98	0.99	**1.05**	1.01
2	1.00	1.00	0.98	1.00	1.01	1.01
3	1.00	1.00	1.00	1.02	1.02	1.03
4	1.00	1.00	0.98	1.03	1.01	**1.07**
5	1.00	0.99	1.09	**1.12**	**1.09**	**1.15**
6	1.00	1.01	1.00	1.00	1.00	**1.06**
7	1.00	1.01	1.01	1.01	1.04	1.00
8	1.00	1.01	1.01	1.01	1.04	1.02
9	1.00	1.00	1.02	1.00	0.98	0.98
10	1.00	1.01	1.02	1.01	1.00	**1.05**
11	1.00	0.99	0.99	1.02	1.01	0.99
12	1.00	1.01	1.01	1.01	1.01	0.99

Table 7. Mean Annual Ratio Between Year-over-Year Monthly Laspeyres and Paasche Indexes for the Modified Israeli CPI Data

Year	1997	1998	1999	2000	2001	2002
Fixed Base	1.00	1.03	1.06	1.03	1.05	.99
Chained	1.00	1.03	1.06	1.12	1.15	1.21

And in table 7 below, we compare the spread between the Laspeyres and Paasche indexes without and with chaining. That is, we compare the fixed base with the chained indexes. Looking at the mean annual ratios in table 7, we see that from year 2000 on, the Laspeyres/Paasche spread is systematically greater for the chained variants. These findings, as in section 4 above for the unmodified Israeli CPI program data, *contradict* the conclusion from the Manual chapter.

A major change in findings occurs with the Lowe (denoted by PLO in figure 3) and Rothwell (PNR) indexes. Now the Rothwell exhibit smaller seasonal movements than the Lowe indexes (means of 1.01 and 1.12, respectively) and are less volatile (see figure 3).

Finally, the seasonally adjusted series of the Lowe, Young and geometric Laspeyres indexes with imputed prices and the Rothwell index seem to perform less well in tracking the trend of the target index values (the centered rolling year index).[40] The centered rolling year index for the chosen data set still fails to reliably represent the overall price index of fresh fruits with X-11 seasonal adjustment.[41] However, the extreme outliers found in the Seasonally-Adjusted Rothwell compared to the target indexes are absent with the modified Israeli data.

[40] For the seasonally adjusted Lowe index, an R^2 of .1094 is obtained for regression on the centered rolling year series (the lowest fit); for the seasonally adjusted Young index, the R^2 is .1274 and for the seasonally adjusted geometric Laspeyres index, the R^2 is .2197. For the seasonally adjusted Rothwell index, the R^2 is .1477.

[41] The R^2 value is .0026.

7.   Concluding Remarks

This paper has three objectives: (1) to summarize the methods and findings of the chapter on the treatment of seasonal products from the new international PPI and CPI Manuals, (2) to describe some of the methods used in the Israeli CPI to overcome seasonal fluctuations (and bias) in a month-to-month index, and (3) to examine some of the conclusions from the Manual chapter by simulating the methods with real Israeli CPI data.

Figure 3. Lowe and Normalized Rothwell Indexes for the Modified Israeli CPI Data

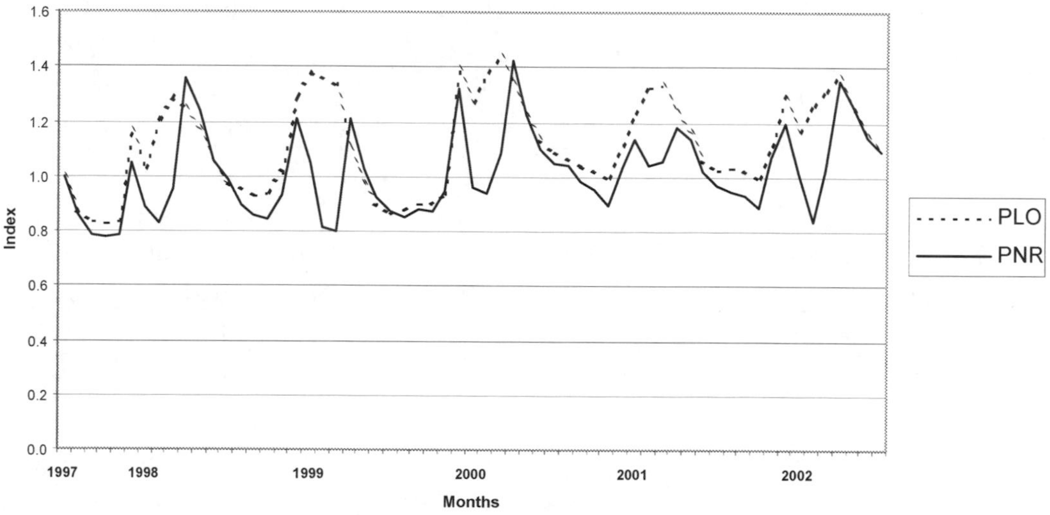

Using real data from the Israeli CPI led to findings that mostly support those reported in the Manual chapter, but there are interesting exceptions. The exceptions are the focus of our report. One conclusion is that the methods presented in the Manual chapter should be compared using fuller data sets and in many countries around the world. This kind of empirical research can improve the methods used for seasonal products. In this regard, analytical series (i.e., unofficial alternative series produced and made available to researchers and other interested users by official statistics agencies) have an important role to play. Computing analytical series on a current basis will enable comparisons that can lead to enhanced procedures in the production of price indexes. Setting rules for modifications in a way that will approach the results obtained by the theoretical dataset may help to treat these problems in a more effective manner. In addition, the investment in analytical series is once only.

Appendix A.   Formulas for Methods of Treatment of Seasonal Products

In this appendix, two sets of the equation number are provided for the convenience of readers interested in studying the fuller presentations of these methods in Diewert and Armknecht (2004) and in Diewert, Armknecht and Nakamura (2007). The same numbering is used as in the latter reference except that an A has been added as a prefix, and the equation numbers from the first of two related reference works are shown in square brackets.

A.1 Year-over-year monthly indexes

For each month $m = 1,2,\ldots,12$, let $S(m)$ denote the set of products that are available for purchase in each year $t = 1,2,\ldots,T$. Let $p_n^{t,m}$ and $q_n^{t,m}$ denote the price and quantity of product n that is available in month m of year t for n belongs to $S(m)$. Then the year-over-year monthly Laspeyres, Paasche and Fisher indexes going from month m of year t to month m of year t+1, in price relative and monthly revenue share form, can be defined as follows:

$$(A-1)[22.4] \qquad P_L = \sum_{n \in S(m)} s_n^{t,m} \left(p_n^{t+1,m} / p_n^{t,m} \right), \qquad\qquad m=1,2,\ldots,12,$$

$$(A-2)[22.5] \qquad P_P = \left[\sum_{n \in S(m)} s_n^{t+1,m} \left(p_n^{t+1,m} / p_n^{t,m} \right)^{-1} \right]^{-1}, \qquad\qquad m=1,2,\ldots,12,$$

$$(A-3)[22.6] \qquad P_F = \sqrt{P_L P_P}.$$

where the monthly revenue share for product $n \in S(m)$ for month m in year t is defined as:

$$s_n^{t,m} = \frac{p_n^{t,m} q_n^{t,m}}{\sum\limits_{i \in S(m)} p_i^{t,m} q_i^{t,m}}, \qquad\qquad m=1,2,\ldots,12,\ n \in S(m)\,;\, t = 0,1,\ldots,T$$

Approximate year-over-year monthly Laspeyres and Paasche indexes are defined as:

$$(A-4)[22.8] \qquad P_{AL} = \sum_{n \in S(m)} s_n^{0,m} \left(p_n^{t+1,m} / p_n^{t,m} \right), \qquad\qquad m=1,2,\ldots,12;$$

$$(A-5)[22.9] \qquad P_{AP} = \left[\sum_{n \in S(m)} s_n^{0,m} \left(p_n^{t+1,m} / p_n^{t,m} \right)^{-1} \right]^{-1}, \qquad\qquad m=1,2,\ldots,12;$$

Where $s_n^{0,m}$ is the base period monthly revenue share.

Using the approximate Laspeyres and Paasche indexes, the approximate Fisher year-over-year monthly indexes are defined by[42]

---

[42] If the monthly expenditure shares for the base year, $s_n^{0,m}$, are all equal, then the approximate Fisher index defined by equation (A-6) reduces to Fisher's (1922, p. 472) formula 101. Fisher (1922, p. 211) observed that this index was empirically very close to the unweighted geometric mean of the price relatives, while Dalén (1992, p. 143) and Diewert (1995, p. 29) showed analytically that these two indexes approximate each other to the second order.

(A-6)[22.10] $P_{AF} = \sqrt{P_{AL}P_{AP}}$.

A.2   Year-over-year annual indexes

Using the notation introduced above, the Laspeyres and Paasche annual (chain link) indexes comparing the prices of year t with those of year t+1 can be defined as follows:

$$(A\text{-}9)[22.16] \qquad P_L = \sum_{m=1}^{12} \sum_{n \in S(m)} \sigma_m^t s_n^{t,m} \left(p_n^{t+1,m} / p_n^{t,m} \right);$$

$$(A\text{-}10)[22.17] \qquad P_P = \left[\sum_{m=1}^{12} \sum_{n \in S(m)} \sigma_m^{t+1} s_n^{t+1,m} \left(p_n^{t+1,m} / p_n^{t,m} \right)^{-1} \right]^{-1},$$

where the revenue share for month m in year t is defined as:

$$\sigma_n^t = \frac{\displaystyle\sum_{n \in S(m)} p_n^{t,m} q_n^{t,m}}{\displaystyle\sum_{i=1}^{12} \sum_{j \in S(i)} p_j^{t,i} q_j^{t,i}}, \qquad\qquad m = 1,2,\dots,12; \ t = 0,1,\dots,T.$$

The current year weights, $s_n^{t,m}$ and σ_m^t and $s_n^{t+1,m}$ and σ_m^{t+1} can be approximated by the corresponding base year weights, $s_n^{0,m}$ and σ_m^0.

There is no need to restrict attention to calendar year comparisons: any 12 consecutive months of data could be compared to the price and quantity data of the base year, provided that the January data in the non-calendar year is compared to the January data of the base year, the February data of the non-calendar year is compared to the February data of the base year, ..., and the December data of the non-calendar year is compared to the December data of the base year. Alterman, Diewert and Feenstra (1999, p. 70) call these indexes *rolling year indexes*.

A.3   Maximum overlap month-to-month price indexes

Let there be N products that are available in some month of some year and let $p_n^{t,m}$ and $q_n^{t,m}$ denote the price and quantity of product n that is in the marketplace in month *m* of year *t* (if the product is unavailable, let $p_n^{t,m}$ and $q_n^{t,m}$ be 0). Let $p^{t,m} \equiv [p_1^{t,m}, p_2^{t,m}, \dots, p_N^{t,m}]$ and $q^{t,m} \equiv [q_1^{t,m}, q_2^{t,m}, \dots, q_N^{t,m}]$ be the month m and year *t* price and quantity vectors, respectively. Let $S(t,m)$ be the set of products that is present in month *m* of year *t and the following month*.

Define the revenue shares of product n in month m and m+1 of year t, using the set of products that are present in month m of year t and the subsequent month, as follows:

$$(A\text{-}12)[22.23] \quad s_n^{t,m}(t,m) = \frac{p_n^{t,m} q_n^{t,m}}{\sum_{i \in S(t,m)} p_i^{t,m} q_i^{t,m}}, \qquad m=1,2,\ldots,11; \ n \in S(t,m),$$

$$(A\text{-}13)[22.24] \quad s_n^{t,m+1}(t,m) = \frac{p_n^{t,m+1} q_n^{t,m+1}}{\sum_{i \in S(t,m)} p_i^{t,m+1} q_i^{t,m+1}}, \qquad m=1,2,\ldots,11; \ n \in S(t,m),$$

where $s_n^{t,m+1}(t,m)$ must be distinguished from $s_n^{t,m+1}(t,m+1)$. The revenue share $s_n^{t,m+1}(t,m)$ is the share of product n in month m+1 of year t with n restricted to the set of products that are present in month m of year t and the subsequent month, whereas $s_n^{t,m+1}(t,m+1)$ is the share of product n in month m+1 of year t with n restricted to the set of products that are present in month m+1 of year t and the subsequent month.

If product n is present in month m of year t and the following month, define $s_n^{t,m}(t,m)$ using (a); if this is not the case, define $s_n^{t,m}(t,m) = 0$. Similarly, if product n is present in month m of year t and the next one, define $s_n^{t,m+1}(t,m)$ using (b); if not, define $s_n^{t,m+1}(t,m) = 0$.

Using these share definitions, Laspeyres and Paasche formulas can be written in revenue share and price form as follows[43]:

$$(A\text{-}14)[22.25] \quad P_L = \sum_{n \in S(t,m)} s_n^{t,m}(t,m)\left(p_n^{t+1,m} / p_n^{t,m}\right), \qquad m=1,2,\ldots,11,$$

$$(A\text{-}15)[22.26] \quad P_P = \left[\sum_{n \in S(t,m)} s_n^{t,m+1}(t,m)\left(p_n^{t+1,m} / p_n^{t,m}\right)^{-1}\right]^{-1}, \qquad m=1,2,\ldots,11.$$

A.4   Annual basket indexes

The Lowe index for month m is defined by the following formula:

$$(A\text{-}17)[22.28] \quad P_{LO} = \frac{\sum_{n=1}^{N} p_n^m q_n}{\sum_{n=1}^{N} p_n^0 q_n}$$

---

[43] It is important that the revenue shares that are used in an index number formula add up to unity. The use of unadjusted expenditure shares would lead to a systematic bias in the index number formula.

where $p^0 \equiv [p_1^0, p_2^0, \ldots, p_N^0]$ is the price vector for the price reference period, $p^m \equiv [p_1^m, p_2^m, \ldots, p_N^m]$ is the current month m price vector, and $q \equiv [q_1, \ldots, q_N]$ is the weight reference year quantity vector.

The Young (1812) index is defined as follows:

$$(A\text{-}18)_{[22.30]} \quad P_Y = \sum_{n=1}^{N} s_n (p_n^m / p_n^0)$$

where $s \equiv [s_1, \ldots, s_N]$ is the weight reference year vector of revenue shares.

The geometric Laspeyres index is defined as follows:

$$(A\text{-}19)_{[22.32]} \quad P_{GL} = \prod_{n=1}^{N} (p_n^m / p_n^0)^{s_n}$$

Thus the geometric Laspeyres index makes use of the same information as the Young index except that a geometric average of the price relatives is taken instead of an arithmetic one.

It is of interest to compare the above three indexes that use annual baskets to the fixed base Laspeyres rolling year indexes. However, the rolling year index that ends in the current month is centered five and a half months backwards. Hence the above annual basket type indexes may be compared with an arithmetic average of two rolling year indexes that have their last month 5 and 6 months forward. This latter *centered rolling year index* is labeled P_{CRY}.

A.5   Bean and Stine Type C or Rothwell indexes

The Bean and Stine Type C (1924, p. 31) or Rothwell (1958, p. 72) index makes use of seasonal baskets in the base year, denoted as the vectors $q^{0,m}$ for the months m = 1,2,…,12. The index also makes use of a vector of base year unit value prices, $p^0 \equiv [p_1^0, \ldots, p_5^0]$ where the nth price in this vector is defined as:

$$(A\text{-}20)_{[22.33]} \quad p_n^0 \equiv \frac{\sum_{m=1}^{12} p_n^{0,m} q_n^{0,m}}{\sum_{m=1}^{12} q_n^{0,m}};$$

The *Rothwell price index* for month m in year t can now be defined as follows:

$$(A\text{-}21)[22.34] \quad P_R = \dfrac{\displaystyle\sum_{n=1}^{N} p_n^{t,m} q_n^{0,m}}{\displaystyle\sum_{n=1}^{N} p_n^{0} q_n^{0,m}}, \qquad\qquad m = 1,\ldots,12.$$

To make the different series more comparable, the normalized Rothwell index P_{NR} is introduced, this index is equal to the original Rothwell index divided by its first observation.

A.6   Forecasting rolling year indexes using month-to-month annual basket indexes

For each of the series -- Lowe, Young and geometric Laspeyres -- a seasonal adjustment factor (SAF) is defined, as the centered rolling year index P_{CRY} divided by P_{LO}, P_Y and P_{GL}, respectively for the first 12 observations. Now for each of the three series, repeat these 12 seasonal adjustment factors for the remaining observations. These operations will create 3 SAF series for all the observations (label them SAF_{LO}, SAF_Y and SAF_{GL}, respectively).

Finally, define seasonally adjusted Lowe, Young and geometric Laspeyres indexes by multiplying each unadjusted index by the appropriate seasonal adjustment factor.

$$(A\text{-}22)[22.35] \quad P_{LOSA} \equiv P_{LO}SAF_{LO}; P_{YSA} \equiv P_Y SAF_Y; P_{GLSA} \equiv P_{GL}SAF_{GL}.$$

A seasonally adjusted version of the Rothwell index presented in the paper may also be defined in the same way.

Appendix B.   Seasonal Data Set for Fresh Fruit

Table B-1. Prices for Fresh Fruits (New Israeli shekel per kilo)

Year	Month	Lemons	Apricots	Avocado	Watermelon	Persimmon	Grapefruit	Bananas
1997	1	3.42	0	3.42	0	5.81	2.81	3.79
	2	3.34	0	3.71	0	5.81	2.74	3.88
	3	3.43	0	3.78	0	6.67	2.78	3.76
	4	3.89	0	4.03	0	0	2.9	4.24
	5	4.35	0	5.07	3.65	0	2.81	5.39
	6	6.76	8.81	6.44	2.03	0	3.01	6.77
	7	7.7	8.01	7.25	1.56	0	3.41	9.73
	8	9.15	0	0	1.46	0	3.63	9.43
	9	8.36	0	7.65	1.56	0	4.48	7.57
	10	6.47	0	5.65	0	6.7	4.31	7
	11	4.79	0	4.35	0	5.34	3.61	6.74
	12	3.9	0	3.95	0	5.44	2.9	5.86
1998	1	3.51	0	3.82	0	5.75	2.69	4.49
	2	3.45	0	3.72	0	5.88	2.42	4.09
	3	3.42	0	3.78	0	0	2.46	4
	4	3.68	0	3.98	0	0	2.57	3.98
	5	4.19	0	4.6	3.34	0	2.95	3.97
	6	5.9	6.11	5.18	1.67	0	3.39	5.01

W. Erwin Diewert, Yoel Finkel and Yevgeny Artsev

Year	Month	Lemons	Apricots	Avocado	Watermelon	Persimmon	Grapefruit	Bananas
	7	6.38	6.64	5.81	1.57	0	3.77	7.12
	8	7.39	0	9.16	1.74	0	3.7	7.52
	9	7.58	0	8.79	0	0	4.74	5.88
	10	7.06	0	6.34	0	7.85	4.36	5.71
	11	5.88	0	5.44	0	6.71	4.16	4.76
	12	4.94	0	5.71	0	7.1	3.37	4.19
1999	1	4.55	0	6.28	0	7.61	3.2	3.89
	2	4.22	0	6.14	0	0	3	3.75
	3	4.17	0	6.5	0	0	3.05	3.67
	4	4.62	0	7.56	0	0	3.22	4.16
	5	5.47	0	10.58	2.47	0	3.45	5.07
	6	7	8.82	13.66	1.7	0	3.88	6.14
	7	7.88	0	0	1.4	0	0	6.36
	8	7.96	0	0	1.42	0	4.13	5.94
	9	7.19	0	8.42	0	0	4.4	4.69
	10	5.68	0	5.84	0	7.5	4.33	4.3
	11	4.85	0	4.95	0	6.23	3.73	4.06
	12	4.32	0	4.64	0	6.41	3.4	3.81
2000	1	4.06	0	4.56	0	7.14	3.29	4.07
	2	3.83	0	4.35	0	7.66	3.19	4.4
	3	3.69	0	3.85	0	0	3.1	4.58
	4	3.49	0	3.67	0	0	3.27	5.13
	5	4.24	0	4.48	2.74	0	3.44	7.58
	6	5.7	7.32	5.56	1.65	0	3.87	7.58
	7	8.15	7.61	6.55	1.76	0	4.24	8.12
	8	10.92	0	9.04	1.93	0	0	7.85
	9	7.84	0	9.26	1.93	0	0	6.12
	10	6.18	0	6.55	0	7.41	5.65	5.83
	11	5.3	0	5.09	0	6.11	4.26	5.71
	12	4.65	0	4.93	0	6.02	3.73	5.49
2001	1	4.15	0	5.03	0	6.35	3.41	5.33
	2	3.86	0	4.86	0	7.01	3.19	5.11
	3	3.70	0	5.04	0	0	3.17	4.84
	4	3.91	0	5.14	0	0	3.32	4.45
	5	4.4	0	6.73	0	0	3.59	4.66
	6	5.78	8.45	8.33	2.21	0	3.75	5.31
	7	6.46	8.86	0	1.97	0	4.66	6.56
	8	6.69	0	0	1.96	0	5.69	6.42
	9	5.62	0	8.88	0	0	0	5.42
	10	5.21	0	6.69	0	7.77	0	5.4
	11	4.57	0	4.97	0	6.75	4.12	4.91
	12	4.31	0	4.75	0	6.82	3.9	4.56
2002	1	4.1	0	4.97	0	7.15	3.56	4.65
	2	3.91	0	4.62	0	7.76	3.48	4.67
	3	3.67	0	4.32	0	0	3.44	4.54
	4	3.94	0	4.7	0	0	3.64	5.72
	5	4.05	10.6	4.74	2.89	0	3.75	5.94
	6	4.21	6.46	5.07	1.99	0	4	6.2
	7	5.84	6.51	0	1.6	0	3.83	7.81
	8	6.58	0	0	1.91	0	0	7.64
	9	6.19	0	9.61	0	0	5.69	6.8
	10	5.48	0	6.32	0	7.93	5.11	6.52
	11	4.8	0	6.22	0	6.28	4.23	5.84
	12	4.22	0	6.33	0	5.91	3.76	5.36

Table B-2. Expenditures for Fresh Fruits[44]

Year	Month	Lemons	Apricots	Avocado	Watermelon	Persimmon	Grapefruit	Bananas
1997	1	1.7	0.1	4.3	0	1.1	0.3	17.7
	2	2.5	0	3.6	0.3	0.9	1.7	14.8
	3	1.9	0	3.7	0.7	0.2	1.4	15.3
	4	2.4	0.1	3	3.4	0	1.4	17.5
	5	2.1	0.2	2.7	11	0	1.5	11.8
	6	3.2	6.4	2.3	28.9	0	1.6	6.2
	7	2,2	7.4	1.6	27.8	0.1	0.8	1
	8	2.9	0.8	0.5	22.2	0	0.7	1.5
	9	2.8	0	0.5	13.3	0	0.5	2.4
	10	2.8	0	1.7	2.7	1.6	0.6	6.7
	11	2.4	0	3.5	0.4	3.6	1.2	13.3
	12	2.2	0.1	5.1	0.2	3.6	0.9	15
1998	1	1.7	0	3.8	0	3	0.7	14.4
	2	2.2	0	4.8	0	1.9	0.8	16.9
	3	2.6	0.1	3.8	0.6	0.7	1	17.4
	4	2.8	0.2	3.2	2.6	0.1	1.7	17.5
	5	2.6	1.1	2.8	22.2	0.1	0.7	12.5
	6	2.4	10.4	1.6	26	0	0.4	7.2
	7	3.7	6.9	1.4	23.6	0	0.7	3.2
	8	2.6	0.3	0.8	24.6	0.2	0.7	3.2
	9	2.9	0.1	1.1	11.7	0.2	1.1	4.5
	10	3.6	0.1	2.1	1.8	0.8	0.4	8.9
	11	3.2	0	4.3	0.3	3.4	1.2	13.8
	12	2.8	0	4	0.2	2.7	0.9	14.7
1999	1	2.1	0.1	4.3	0	1.5	1	16.1
	2	2.4	0.1	4.3	0.1	1.7	1.1	14.2
	3	2.1	0	4.4	0.4	0.3	1.1	15
	4	3	0.1	4	4.3	0.2	1.2	13.6
	5	3.2	2.2	2.2	21	0.3	1.7	11.5
	6	2.8	11	1.9	26.7	0	0.8	6.7
	7	3.1	6	0.4	25.7	0	0.8	4
	8	2.6	0.5	0.2	19.4	0.1	0.4	3.7
	9	2.8	0.2	1.1	9.4	0.4	0.6	6.1
	10	2.8	0	2.6	1.4	1.6	0.9	8.3
	11	2.5	0.3	5.2	0.2	3.7	1.4	12.7
	12	2.6	0	4.4	0	3.4	0.7	12.3
2000	1	2.2	0.2	3.7	0	2.9	1	11
	2	2.7	0	4.2	0	2.3	1	13.6
	3	3.1	0	3.6	0.1	0.6	1.4	12.7
	4	2.6	0	3.2	3.6	0.1	1	14.2
	5	3.1	1.2	3	18	0	1.1	8.5
	6	2.4	8.9	1.6	25.4	0.1	0.6	4.7
	7	3.2	7.1	1.6	25.7	0	0.2	2
	8	3.8	0.4	1.1	21.3	0	0.5	2.5
	9	2.6	0.1	1.1	9.9	0.1	0.3	4.6
	10	2.9	0.1	2.5	1.8	1.5	0.6	9.4
	11	3.1	0	5	0.7	3.9	1	11.3

[44] The given data set of expenditures has been further adjusted for the purpose of calculations: in the months where the price for the good is equal to 0, we assume that the expenditure also equals 0.

Year	Month	Lemons	Apricots	Avocado	Watermelon	Persimmon	Grapefruit	Bananas
	12	2.6	0.3	4	0.2	3.5	0.9	13.7
2001	1	2.3	0	4.2	0	4.1	1.4	13.5
	2	2.9	0.2	3.7	0.2	2	0.9	14
	3	2.6	0.2	3.6	0.8	1.7	1.2	13.8
	4	2.9	0.1	3	5.9	0.1	0.8	13.7
	5	2.4	2.5	2.5	21.1	0	0.7	10.1
	6	2.8	10.1	2.3	23.3	0	0.9	5.8
	7	3	3.6	2.1	23.6	0	0.4	4
	8	3.3	0.1	1.1	17	0	0.3	3
	9	3.4	0.1	1.4	5.2	0.2	0.1	4.8
	10	3.7	0.2	4.1	1.8	2.4	0.6	9.4
	11	3.1	0	6.3	0.5	4.4	1	13.2
	12	2.5	0.1	5	0.5	3.4	0.8	13.5
2002	1	1.8	0.2	16	0	3.2	1.2	12.7
	2	3	0.1	15	0.5	1.9	1.3	16.4
	3	3.5	0.1	14.2	0.7	1.1	1.1	14.4
	4	3.7	0.1	14.2	9.9	0.4	1.1	14.5
	5	2.8	4	13.6	17.3	0.1	1.2	11
	6	2.8	10.6	13.1	21.6	0	0.7	6.9
	7	3.3	3.8	16	25.1	0	0.7	3.4
	8	3.9	0.3	20.5	18.4	0	0.1	3.2
	9	3.4	0.1	16.8	10.6	0.2	0.4	3.8
	10	2.8	0	17.3	1	2.1	0.4	7.3
	11	2.8	0	16.7	0.3	4.5	0.7	11.5
	12	2.8	0	21.4	0.4	5	0.9	14.7

Appendix C. Seasonal Data Set for Fresh Vegetables

Table C-1. Prices for Fresh Vegetables (New Israeli shekel per kilo)

Year	Month	Cabbage	Cauliflower	Cucumbers	Potatoes	Carrots	Lettuce	Eggplants
1997	1	2.09	3.1	3.21	2.37	3.16	3.01	3.28
	2	2.5	3.77	5	2.54	3.16	3.05	6.31
	3	2.67	3.92	5.49	3.23	3.26	3.14	6.49
	4	2.34	4.04	4.46	3.17	3.26	3.12	5.55
	5	2.4	3.63	2.98	2.91	3.13	3.18	4.07
	6	2.24	4.1	2.56	2.64	3.02	3.26	3.33
	7	2.12	4.5	2.96	2.56	3.07	3.25	2.63
	8	2.61	4.54	2.96	2.93	3.33	3.46	2.82
	9	2.83	4.51	2.73	2.93	3.55	3.45	2.74
	10	2.71	4.19	3.35	3.05	3.86	3.53	2.99
	11	2.55	4	3.44	3.04	3.52	3.61	3.12
	12	2.45	3.8	3.27	2.86	3.11	3.44	3.03
1998	1	2.36	3.4	3.11	2.71	2.81	3.29	3.21
	2	2.28	3.13	2.99	2.58	2.76	3.1	3.61
	3	2.18	3.54	3.47	2.42	2.67	3.17	4.12
	4	2.18	3.51	4.14	2.46	2.77	3.18	4.64
	5	2.12	4.24	3.26	2.44	2.84	3.28	5.03
	6	2.27	4.8	2.67	2.34	3.12	3.32	3.14
	7	2.33	4.88	2.69	2.36	3.39	3.39	2.94
	8	3.76	5.65	3.35	2.65	3.88	3.99	2.95

Year	Month	Cabbage	Cauliflower	Cucumbers	Potatoes	Carrots	Lettuce	Eggplants
	9	7.4	7.24	3.75	2.94	4.27	5.1	3.33
	10	6.38	6.18	3.53	3.25	4.54	5.04	3.43
	11	3.84	5.56	3.09	3.32	4.14	4.23	3.32
	12	3.05	4.89	4.43	3.26	3.72	3.7	3.16
1999	1	3.21	3.99	3.25	3.18	3.59	3.26	4.39
	2	2.72	3.4	3.19	3.09	3.47	3.26	4.8
	3	2.27	3.98	3.05	2.81	3.21	2.89	4.15
	4	2.34	3.46	3.15	2.76	3.18	2.91	3.8
	5	2.2	3.54	2.78	2.45	3.12	3.07	3.38
	6	2.24	4.15	2.86	2.4	3.28	3.16	3.2
	7	2.33	5.61	3.05	2.39	3.38	3.28	3.07
	8	2.67	6.02	2.99	2.71	3.29	3.5	3.17
	9	2.93	5.33	3.51	2.77	3.31	3.68	3.13
	10	2.86	4.95	4.34	2.86	3.58	3.72	3.22
	11	2.65	5	3.67	2.97	3.59	3.56	3.03
	12	2.76	5.24	5.02	3.57	3.74	3.52	3.88
2000	1	2.6	3.69	4.33	3.18	3.86	3.5	4.45
	2	2.56	3.82	4.45	2.98	3.88	3.6	6.38
	3	2.44	4.44	4.18	2.9	3.7	3.29	5.67
	4	2.24	3.89	3.16	2.53	3.25	3	4.85
	5	2.28	3.79	2.68	2.52	3.38	3.27	4.51
	6	2.29	4.25	2.95	2.44	3.24	3.43	3.28
	7	2.86	5.09	3.33	2.61	3.28	3.45	2.85
	8	3.71	5.42	2.96	3.09	3.49	3.68	2.94
	9	3.65	5.1	3.21	3.14	3.69	3.84	2.96
	10	3.25	5.09	4.02	3.3	3.99	3.79	3.31
	11	3.03	5.32	4.26	3.21	3.89	3.77	3.41
	12	3.02	4.54	3.87	2.99	3.85	3.73	3.31
2001	1	2.96	4.16	3.06	2.67	3.63	3.63	3.31
	2	2.81	4.1	3.26	2.45	3.41	3.53	3.52
	3	2.65	4.14	3.13	2.34	3.21	3.3	3.62
	4	2.57	4.49	3.47	2.58	3.36	3.39	4.57
	5	2.5	4.46	3.5	2.88	3.55	3.49	4.14
	6	2.52	4.8	3.24	3.1	3.73	3.62	3.72
	7	2.55	5.12	3.35	3.43	3.9	3.56	3.4
	8	2.71	5.25	4.64	3.76	3.99	3.61	3.54
	9	2.87	6.21	5.18	3.77	4.26	3.93	4.11
	10	3.01	5.51	4.03	4.08	4.38	3.88	3.75
	11	2.95	5.1	3.7	4.29	4.23	3.89	3.65
	12	3.46	4.66	4.29	3.94	4.12	3.91	3.72
2002	1	3.38	4.64	5.96	3.51	3.97	3.95	5.19
	2	3.3	4.45	4.86	3.6	4.03	3.83	6.34
	3	2.97	4.17	3.75	3.44	3.93	3.53	4.74
	4	2.91	4.17	3.87	3.42	3.94	3.57	4.95
	5	2.6	4.24	3.09	3.27	3.83	3.57	4.4
	6	2.56	4.68	3.41	3.17	3.75	3.62	3.55
	7	2.44	5.51	3.41	3.07	3.63	3.52	3.22
	8	3.49	6	3.99	3.16	3.82	3.98	3.63
	9	4.72	6.38	4.11	3.33	4.06	4.31	3.79
	10	4.54	5.15	4.66	3.28	4.3	4.08	3.64
	11	3.36	5.5	4.53	3.03	4.18	3.93	3.24
	12	3.07	5.04	4.25	3.03	4.08	3.69	4.01

Table C-2. Expenditures for Fresh Vegetables

Year	Month	Cabbage	Cauliflower	Cucumbers	Potatoes	Carrots	Lettuce	Eggplants
1997	1	5.1	3	15.6	21.5	5.2	2.9	3.9
	2	4.2	3.1	13.3	16.4	4.4	2.7	3.1
	3	3.8	2.6	15.1	19.1	4.4	2.4	4.2
	4	4.1	2.2	17	21.1	4.8	3.4	2.8
	5	3.1	1.4	14.3	22.1	4.2	3.8	2.2
	6	3.1	1.2	12.2	18.6	4	2.2	3.9
	7	3.3	1.6	12	16.7	3.3	2.2	4
	8	2.5	1.1	11.8	16.9	3	1.8	4.7
	9	2.1	1.2	9.9	18.5	3.8	2.3	3.1
	10	3.4	2.2	12.2	21.2	4.5	2.6	3.6
	11	4.1	2	13.3	20	4.6	2.5	3.9
	12	3.9	2.4	11.2	17.5	4.1	2.4	3.3
1998	1	3.3	2.6	10.2	19.9	4.4	3.1	1.6
	2	4.3	2.7	12.9	19.9	4.1	2.9	3.7
	3	3.9	2.3	13.4	18	4.1	2.7	2.9
	4	3.2	2	15.2	18.7	3.7	4.1	3.9
	5	3.4	1.9	15.2	18.3	3.9	3.2	4.1
	6	2.9	1.3	13.2	16.6	3.6	1.8	4.4
	7	2.7	1.6	13.1	14.2	3.6	2.2	4.1
	8	2.8	1.4	12.6	17	3.3	2.1	3.4
	9	3.7	1.7	16.1	19.5	4	2.9	3.8
	10	6.4	2.1	15.5	19.2	4.2	3.5	4.9
	11	5.2	2.3	12.8	19.5	5.4	3.3	4.2
	12	4	2.8	11.5	19	4.7	3.4	3
1999	1	5.2	4	10.3	19.8	5.8	3.3	3.1
	2	5	3.1	11.6	19	4.6	2.9	3.9
	3	4.2	1.9	12.4	18.7	4.4	3.4	2.4
	4	4.2	2.9	13.3	20	4.3	3.7	2.5
	5	3.6	1.9	12.8	19.6	4.3	3.2	4.2
	6	3.7	1.2	15.2	18.8	4.1	3.3	4.5
	7	3.1	1.1	13.9	16.3	4.3	2.7	4.5
	8	2.8	1.2	11.6	17	4	1.8	4.7
	9	3.7	1.8	14.8	19.6	4	3.1	4.8
	10	3.3	2	13.1	16.1	3.9	3	4.3
	11	3.7	2.1	13.2	17.9	4.1	3.7	3.2
	12	4.5	2.8	16.3	22.3	4.7	2.9	3.8
2000	1	3.1	1.4	10	20.2	5.2	2.7	1.9
	2	4.4	2.6	13.8	21.6	7.2	3.3	3.1
	3	3.8	2.4	12.8	20	4.6	3.3	4
	4	3.7	2.7	13.4	19.2	4.5	4.1	3
	5	4.2	2.1	12.5	19.1	4.2	4.4	3.5
	6	3.5	1.3	12.5	14.4	4.2	3.4	3.8
	7	3.4	0.9	12.5	17.2	4.3	2.8	3.3
	8	4.7	1.3	12.6	17.6	3.5	3.1	3.7
	9	3.9	1.2	13.8	19.6	3.9	3.3	3.6
	10	5.5	2.9	14.4	22.7	5.6	4.5	4.9
	11	4.3	1.7	13.5	19.5	5.3	3.9	3.6
	12	4.1	2.7	13.3	20.5	4.6	3.6	3.4
2001	1	4.6	2.5	10.5	19.9	5	4.8	2.2
	2	4.1	2.2	10.7	15.8	4.9	3.9	3
	3	4.8	2.5	11.4	18	4.9	3.8	3.4
	4	3.6	2.8	13.1	19.2	4.2	3.8	3.4
	5	3.2	1.1	13.1	15.7	3.9	3.6	3.6

W. Erwin Diewert, Yoel Finkel and Yevgeny Artsev

Year	Month	Cabbage	Cauliflower	Cucumbers	Potatoes	Carrots	Lettuce	Eggplants
	6	3.4	1.2	12	16.6	4.6	3.3	3.3
	7	4.1	1.5	12.5	17.6	5.3	3.7	3.8
	8	3.9	1.3	14.7	20.7	5	3.1	4.2
	9	4.4	1.9	16.2	22.3	4.8	3.6	4.7
	10	5.3	2.4	15.4	21	5.6	4.4	4.3
	11	4.5	2.7	14.5	25.5	5.9	4.8	3.5
	12	5	2.9	13.1	23.1	6.1	4.3	2.7
2002	1	4.8	2.9	13.6	22.7	5.5	3.9	2.8
	2	6.3	3.4	19.1	23.2	4.7	5.6	3.4
	3	5.3	2.9	14.5	21.5	5	5	3.2
	4	5.3	2.7	14.2	22.7	5.2	5.6	5.2
	5	4.4	1.8	13.6	19.4	4.7	4.7	3.6
	6	4.4	1.8	13.5	18.2	4.3	4.3	4.7
	7	4	0.9	13.9	16.8	4.8	4.4	4.3
	8	4.8	2.5	14.7	19.3	3.6	4.1	3.9
	9	4.5	1.3	13.3	17.9	4.9	4.3	3.2
	10	5.3	1.9	15.2	20.1	4.4	5.2	3.1
	11	5.3	2.4	16.3	18.4	6.7	4.5	3.9
	12	4.7	3.1	14.9	20.8	5.8	4.2	3.8

References

Alterman, W.F., W.E. Diewert and R.C. Feenstra (1999), *International Trade Price Indexes and Seasonal Commodities*, Bureau of Labor Statistics, Washington D.C.

Armknecht, P.A., ed. (2004), *Producer Price Index Manual: Theory and Practice* (*PPI Manual*), published by the International Labour Office, International Monetary Fund, Organisation for Economic Co-operation and Development, Eurostat, United Nations, and The World Bank. Chapters and whole can be downloaded for free at http://www.imf.org/external/np/sta/tegppi/index.htm

Artsev, Y., V. Roshal and Y. Finkel (2006), "Consumer Price Indices – Measuring Across Households," working paper, Israeli Central Bureau of Statistics, presented at the 9th Ottawa Group Meeting on Prices.

Baldwin, A. (1990), "Seasonal Baskets in Consumer Price Indexes," *Journal of Official Statistics* 6 (3), 251-273.

Balk, B.M. (1980a), "Seasonal Products in Agriculture and Horticulture and Methods for Computing Price Indices," Statistical Studies no. 24, The Hague: Netherlands Central Bureau of Statistics.

Balk, B.M. (1980b), "Seasonal Commodities and the Construction of Annual and Monthly Price Indexes," *Statistische Hefte* 21 (2), 110-116.

Balk, B.M. (1980c), "A Method for Constructing Price Indices for Seasonal Commodities," *Journal of the Royal Statistical Society A* 143, 68-75.

Balk, B.M. (1981), "A Simple Method for Constructing Price Indices for Seasonal Commodities," *Statistische Hefte* 22, 72-78.

Balk, B.M. and W.E. Diewert (2011), "The Lowe Consumer Price Index and Its Substitution Bias," in Diewert, W.E., Balk, B.M., Fixler, D., Fox, K.J. and Nakamura, A.O. (eds.), *Price and Productivity Measurement: Volume 6 -- Index Number Theory*, Trafford Press.

Bean, L. H. and O. C. Stine (1924), "Four Types of Index Numbers of Farm Prices," *Journal of the American Statistical Association* 19, 30-35.

Burck, L. and Y. Gubman (2003), "Pre-adjustment in X12-ARIMA," working paper of the Israel Central Bureau of Statistics. http://www.fcsm.gov/03papers/Burck.pdf

Burck L. and E. Salama (2003), "Seasonal and Prior Adjustment Factors for 2003," *Current Statistics* 7, Central Bureau of Statistics, Israel

Crump, N. (1924), "The Interrelation and Distribution of Prices and their Incidence Upon Price Stabilization," *Journal of the Royal Statistical Society* 87, 167-206.

Dalén, J. (1992), "Computing Elementary Aggregates in the Swedish Consumer Price Index," *Journal of Official Statistics* 8, 129-147.

Diewert, W.E. (1983), "The Treatment of Seasonality in a Cost of Living Index", in W.E. Diewert and C. Montmarquette (eds.), *Price Level Measurement*, Statistics Canada, 1019-1045. http://www.econ.ubc.ca/diewert/living.pdf. An excerpt of this original paper is published as chapter 8 Diewert, W.E., Balk, B.M., Fixler, D., Fox, K.J. and Nakamura, A.O. (eds.) (2011), *Price and Productivity Measurement: Volume 2 -- Seasonality*, Trafford Press.

Diewert, W.E. (2011), "Axiomatic and Economic Approaches to Elementary Price Indexes," in Diewert, W.E., Balk, B.M., Fixler, D., Fox, K.J. and Nakamura, A.O. (eds.), *Price and Productivity Measurement: Volume 6 -- Index Number Theory*, Trafford Press.

Diewert, W.E. (1996), "Seasonal Commodities, High Inflation and Index Number Theory," Discussion Paper 96-06, Department of Economics, University of British Columbia, Vancouver, Canada, V6T 1Z1.

Diewert, W.E. (1998), "High Inflation, Seasonal Commodities and Annual Index Numbers," *Macroeconomic Dynamics* 2, 456-471.

Diewert, W.E. (1999), "Index Number Approaches to Seasonal Adjustment," *Macroeconomic Dynamics* 3, 1-21.

Diewert, W.E. (2002), "Harmonized Indexes of Consumer Prices: Their Conceptual Foundations," *Swiss Journal of Economics and Statistics* 138 (4), 547-637.

Diewert, W.E. and P.A. Armknecht (2004), "The Treatment of Seasonal Products," chapter 22 in the *CPI Manual* edited by Hill (2004) and also in the *PPI Manual* edited by Armknecht (2004). Available for free download at http://www.imf.org/external/np/sta/tegppi/ch22.pdf

Diewert, W.E., P.A. Armknecht and A.O. Nakamura (2011), "Methods for Dealing with Seasonal Products in Price Indexes," chapter 2 in W.E. Diewert, B.M. Balk, D. Fixler, K.J. Fox, and A.O. Nakamura (eds.), *Price and Productivity Measurement: Volume 2 -- Seasonality*, Trafford Press.

Feenstra, R.C. and M.D. Shapiro (2003), "High-Frequency Substitution and the Measurement of Price Indexes," in Robert Feenstra and Matthew Shapiro (eds.), *Scanner Data and Price Indexes*, National Bureau of Economic Research Studies in Income and Wealth, University of Chicago Press, 123-146.

Fisher, I. (1922), The Making of Index Numbers, Boston: Houghton Mifflin Co.

Hill, T.P., ed. (2004), *Consumer Price Index Manual: Theory and Practice* (*CPI Manual*), published by the International Labour Office, International Monetary Fund, Organisation for Economic Co-operation and Development, United Nations, and The World Bank. Available for free download in whole or by chapter at http://www.ilo.org/public/english/bureau/stat/guides/cpi/index.htm.

Hill, T.P. (2011), "Lowe Indices," in W.E. Diewert, B.M. Balk, D. Fixler, K.J. Fox, and A.O. Nakamura (eds.), *Price and Productivity Measurement: Volume 6 -- Index Number Theory*, Trafford Press.

Karshai, R. (1992), The Consumer Price Index, *Technical Publication Series* No. 60, Central Bureau of Statistics, Israel.

Lowe, J. (1823), The Present State of England in Regard to Agriculture, Trade and Finance, second edition, London: Longman, Hurst, Rees, Orme and Brown.

Mendershausen, H. (1937), "Annual Survey of Statistical Technique: Methods of Computing and Eliminating Changing Seasonal Fluctuations," *Econometrica* 5, 234-262.

Rothwell, D.P. (1958), "Use of Varying Seasonal Weights in Price Index Construction," *Journal of the American Statistical Association* 53, 66-77.

Sabag, M. and Y. Finkel (1994), "The Israeli CPI: Alternative Computing Methods for an Item Price Index," *Statistical Journal of the United Nations ECE* no. 11, 95-118

Turvey, R. (1979), "The Treatment of Seasonal Items in Consumer Price Indices," *Bulletin of Labour Statistics*, Fourth Quarter, International Labour Office, Geneva, 13-33.

Young, A. (1812), *An Inquiry into the Progressive Value of Money in England as Marked by the Price of Agricultural Products*, London.

Chapter 5

THE REDESIGN OF THE CANADIAN FARM PRODUCT PRICE INDEX

Andrew Baldwin[1]

1. Background

The Farm Product Price Index (FPPI) is a monthly series that measures the changes in prices that farmers receive for the agriculture commodities they produce and sell. The price index has separate crop and livestock indexes, a variety of commodity-group indexes such as cereals, oilseeds, specialty crops, cattle and hogs, and an overall index -- all available monthly and annually for the provinces and for Canada. The index expresses current farm prices from Statistics Canada's Farm Product Prices Survey as a percentage of prices prevailing in the base period (currently1997=100). Its primary purpose is to serve as a measure of Canadian agricultural commodity price movement and as a means to deflate agricultural commodity prices.

Prices are based on either administrative data sources, or monthly surveys of agricultural producers or commodity purchasers. Commodities are priced at point of first transaction. The fees deducted before a producer is paid are excluded (e.g., storage, transportation and administrative costs), but bonuses and premiums that can be attributed to specific commodities are included. Commodity-specific program payments are not included in the price.

The FPPI is based on a five-year basket that is updated every year. This captures the continual shift in agricultural commodities produced and sold. The annual weight base is derived from the farm cash receipts series. There is a two-year lag in the years used to construct the basket because of the availability of farm cash receipts data and to reduce the revisions made to the index. Therefore, the years used to construct the basket for year y are y-6 to y-2.

The seasonal weighting pattern was derived using the monthly marketings from 1994 to 1998. This weighting pattern remains constant and will only be updated periodically such as during intercensal revisions or when the time base is revised. The methodology of the index and the price series which construct the index have been designed to control errors and to reduce the potential effects of these. However, both administrative and survey data are subject to various

[1] The author is with Statistics Canada, and can be reached at Andy.Baldwin@statcan.ca. He was the technical consultant on the revival of the FPPI. The opinions expressed are his own and do not necessarily reflect the official policy of Statistics Canada. The author thanks the other members of the FPPI Redesign Team: Gail-Anne Breese, Patricia Conor, Paul Murray and Bernie Rosien. He also thanks Erwin Diewert of the University of British Columbia, Alice Nakamura of the University of Alberta, Mike Trant, previously with Statistics Canada, and especially his discussant Bert Balk of Statistics Netherlands.

Citation for this chapter:
A. Baldwin (2011), "The Redesign of the Canadian Farm Product Price Index,"
chapter 5, pp. 79-104 in
W.E. Diewert, B.M. Balk, D. Fixler, K.J. Fox and A.O. Nakamura (eds.),
PRICE AND PRODUCTIVITY MEASUREMENT: Volume 2 -- Seasonality. Trafford Press.

© Alice Nakamura, 2011. Permission to link to, or copy or reprint, these materials is granted without restriction, including for use in commercial textbooks, with due credit to the authors and editors.

kinds of error. Survey data are mainly subject to response and data capture errors. In reporting prices each month, farm survey respondents are asked to report the average prices prevailing in their neighborhood, taking into account the various grades of each commodity marketed. Thus, average prices reported by these respondents may differ from month to month due to changes in price, quality or both. The agencies providing administrative data are considered to be the best sources available, and data received from them are judged to be of very good quality.

The FPPI is not adjusted for seasonality, but seasonal baskets are used since the marketing of virtually all farm products is seasonal. The index reflects the mix of agriculture commodities sold in each given month. The FPPI allows the comparison, in percentage terms, of prices in any given time period to prices in the base period.

2.   The Main Elements of the FPPI Redesign

The Farm Product Price Index (FPPI) was discontinued with the March 1995 estimates when it was still on a 1986 time base. It was then revived in April 2001 due to the continuing demand for an index of prices received by farmers. The time base of the index was changed from 1986 to 1997, since the System of National Accounts (SNA) switched to estimates at 1997 prices. In its initial updating the FPPI was calculated up to March 2001, including all of the months from April 1995 forward for which no official estimates have been published. The indexes were also revised back to 1992, incorporating substantial changes in the way they are put together. There was no change in methodology for the indexes before 1992. Though the index levels of the 1997=100 series will be different from those of the 1986=100 series, the percent changes for the period ending in December 1991 will remain unchanged.

The methodology changes made with the revival of the FPPI are the most substantial in its history. There are five main changes:

(1)   The new index is an annually reweighted chain price index, so the annual weighting pattern is updated every year. The weighting pattern for an index is also called its basket. The old index was a fixed-basket price index for the most recent period, and its basket was updated only after ten or more years had elapsed.

(2)   The new index follows a seasonal-basket concept, where the volume shares of the various commodities are different in each of the twelve months of the calendar year. The old index followed a fixed-basket concept, where those shares were the same for all months of the year. Now there are 12 different baskets used in calculating the months of a calendar year in the FPPI, where before there was only one.

(3)   In the new index, consistent with its seasonal basket concept, the annual index number for a given year is a weighted average of the corresponding monthly index numbers. In the old index, consistent with its fixed-basket concept, the annual index number was the mean or simple average of the corresponding monthly index numbers.

(4)   In the new index, goods for which there are receipts but no marketings have their price movement proxied by a group index (e.g. maple products take their price movement from total crops). In the old index, such goods were simply omitted and had no impact on the overall index.

(5)   In the new index, each annual basket will be based on marketings for an average of five years; the last annual basket for the old index was based on marketings for an average of four years from 1981 to 1984.

Probably no index redesign in the history of Statistics Canada has marked such a substantial and salutary break with the past. It is the first Statistics Canada index to be calculated with monthly baskets since 1973, when the consumer price index abandoned the monthly-basket approach it previously used for seasonal food groups. It is the first Statistics Canada index ever to implement the Rothwell formula for seasonal commodities, the monthly-basket formula most commonly used by official statistical agencies. It is the first Statistics Canada index for a goods-producing industry with annual chain linking, and the first index in North America, perhaps in the world, to combine annual chaining with a monthly-basket-formula for all aggregate and sub-aggregate indexes (the U.S. counterpart of the FPPI changes baskets every year, but is not a chain price index; there is no linking involved). It is the first annually chained index calculated by Statistics Canada that allows one to calculate a measure of pure price change for all consecutive months or quarters or years. For example, the monthly new housing price index does not allow this for all months or for any years. Finally, while the old FPPI was only linked back to 1981 on a monthly basis, the new index is linked back to 1935, making it by far the longest continuous series in Statistics Canada's industrial price index program; by contrast, the industry product price indexes only stretch back to 1956.

3.   The Rothwell Formula

The seasonal basket formula used in the revised FPPI is a variant of what is usually called the Rothwell formula, after Doris Rothwell (1958), an economist with the U.S. Bureau of Labor Statistics, who proposed it for the U.S. consumer price index (CPI). However the formula was originally proposed decades previously by two economists with the U.S. Bureau of Agricultural Economics, Louis H. Bean and O.C. Stine (1924) as an index number for farm prices. Thus the formula adopted was originally designed an indicator of farm price movements.

The Rothwell formula must be used to calculate indexes of fresh fruits and vegetables in the harmonized indexes of farm product prices of the European Community.[2] Dick Carter, who now works for Statistics Canada, and E. T. Richards (1975) introduced it as the formula for the United Kingdom's agricultural price indexes in 1972. It is also used to calculate series for seasonal commodity groups in the CPIs of other countries, including Japan, France and the United Kingdom.

Restrictively defined, the Rothwell formula is the monthly-basket counterpart to the Laspeyres formula, and with a 1997 base year, is defined as:

$$(3.1) \quad P_{y,m/97}^{R(I)} = \frac{\sum p_{y,m}^{j} q_{97,m}^{j}}{\sum p_{97}^{j} q_{97,m}^{j}},$$

---

[2] See Eurostat (1985), chapter II, section G and Annex V.

where $P_{y,m/97}^{R}$ is the Rothwell index number for the mth month of year y, $p_{y,m}^{j}$ is the price of the jth commodity in the mth month of year y, $q_{97,m}^{j}$ is the quantity produced (or in the FPPI case, marketed) of the jth commodity in the mth month of base year 1997, and p_{97}^{j} is the average price of the jth commodity in base year 1997, defined as a unit value:

$$(3.2) \quad p_{97}^{j} = \frac{\sum_{m=1}^{12} p_{97,m}^{j} q_{97,m}^{j}}{\sum_{m=1}^{12} q_{97,m}^{j}}.$$

The formula is shown with base year 1997 since this is the base year of the revised FPPI.

It can be seen that in the special case where $q_{97,m}^{j} = q_{97}^{j}/12; m = 1,2,...12$, the Rothwell index reduces to the corresponding Laspeyres index:

$$(3.3) \quad P_{y,m/97}^{R(I)} = \frac{(1/12)\sum p_{y,m}^{j} q_{97}^{j}}{(1/12)\sum p_{97}^{j} q_{97}^{j}} = \frac{\sum p_{y,m}^{j} q_{97}^{j}}{\sum p_{97}^{j} q_{97}^{j}} = P_{y,m/97}^{L},$$

or in other words, the Laspeyres index is a special case of the Rothwell index.

More broadly defined, the Rothwell formula is the monthly-basket counterpart to the fixed-basket formula, and with a 1997 base year, is given by:

$$(3.4) \quad P_{y,m/97}^{R(II)} = \frac{\sum p_{y,m}^{j} q_{c,m}^{j}}{\sum p_{97}^{j} q_{c,m}^{j}},$$

where $q_{c,m}^{j}$ is the quantity marketed of the jth commodity in the mth month of period c, which is some year or sequence of years not necessarily equal to or inclusive of base year 1997.

It can be seen that in the special case where $q_{c,m}^{j} = q_{c}^{j}/12; m = 1,2,...12$, the second variant of the Rothwell index reduces to the corresponding fixed-basket (FB) index:

$$(3.5) \quad P_{y,m/97}^{R(II)} = \frac{(1/12)\sum p_{y,m}^{j} q_{c}^{j}}{(1/12)\sum p_{97}^{j} q_{c}^{j}} = \frac{\sum p_{y,m}^{j} q_{c}^{j}}{\sum p_{97}^{j} q_{c}^{j}} = P_{y,m/97}^{FB(I)},$$

i.e. a fixed-basket index with a basket from period c (also called a Lowe index),[3] but with 1997 base prices calculated as unit values.

Yet more broadly defined, the Rothwell formula would substitute different base prices:

---

[3] See T.P. Hill (2007) and Balk and Diewert (2007).

$$(3.6) \quad P_{y,m/97}^{R(III)} = \frac{\sum p_{y,m}^j q_{c,m}^j}{\sum \bar{p}_{97}^j q_{c,m}^j},$$

where $\bar{p}_{97}^j$, the 1997 base prices are calculated as:

$$(3.7) \quad \bar{p}_{97}^j = \frac{\sum\limits_{m=1}^{12} p_{97,m}^j q_{c,m}^j}{\sum\limits_{m=1}^{12} q_{c,m}^j}.$$

Note that this calculation requires an imputation for the commodity price in any month m where there are marketings in period c but not in base year 1997, and will ignore any monthly price in base year 1997 representing actual marketings if there were not also marketings of the same commodity in the same calendar month of the basket reference period, both of which are avoided using formula II. This is inevitable since any other seasonal weighting pattern will be less representative of base year 1997 than its own weighting pattern.

On the other hand, if one is going to use one seasonal weighting pattern for all other years, it is hard to justify using a different pattern for base year 1997, especially since this would lead to the absurdity that the annual index for 1997 in the second variant would be:

$$(3.8) \quad P_{97/97}^{R(II)} = \frac{\sum \bar{p}_{97}^j q_c^j}{\sum p_{97}^j q_c^j} \neq 1.$$

Of course no statistical agency would publish such an estimate; the 1997 value would be normalized to one, inducing a slight break between December 1997 and January 1998. It would be pointless to apply the rebasing factor used to normalize 1997 to all years of the series, since then the annual series for variant II would be identical with the annual series for variant III:

$$(3.9) \quad P_{y/97}^{R(II)} = (1 / \frac{\sum \bar{p}_{97}^j q_c^j}{\sum p_{97}^j q_c^j}) \frac{\sum \bar{p}_y^j q_c^j}{\sum p_{97}^j q_c^j} = \frac{\sum p_{97}^j q_c^j}{\sum \bar{p}_{97}^j q_c^j} \times \frac{\sum \bar{p}_y^j q_c^j}{\sum p_{97}^j q_c^j} = \frac{\sum \bar{p}_y^j q_c^j}{\sum \bar{p}_{97}^j q_c^j},$$

although the monthly series would still differ somewhat:

$$(3.10) \quad P_{y,m/97}^{R(II)} = (1 / \frac{\sum \bar{p}_{97}^j q_c^j}{\sum p_{97}^j q_c^j}) \times \frac{\sum p_{y,m}^j q_{c,m}^j}{\sum p_{97}^j q_{c,m}^j} = \frac{\sum p_{97}^j q_c^j}{\sum \bar{p}_{97}^j q_c^j} \times \frac{\sum p_{y,m}^j q_{c,m}^j}{\sum p_{97}^j q_{c,m}^j} \neq \frac{\sum \bar{p}_y^j q_c^j}{\sum \bar{p}_{97}^j q_c^j}.$$

As a practical matter, consumer price indexes not subject to revision must always use the most broadly defined Rothwell formula, as is also the case for industry price indexes if they do not allow revisions over many months (11 months, if not more). Perhaps this is why most of the literature does not really bother to distinguish between these different variants and they are all treated as representing the Rothwell formula. Szulc (1983, p.560) rightly complains about the lax terminology that would equate any fixed-basket index with a Laspeyres index, and the errors of reasoning into which this can lead one. However there do not seem to be the same dangers

Andrew Baldwin

associated with calling variant III a Rothwell index rather than say, a monthly-basket Lowe index with basket-weighted base prices or with calling variant II a monthly-basket Lowe index with unit values as base prices, although the three different variants do have somewhat different characteristics.

In the FPPI, only variant III of the Rothwell formula is used, although with its extended revision period it would be possible to use variant II instead.

4. The Previous FPPI (1986=100)

The FPPI that was discontinued with the release of March 1996 data had the formula:

$$(4.1) \quad P^{FB}_{y,m/86} = \frac{\sum p^j_{y,m} q^j_{81-84}}{\sum p^j_{86} q^j_{81-84}}; y = 1981,1982,$$

where $P^{FB}_{y,m/86}$ stands for the index for the mth month of year y with a 1986 base, and the FB superscript indicates that it is a fixed-basket index, and $p^j_{86} q^j_{81-84}$ is the hybrid expenditure representing expenditures for commodity j from 1981 to 1984 revalued at 1986 prices. To reduce the burden of notation, hereafter, unless required to remove ambiguity, summation over commodities will be assumed, and the commodity superscript will be omitted.

Note that, although a fixed-basket formula was used, the historical FPPI was not a Laspeyres price index. The Laspeyres equivalent of formula (1) would be:

$$(4.2) \quad P^{FB}_{y,m/86} = \frac{\sum p^j_{y,m} q^j_{86}}{\sum p^j_{86} q^j_{86}}; y = 1981,1982,...,$$

which has the obvious disadvantages, compared to (4.1), that the weighting pattern would almost certainly not be representative of some agricultural commodities that would have unusually low levels of output in 1986, and one would have to wait on 1986 receipts data before implementing (4.2); i.e., there would be smaller revisions using equation (4.1), since when the initial estimates for 1986 marketings became available the marketings for 1981-84 had already been revised several times.

5. The New FPPI (1997=100)

The new annual FPPI is defined as

$$(5.1) \quad P^{ch}_{y/97} = P^{ch}_{y-1/97} \times \frac{\sum p^j_y (\sum_{k=1}^{5} q^j_{y-1-k})}{\sum p^j_{y-1} (\sum_{k=1}^{5} q^j_{y-1-k})}.$$

The new index's basket is updated every year, whereas the old index's basket was updated every 10 years at most. A basket update no longer implies a change in the base year of the index, as it did in the old index, so it is no longer necessary to rebase the entire historical series every time a new basket is introduced. However, the observations for the new index do not have the nice properties of a fixed-basket index, as they did with the old index. For example, for the year 1999, one calculates an unlinked series with the year 1998 as base, and a basket based on marketings in 1993-97 for all of the months from January 1998 to December 1999. This is an update from the basket used to calculate 1998, when the basket was based on marketings in 1992-96. With each January updating a year is dropped and a year is added in calculating a new index basket.

The unlinked estimate for 1999 is then multiplied by the chain price index number for 1998 on a 1997 base to get the chain index number for 1999 on a 1997 base. The basket is updated but there is no change in the base year of the index, and there are no revisions to previous years of the series.

It is tempting to call the procedure for updating the basket a five-year moving average, but it is a little misleading to do so, since from one year to another the farm cash receipts are evaluated at different prices. The receipts for 1992-96 are evaluated at 1997 prices, those for 1993-97 at 1998 prices. Evaluating 1993-97 receipts at 1998 prices means that for each commodity receipts for 1993 are deflated by a price index for 1993, receipts for 1994 are deflated by a price index for 1994, and so forth, where all price indexes used as deflators are on a 1998 base. The unlinked series for 1999 is then a fixed-basket index with a 1998 base and a 1993-97 basket. It would only be correct to speak of a five-year moving average of marketings if all baskets were evaluated at the same prices, but this is not so for the calculation of the index.

In the new FPPI, baskets are updated in a far more timely way than they were in the old FPPI. The last time the old index was updated, it was to a 1981-84 basket, an updating that occurred in December 1986. The movement of the old index was revised backward to 1981 based on the new index basket, and the index was rebased to 1981. There was no linking involved to calculate the index from January 1981 forward, since it was essentially a direct fixed-basket index with a 1981-84 basket and a 1981 base period.

On the other hand, it was necessary to backward link the historical series, prior to 1981, so that it too was available on a 1981 base. Because of this linking process, the indexes for the period 1971-80 no longer had the nice properties of a fixed-basket index that they possessed on a 1971 base. For example, it was no longer necessarily true that an aggregate index would have a value somewhere between that of its smallest and largest component series. But the direct fixed-basket index, from 1981 forward, did have these properties.

Because it is a chain index, any time the new index has its time base changed (for example, from 1997 to 2002), it will be a simple arithmetic operation, not involving any change in basket. Also, because there is a two-year lag between the last year of the five-year basket and the year that the index is updated to incorporate it, there is never any need to revise the index because of basket updatings.

There are many advantages to the new basket update procedures. The most obvious advantage is operational. There is considerably less work involved in any given basket updating than there was previously, and because they occur every year, they are easier to accommodate in the production schedule. Any decision to move to a new base period can also be easily accommodated because only an arithmetic rebasing of the chain price indexes is required.

However, the more important advantage is conceptual. The FPPI is used as both a short term and a long term indicator of price changes. People interested in making price comparisons from year to year and in following the evolution of price movements over decades both make use of the FPPI. In order to make long term comparisons feasible it is necessary for the index basket to be updated from time to time. An index of farm product prices based on a 1935-39 basket would not be very useful for analyzing farm price movements in the 21st century. On the other hand, any change in basket inevitably creates a discontinuity in the monthly or annual movements of the series.

Infrequent basket changes reduce the number of discontinuities in the series, but make them more important when they occur. Moreover, infrequent basket changes create problems of their own. It may be necessary to proxy a price index for a commodity in a province where it is no longer produced. On the other hand it is not possible to introduce a new product until there is a new basket updating, which may not occur until long after a new commodity has obtained a substantial market share. With annual updating of baskets, new commodities can be added to a basket and old items deleted from it in any year.

Generally speaking, a chain price index should be constructed so that the basket used in its initial year is representative of that year, the basket used in its terminal year is representative of that year and the baskets lying between smoothly between the initial and terminal baskets, being approximately linear combinations of the two baskets. The chain price index formula used in the FPPI satisfies these criteria. A 1986-90 basket is reasonably representative of 1992 and a 1995-99 basket of 2001, while the use of a five-year basket reference period ensures that the interim baskets change smoothly from the initial to the terminal basket.

It would not be desirable to link in basket changes that were quickly reversed in later updatings. This would happen if, for example, one linked monthly, so that every twelfth update one would approximately circle back to the initial basket. It would also happen if there were only a single year determining the weighting pattern. The basket for a given year y that experienced normal weather conditions following a year in which there was a severe drought would have more in common with the baskets of earlier years than with the basket for the previous year.

Any index basket must have its expenditures expressed in terms of the constant prices of its base period in the case of a direct index, or of its link period, in the case of a chain index. The Industry Product Price Index (IPPI) basket is based on 1992 expenditures and they are not re-expressed in the prices of any other year. This is because from 1992 forward the IPPI is a direct Laspeyres index and its basket reference year and its base year are one and the same. There is no need to re-express its expenditure weights in terms of prices of another year.

The FPPI is not a direct Laspeyres index, but a chain index, and at the annual level, a chain fixed-basket index. The link year for the 1994-98 basket is 1999, so all expenditures before

1999 are re-expressed at 1999 prices. In general, any five-year basket whose initial year is y-5 has its expenditures re-expressed at prices of year y.

This ensures a measure of price change for consecutive years that involves only the prices of those years, and does not depend in any way on the prices of the five preceding years.

The FPPI practice is identical with that of the consumer price index. Its most recent basket reference year is 1996, but since the 1996 basket is only linked into the index at December 1998, 1996 expenditures are re-expressed at December 1998 prices.

A direct comparison of the baskets for two different years is an apples with oranges comparison if it is based on the weighting patterns used in the actual FPPI calculation. The 1992-96 basket is evaluated at 1997 prices, while the 1993-97 basket is evaluated at 1998 prices. If a comparison between the two weighting patterns shows a substantial increase in the basket share of a particular commodity for the more recent basket it is unclear if it due to a rise in that commodity's share of the volume of marketings from 1992-96 to 1993-97, or merely due to an increase in its price relative to other commodities from 1997 to 1998.

Any comparison of index baskets should be based on a common set of prices. In a comparison between the new index basket and the previous basket one would generally re-evaluate the basket used for the previous year at the same prices used to evaluate the current year basket. For example, for the 2002 update, a 1996-2000 basket is evaluated at 2001 prices. A comparison with the previous 1995-99 basket at 2000 prices is inappropriate; instead the previous basket should be evaluated at 2001 prices to match the current basket.

An acceptable alternative would be to evaluate both baskets at base year prices (that is, at 1997 prices), especially if three or more baskets were being compared. Just because farm prices are so volatile, there would be some merit in basing comparisons for several baskets on a multi-year base period, say 1996-99 prices rather than 1997 prices.

The FPPI contains many commodities that are unavailable in December (e.g. apricots, broccoli, cauliflower). It is not possible to link at December for these series without imputing a December price for them, and it would be better to avoid linking based on imputed prices.

One reason the CPI links at December is to ensure that the December-to-January movement is a measure of pure price change, that is, if all prices show the same rate of change from December to January, the total index will show the identical rate of change. A special case of this would be if all prices in January were the same as those in December; then the total index should show zero change. Linking at December ensures that December and January prices are both measured in terms of the new basket, whereas linking at the year would distort the comparison because of the shift from the old to the new basket. (Whether this objective is achieved, given the number of seasonally disappearing commodities in the CPI, is a moot point.)

However, in the FPPI the December to January comparison is distorted by the shift from one monthly basket to the next in any case, so this reason for linking at December does not exist. The question then becomes whether it is more important to link at December and preserve the December-to-December movement as a measure of pure price change or to link at the year, and preserve the year-to-year movement as a measure of pure price change. As was just mentioned many agricultural commodities have no marketings in December, so the year-to-year measure is much more representative of agricultural production in general than the December-to-December movement. The obvious choice for the FPPI is to link at the year.

It is not necessary to have monthly data for the earlier year to correctly calculate the chain index. This is done for analytical purposes. In a monthly-basket index the 12-month ratios of the index numbers (e.g. January over January, February over February, etc.) should be measures of pure price change, that is, if there is no change in any of the prices from one month to the next, the index change should be nil. While there is a change in the index basket from one month to the next, there is no change in the index basket between the same calendar months of consecutive years. Unfortunately, this is not the case in the FPPI because it is an annually-chained index, so the basket does change between the same calendar months of consecutive years. We calculate the chain links as 24-month spans so that we can decompose the 12-month change in the index between a pure price change component (i.e. what the change would be if the index kept its original basket) and a component for the interaction between price change and basket change. It means that every year is essentially calculated twice: The year 1999 will be calculated initially based on a 1994-98 basket, and these estimates will become part of the FPPI. It will be calculated again based on a 1995-99 basket, and these estimates will only be used to analyze price movements between 1999 and 2000.

There would be some merit in calculating each unlinked span for an extra year, so that if the basket went from year y-5 to y-1 it would be calculated over the years from y-1 to y, even though it would only be used as the basket for year y. This would mean that each year-over-year change would be comparable with a previous year-over-year change based on the same basket. Also, the pure price change component of each 12-month change would be comparable to a 12-month change for the previous year based on the identical basket.

This was not implemented because it is already a fair amount of extra work to calculate all unlinked series over a 24-month span, and it would have no influence on the quality of the index itself, only the quality of the analysis. Nevertheless, this is something that might be implemented in the future.

Prior to the revision of the FPPI, Statistics Canada calculated other industry price indexes that were chained annually. The New Housing Price Index (NHPI), for example, has its basket updated every year to reflect building completions for the last three years at base year constant prices, and these are used to weight component price indexes with the same base year for the thirteen months from December to December only, linking being at December rather than at the year. Since linking is at December, the December-to-December movement is a measure of pure price change, but the same is not true for any calendar month. There is no way to know how much of the 12-month change in the NHPI is due to pure price change because of the short span of the calculation. Consequently, analysts are forced either to ignore the 12-month changes in the index, or to treat them as if they were measures of pure price change, even though this is not so.

Likewise, the year-to-year movement of the NHPI does not represent a measure of pure price change, unlike the year-to-year movement of the FPPI. There is no way of knowing how the change from one basket to another distorts this year-to-year movement, as one would know if each consecutive unlinked NHPI series were calculated over a 24-month span, like the FPPI.

At the annual level, the FPPI is a chain fixed-basket price index, but not a chain Laspeyres price index. If it were a true chain Laspeyres index the choice of base period would impact on the series movement, since a single-year base period would imply a single-year basket.

6. The New Monthly FPPI (1997=100)

The new monthly FPPI is defined as

$$(6.1) \quad P^{ch}_{y,m/97} = P^{ch}_{y-1/97} \times \frac{\sum p^j_{y,m}(\sum_{k=1}^{5} \hat{q}^j_{y-1-k,m})}{\sum p^j_{y-1}(\sum_{k=1}^{5} q^j_{y-1-k})}.$$

For each product, for each province, the average of marketings for the five years of 1994-98 are calculated for each month of the year. Then the 12 monthly shares for the province-product pair are calculated. To obtain the monthly revenue weight for a given province-pair, the annual revenue weight for a particular year is multiplied by the relevant monthly share. The sum of these monthly weights equals the annual weight.

Algebraically:

$$(6.2) \quad (\sum_{k=1}^{5} \hat{q}^j_{y-1-k,m}) = w^j_m \times (\sum_{k=1}^{5} q^j_{y-1-k}),$$

where

$$(6.3) \quad w^j_m = \sum_{y=1994}^{1998} q^j_{y,m} / \sum_{y=1994}^{1998} q^j_y.$$

The annual price of a commodity is defined as

$$(6.4) \quad p^j_y = \frac{\sum p^j_{y,m}(\sum_{k=1}^{5} \hat{q}^j_{y-1-k,m})}{(\sum_{k=1}^{5} \hat{q}^j_{y-1-k,m})}.$$

Note that this is not a unit price (i.e. the revenues for a given year divided by same year marketings), like the annual prices to be found in a Balk index (discussed below).

One of the major strengths of the new approach is its handling of seasonally disappearing commodities. Using the old annual-basket approach, commodities, for example, sweet corn and strawberries had the same basket share in every month of the year. One had to impute prices for such commodities in months when there were no marketings. Using a monthly-basket approach, if there were no marketings for a commodity in a given month in 1994-98, then it would simply fall out of the index basket. There would be no need to impute a fictive price for it.

When prices are first established for seasonal fresh fruits and vegetables, they are based on farm income forecast work carried out by Agriculture and Agri-Food Canada (AAFC), the provinces and Statistics Canada. At the end of the season a survey is conducted to obtain the amount of the commodity harvested and the dollar value received for the crop. Based on these data, an average price for the season is established. Farmers sell their product at whatever the market offers, however, it would be prohibitively costly to collect monthly prices for the wide range of commodities to which prices must be assigned. One price for the season is established and farm cash receipts data are calculated from that price using an established marketing pattern for each of the commodities.

If there were no marketings for a seasonal commodity in a given month in 1994-98 but there were some thereafter, there would be a shift in the overall seasonal pattern of production of an agricultural commodity that is substantial enough to make the season last an additional month, though this does not happen very often. But if this did happen, the monthly weighting patterns for fresh vegetables would be updated when we move to a 2001 base, to adjust to the new seasonal profile of marketings.

Until then, we would simply ignore any prices for fresh corn in November and they would have no impact on our index. In the existing weighting pattern, even the month of October has only a 5% share of marketings of fresh corn for the province of Ontario, and November has nothing. So any marketings of corn in November would likely account for much less than 5% of the corn total. Assuming a marketings share of 0%, as is done now, is much closer to reality than assuming a share of 8⅓% (one twelfth), as under the old fixed-basket approach.

If there were marketings for fresh corn in November 2001 but not for any other year in the decade, such marketings might be reflected in an updated seasonal weighting pattern if the year 2001 were part of it. Obviously if one only has November marketings of fresh corn about once every 10 years, there would be little cause to extend the in-season months for fresh corn to include November and one would probably be well advised to edit out such expenditures from the seasonal weighting pattern.

What about the opposite problem? Suppose that, due to an early frost, there are no marketings of corn in October? This kind of scenario is more likely to occur than the one we just discussed. In this case, there would be no market price for corn but it would still have a basket share in the October index, so an imputed price would have to be assigned to it.

In such situations, the imputed price would be the weighted average price for the months through September. Though one could argue for other solutions, such an imputation is simple, does not depend on price information external to the stratum or the commodity in question, and gives the same annual price one would obtain by simply ignoring October in calculating the annual price. Also, as noted, only one annual price is calculated now for seasonally disappearing commodities, so it is logical to impute this price in a month where there are no marketings.

Only one annual price is calculated for seasonally disappearing commodities so this is the price that would be assigned. If sufficient resources ever became available to have monthly pricing for some of these commodities, then another imputation procedure would be needed.

In the official Consumer Price Index, imputation for seasonally disappearing commodities is based on the price movement of continuously priced items in the same group as the target series. This amounts to a poor man's version of seasonal weighting. If the FPPI had monthly pricing for seasonally disappearing items, it could seek to impute prices for out-of-season months more in line with the economic notion of shadow or scarcity prices.

All farm commodities without exception have seasonal marketing patterns and on this basis it makes sense to calculate the whole index as a seasonal-basket index. The European

Union (EU) approach, which requires that fresh fruit and fresh vegetables have fixed-basket shares within the overall index has the drawback of not being consistent in aggregation. If one reformulates such an index in terms of greenhouse products and field products for example, and aggregates to a total, one will not get the same result as using the primary commodity classification. This problem does not exist for the FPPI aggregation; one gets the same overall index however one chooses to reorganize groups and subgroups of commodities because they are all generated from the same underlying seasonal weighting patterns.

Even if one were to adopt a more restrictive definition of seasonal commodities it is difficult to justify limiting it to fresh fruit and vegetables as the EU does. What about Christmas trees which are far more seasonal in their marketings than virtually any item of fresh produce?

It should be remembered that in defining their standard for harmonization the EU was constrained by the fact that its standard must be implemented by a country like Luxemburg with both limited resources for calculating farm product price indexes and limited interest, given their modest agricultural bases, in doing so. Also, virtually none of the countries in the EU, with the possible exception of Finland, would have such an extreme seasonal profile of production as Canada. In many European countries field production can generate two or more crops a year, something that Canadian farmers can only dream about.

In Canada, the input counterpart of the FPPI is the farm input price index (FIPI). The FIPI is now an annual price index so for now at least a seasonal-basket price index is a moot point. The source of weights for the FIPI when it was a quarterly index was Farm Operating Expenses and Depreciation Charges for 1992. This was an annual survey and so did not provide the weighting information required to calculate a seasonal-basket index. This being said, many of the expenses associated with farming (fertilizer use, seeding) are seasonal, and this would argue for a seasonal-basket approach to the FIPI if the quarterly FIPI were restored and redesigned in the manner of the FPPI. Yet many of the expenses associated with farming (mortgage and non-mortgage interest, farm rent) are decidedly non-seasonal, so a top-to-bottom seasonal-basket approach such as has been implemented in the FPPI redesign would not appropriate for the FIPI.

7.   Price Imputations for Seasonally Disappearing Commodities

It is sometimes necessary to make price imputations for seasonally disappearing commodities if one's monthly weighting pattern is based on a typical seasonal profile rather than the monthly marketings of the year in question. The Dutch economist Bert Balk (1980a and 1980b) suggested that the monthly weights for a given year be based on the given year pattern of marketings and the Balk formula actually was implemented by the Netherlands Central Bureau of Statistics for their price index numbers of output and input of goods and services of agriculture, the Dutch counterparts of our own FPPI and farm input price index (FIPI). Using the Balk formula, there is never any need for seasonal imputation, and there are never any monthly prices that go ignored in the index. If marketings for corn exceptionally occur in December then because the weighting is based on current marketings its December prices are incorporated in the December measure. If on the other hand there are no marketings in October, then corn drops out of the index in that month for that year, but not for other months where there are marketings. There is no need to impute an October price for corn if there are no marketings.

From an operational viewpoint, a Balk index is more difficult to calculate than the Rothwell index (the FPPI uses the Rothwell formula) and more subject to revision. It would not be consistent to adopt a basket reference period that does not incorporate the given year but uses a seasonal-basket formula based on the given year seasonal pattern. From a conceptual viewpoint, the greater representativeness of the Balk index is obtained at a price in comparability. Dikhanov (1999, p. 2) has noted that the idea of achieving both comparability and representativeness in a price index is not unlike the Heisenberg Uncertainty Principle in nuclear physics on determining location and speed of an elementary particle: it is impossible to determine both simultaneously. The 12-month changes of the unlinked spans of the FPPI are measures of pure price change; those of the Balk index are distorted by basket shifts. That being said, it would be of considerable interest to recalculate the FPPI according to the Balk formula.

8. Understanding the Monthly Changes

Because the index basket changes from one month to the next, the FPPI does not provide a measure of pure price change for monthly movements. Even if there is no change in prices from one month to the next there can still be a change in the index due to the basket change.

However it is possible to decompose the monthly change in the FPPI, as with the change in a Paasche price index, into a pure price change component and a residual component, for all months except January. The December-to-January change is distorted not only by the switch from one monthly basket to another but from one annual basket to another. However, the December-to-January change of the unlinked series can be decomposed in the same way as the changes for the other months of the year.

The pure price change component measures what the change in the FPPI would be if there were no change in the monthly basket. The October-to-November measure then would be based on the October basket. Because the October basket is used in both months of the year, the calculation of the pure price change component entails the calculation of imputed prices for some commodities that go out of season in November, fresh corn for example.

The monthly price movements of the FPPI do not mean very much, especially for the most seasonal commodity groups like fruits and vegetables, but neither do the monthly movements for a fixed-basket price index. What precisely would the June-to-July movement for a fixed-basket price index for fresh vegetables signify for example? If the price of corn were imputed using the last in-season price then the June-to-July movement for corn would actually reflect the October-to-June movement. If this movement were substantial enough, the measured June-to-July movement for fresh vegetables might actually exceed the June-to-July movements of any of the vegetable items for which prices existed in both June and July. Thus the fixed-basket price index would contradict one of the basic characteristics of an indicator of pure price change: that the aggregate measure should be bounded by its highest and lowest components.

It is only when one reconstructs monthly price movements using the monthly baskets that are building blocks of seasonal-basket price indexes that any meaningful analysis is possible. The mechanics of obtaining monthly measures of price change is discussed in the appendix.

9. Comparing the FPPI in Canada with the U.S. Prices Received by Farmers Index

A major inspiration was the reconstruction of the U.S. Prices Received by Farmers Index. It had a number of features that were emulated in the FPPI redesign:

- A seasonal weighting pattern for the 12 months of the year for all commodities,

- An update of the index basket every year based on marketings for the last five years,

- A considerable increase in the commodity coverage of the index.

Officials in the United States Department of Agriculture (USDA) were most helpful in responding to enquiries about their index, which was of great benefit to the FPPI redesign.

Plans to introduce a seasonal weighting pattern for the FPPI when its basket was next updated had already been made when the index was discontinued in 1995. Nevertheless, the USDA's switch to a seasonal-basket approach was a great encouragement to everyone who worked on the FPPI redesign. It confirmed that a seasonal-basket approach from top to bottom was viable, and it provided an additional incentive (compatibility with the USDA index) for adopting a seasonal-basket approach for the FPPI.

The FPPI is a chain index with a new annual basket linked into the index every year, and where the link is at the year and not at the month. The USDA index is more like a Paasche price index, with a new annual basket slipped into the index every year, without any linking. This means that the annual price change is not a measure of pure price change, as it is in the FPPI.

For each year, the USDA calculates a five-year average of farm cash receipts at current prices, so that the weighting pattern reflects the price structure of all five years. By contrast, the FPPI calculates a five-year average of farm cash receipts at link year prices, as described above. Therefore the weighting pattern of the FPPI reflects the pattern of marketings of the five different years but the price structure only of the base year, while the weighting pattern of the USDA index reflects the pattern of marketings of the five different years, and also the price structure of the five different years.

For example, for the year 2000, the FPPI basket would be based on 1994-1998 farm cash receipts at 1999 prices, which is appropriate to calculating the price change between 1999 and 2000. The USDA weighting pattern would be based on 1994-1998 farm cash receipts at current prices, so the weights reflect 1994-1998 prices. Given that their index formula is more like that of a Paasche price index than anything else, it would make more sense for the USDA to re-express the farm cash receipts at 1990-1992 prices, since the USDA index is at 1990-92=100. But it would be better still if they calculated their index as an annually reweighted chain index, and duplicated the FPPI calculation of annual baskets.

Annual FPPIs are calculated as weighted averages of monthly FPPIs, consistent with the monthly-basket concept of the index. The USDA calculates annual indexes as the means of the monthly indexes, which is inconsistent with its monthly-basket approach to calculating the monthly series, and does not ensure that each month is fairly represented in the annual index.

The FPPI includes commodities for which there are farm cash receipts but no marketings in the index basket, allowing them to influence the relative importance of the category to which they belong (crop or livestock). The USDA index simply excludes such commodities from the index. The index for prices received by farmers has a three-year base period (1990-2); the base period of the FPPI is a single year (1997).

Except for the use of a multi-year base period, all of these differences are improvements on the USDA methodology, and provide a more meaningful indicator of farm price movements.

The USDA methodology notes that "a 3-year ... base period was selected since it provides ... base period prices for comparison purposes that are overall closer to historical price trends than a 1-year period provides." The volatility of farm prices is such that a multi-year base period is to be preferred to any single-year base period.

A 1997 base period was chosen for the FPPI because of the rebasing of SNA expenditure estimates to 1997 constant prices, and the rebasing of most of Statistics Canada's price indexes to 1997=100. It was considered more important to have the FPPI series comparable with other published price indexes than to have a base period that better met its special needs.

This difference between the American and the Canadian index is revelatory of a difference in philosophy between the statistical programs of the two countries. In the United States there are many agencies associated with their statistical program, and there is greater emphasis on delivering products that are useful to their client groups. In Canada there is a centralized statistical agency, Statistics Canada, and there is a greater emphasis on compatibility of all economic statistics with the SNA.

Appendix: Monthly Price Change Analysis for the FPPI

This note discusses the analysis of monthly price changes for the FPPI, which is problematic because the basket changes every month for all commodities. Let the index link for the mth month of 2001 be

$$P_{01,m/00} = \sum_j (\overline{V}^{00j}_{95-99,m} / \sum_j \overline{V}^{00j}_{95-99,m}) \times (p^j_{01,m} / p^j_{00})$$

(A.1)
$$= \sum_j (p^j_{00}\overline{q}^j_{95-99,m} / \sum_j p^j_{00}\overline{q}^j_{95-99,m}) \times (p^j_{01,m} / p^j_{00})$$

$$= \sum_j p^j_{01,m}\overline{q}^j_{95-99,m} / \sum_j p^j_{00}\overline{q}^j_{95-99,m}$$

where $\overline{q}^j_{95-99,m}$ represents average marketings for the jth commodity over 1995-99 for the mth month of the calendar year, $\overline{V}^{00j}_{95-99,m}$ represents the value of these marketings at year 2000 prices, and $p^j_{01,m}$ is the price of the jth commodity in the mth month of 2001.[4] The index link for the m+1st month is then equal to:

---

[4] For this analysis of contributions to change, the discussion is always in terms of chain links and therefore the indexes of interest are the chain links at link period prices. Since the example used in this note relates to the calculation of the April-May 2001 indexes, all of the formulas are in terms of the 2000-2001 link series, which is at

$$P_{01,m+1/00} = \sum_j (V^{00j}_{95-99,m+1} / \sum_j V^{00j}_{95-99,m+1}) \times (p^j_{01,m+1}/p^j_{00})$$

$$\text{(A.2)} \quad = \sum_j (p^j_{00}\bar{q}^j_{95-99,m+1} / \sum_j p^j_{00}\bar{q}^j_{95-99,m+1}) \times (p^j_{01,m+1}/p^j_{00})$$

$$= \sum_j p^j_{01,m+1}\bar{q}^j_{95-99,m} / \sum_j p^j_{00}\bar{q}^j_{95-99,m}$$

The ratio of the two indexes equals:

(A.3)

$$P_{01,m+1/00} / P_{01,m/00} =$$

$$(\sum_j p^j_{01,m+1}\bar{q}^j_{95-99,m+1} / \sum_j p^j_{01,m}\bar{q}^j_{95-99,m})/(\sum_j p^j_{00}\bar{q}^j_{95-99,m+1} / \sum_j p^j_{01}\bar{q}^j_{95-99,m}).$$

It can be seen that the expression in the first set of brackets on the right hand side of (A.3) defines a price index for the m+1st month of year y with the previous month as the base. However the prices are weighted differently in the numerator and the denominator, in each case prices are weighted by marketings for their own month of the calendar year. Therefore even if

$$\text{(A.4)} \quad p^j_{01,m} = p^j_{01,m+1}$$

for all j, the index number would not necessarily be equal to one, that is, even if there were no price changes for any of the components of the index, it might still register a positive or negative price change due to shifts in the quantity weights. Therefore, the monthly change for the price index does not satisfy the proportionality test.

The expression in the second set of brackets on the right hand side of (A.3) defines a volume index for the m+1st month with respect to the mth month at 2000 constant prices. This index will also generally differ from one, if there is a seasonal production profile. It will be equal to one in the special case where $\bar{q}^j_{95-99,m+1} = \bar{q}^j_{95-99,m}$ for all j. In this case, (A.1) will simplify to:

$$\text{(A.5)} \quad P_{01,m+1/00} / P_{01,m/00} = (\sum_j p^j_{01,m+1}\bar{q}^j_{95-99,m} / \sum_j p^j_{01,m}\bar{q}^j_{95-99,m})$$

which is a measure of pure price change, since if (A.4) holds for all j, then (A.5) will equal one.

Let $W^{00,j}_{95-99,m} = \bar{V}^{00,j}_{95-99,m} / \sum_j \bar{V}^{00,j}_{95-99,m}$ and $P^j_{01,m} = p^j_{01,m}/p^j_{00}$. Then, expressing the indexes as weighted averages of price relatives, one can write the difference between the indexes for two consecutive months in terms of the following decomposition:

year 2000 prices. Thus the 00 subscript does not indicate any base year 0, like the 0 subscript that one often sees in index number formulas, but rather the specific link year 2000.

Andrew Baldwin

$$P_{01,m+1/00} - P_{01,m/00} = \sum_j W_{95-99m+1}^{00j} P_{01,m+1/00}^j - \sum_j W_{95-99m}^{00j} P_{01,m/00}^j$$

(A6)
$$= \sum_j W_{95-99m}^{00j}(P_{01,m+1/00}^j - P_{01,m/00}^j) + \sum_j (W_{95-99m+1}^{00j} - W_{95-99m}^{00j})P_{01,m+1/00}^j.$$

The first term on the right hand side of the second equals sign is the pure price change component of the change. This is the difference between two index numbers for a fixed-basket index for months m and m+1, with a basket based on the mth month. The second term is the difference in the two baskets at prices of the m+1st month of 2001. It is a measure of the residual change in the index, that is, the interaction between weight change and price change.

People familiar with the literature on the Paasche price index and on implicit price indexes have probably seen a similar decomposition for those indexes. It should be obvious that the same decomposition applies if one looks at the percent change between indexes for two consecutive months rather than the simple difference:

$$100 \times (P_{01,m+1/00} - P_{01,m/00})/P_{01,m/00}$$

$$= 100 \times (\sum_j W_{95-99m+1}^{00j} P_{01,m+1/00}^j - \sum_j W_{95-99m}^{00j} P_{01,m/00}^j)/\sum_j W_{95-99m}^{00j} P_{01,m/00}^j$$

$$= 100 \times \sum_j W_{95-99m}^{00j}(P_{01,m+1/00}^j - P_{01,m/00}^j)/\sum_j W_{95-99m}^{00j} P_{01,m/00}^j$$

$$+ 100 \times \sum_j (W_{95-99m+1}^{00j} - W_{95-99m}^{00j})P_{01,m+1/00}^j /\sum_j W_{95-99m}^{00j} P_{01,m/00}^j$$

Another way of decomposing the difference between the indexes for consecutive months evaluates pure price change in terms of the basket of the later month rather than the earlier one:

(A7) $$\sum_j W_{95-99,m+1}^{00}(P_{01,m+1/00}^j - P_{01,m/00}^j) + \sum_j (W_{95-99,m+1}^{00} - W_{95-99,m}^{00})P_{01,m/00}^j.$$

Again the first term represents pure price change and the second term the interaction between price changes and basket changes. However, the same thing can *not* be said of (A.7) when it is put in percent change form:

$$100 \times \sum_j W_{95-99,m+1}^{00}(P_{01,m+1/00}^j - P_{01,m/00}^j)/\sum_j W_{95-99,m}^{00} P_{01,m/00}^j$$

$$+ 100 \times \sum_j (W_{95-99,m+1}^{00} - W_{95-99,m}^{00})P_{01,m/00}^j /\sum_j W_{95-99,m}^{00} P_{01,m/00}^j$$

It can be seen that the numerator of the first term represents weights for month m+1, while the denominator represents weights for month m, so it does not represent a measure of pure price change, and will be distorted by shifts in the basket from month m to month m+1. Thus, while it might seem that there is no reason to favour the earlier month over the later month in choosing a common basket for price comparison, this is not in fact the case. The reason for this is the conventions governing percent changes; like one of the faces of Janus, they only look backward. For some reason, we have come to look at percent changes always using the earlier period value to scale first differences, never the later period value or some average of them. Thus in decomposing the percent change between month m and month m+1 for a seasonal-basket index, the percent change generated by a fixed-basket index based on the earlier month m is the only appropriate measure of its pure price change component.

The December to January movement, and in general, any sub-annual movement that crosses the December boundary poses special problems for the FPPI since it is a chain index as well as a seasonal-basket index. However, since December 2000 would be calculated based on a 1995-99 basket even though it is not used in calculating its official index (which is based on 1994-98) it is possible to get a measure of pure price change from December 2000 to January 2001 based on a basket for December 1995-99, that is:

$$100 \times \sum_j W^{00j}_{95-99,12} (P^j_{01,1/00} - P^j_{00,12/00}) / \sum_j W^{00j}_{95-99,12} P^j_{00,12/00}.$$

It is obvious that the contribution of any given component to the monthly percent change of the aggregate can be calculated as

$$100 \times (\sum_j W^{00j}_{95-99m+1} P^j_{01,m+1/00} - \sum_j W^{00j}_{95-99m} P^j_{01,m/00}) / P_{01,m/00}.$$

Table A1 below shows such a calculation for a particular case, the FPPI for potatoes in Alberta between April and May of 2001. Two of the three components, accounting for almost 85% of the April basket share, dropped substantially in price in the month of May; only processing potatoes showed an increase in price. Nevertheless, the FPPI for potatoes increased by 12.1% in May -- almost as large an increase as for processing potatoes themselves.

Table A1. Contributions to Percent Change for the Albertan FPPI for Table Potatoes

Commodity	Basket Share		$P_{t/2000}$		%Ch	Cntrbtn to Agg %Ch
	April 2001	May 2001	April 2001	May 2001		
Total Potatoes	100.00%	100.00%	84.77	95.06	12.1%	12.1%
Local and Table Potatoes	12.82%	30.17%	72.54	66.25	-8.7%	12.6%
Seed Potatoes	71.80%	24.84%	81.57	77.50	-5.0%	-46.4%
Processing Potatoes	15.38%	44.99%	109.92	124.07	12.9%	45.9%

Table A1 indicates how this puzzling result was established. There are strong shifts in basket shares for components between April and May, with seed potatoes falling in importance from the dominant component to the least important, and losing more of its basket share to processing potatoes (whose price increased in May) than to local and table potatoes, whose price dropped in the same month.

As a result the contributions to aggregate percent change of all three of the components are much greater in magnitude than their own percent changes, something which can, of course, never be found in the percent changes of a fixed-basket index, where the contribution to percent change is always a fraction of its own percent change. The contribution of processing potatoes to the aggregate percent change is 45.9%, between three and four times its own percentage increase. Local and table potatoes, although it decreased by 8.7% in May, has a positive contribution to change of 12.6%, a function of its increase in basket share from 13% to 30%. Seed potatoes dropped by 5% in May, but its contribution to percent change is –46.4%, the result of its dramatic slide from a 72% to a 25% basket share. However, this negative contribution is swamped by the positive contributions of the other two components.

The more meaningful contribution is probably the contribution of the component to the pure price change portion of the monthly index change, which is

$$(A.8) \quad 100 \times W_{95-99m}^{00j} \times (P_{01,m+1/00}^{j} - P_{01,m/00}^{j})/P_{01,m/00}.$$

Table A2 shows these contributions to percent changes based on an April basket for Alberta potatoes, that is, where $m=4$. Note that the contribution for local and table potatoes is now negative, matching its price decrease for May, and the contributions for the other two components continue to match their signs. None of the contributions is larger in absolute magnitude than its contribution to change, since this cannot happen for a fixed-basket index.

Table A2. Contributions to Percent Change for the Albertan FPPI for Table Potatoes
Pure Price Change Component (Based on an April Basket)
(May Index Number for Total Potatoes Is Not Equal to the Published FPPI Estimate)

Commodity	Basket Share	$P_{t/2000}$ April 2001	$P_{t/2000}$ May 2001	%Ch	Cntrbtn to Agg %Ch
Total Potatoes	100.00%	84.77	83.22	-1.8%	-1.8%
Local and Table Potatoes	12.82%	72.54	66.25	-8.7%	-1.0%
Seed Potatoes	71.80%	81.57	77.50	-5.0%	-3.4%
Processing Potatoes	15.38%	109.92	124.07	12.9%	2.6%

The counterpart to this price change component is the residual component, defined as

$$100 \times (W_{95-99m+1}^{00j} - W_{95-99m}^{00j}) P_{01,m+1/00}^{j} / P_{01,m/00}.$$

Table A3 shows the calculation of these components for the Alberta table potatoes example. Note that the largest basket change, by far, is for seed potatoes, whose basket share goes from almost three quarters to less than one quarter, while the next largest basket change, for processing potatoes, is substantially smaller and in the opposite direction. However, because the May 2001 index number for processing potatoes is about 60% greater than the corresponding index number for seed potatoes, the two components have contributions to residual change that largely cancel each other out so the residual change for the index largely reflects the positive impact of the local and table potatoes component.

Table A3. Contributions to Percent Change for the Albertan FPPI for Table Potatoes
Residual Component (Where Pure Price Change Is Based on an April Basket)

Commodity	April Basket Share	May Basket Share	Price Index(2000=100) Apr-01	May-01	Cntrbtn to Agg Ch
TOTAL POTATOES	100.00%	100.00%	84.77	95.06	13.96%
Local and Table Potatoes	12.82%	30.17%	72.54	66.25	13.56%
Seed Potatoes	71.80%	24.84%	81.57	77.50	-42.93%
Processing Potatoes	15.38%	44.99%	109.92	124.07	43.33%

Further note that the total contribution for the residual component is 13.96%, which when added to the total pure price change component based on the April basket at -1.83% gives the 12.13% increase of the official FPPI index.

If one makes a calculation based on a May basket, one can no longer speak about a pure price change component of the FPPI monthly movement, because when the May basket is used to evaluate both April and May, the May estimate is equal to the FPPI estimate, but the April estimate is not. Since the April estimate is the denominator of the expression for percent change, and hence for any contributions to percent change from April to May, the April to May change using a May basket does not represent the pure price change part of the FPPI change, or at least not in an additive sense. The formula for percent contribution to change shown in (A8) above, should be rewritten as

$$(A.9) \quad 100 \times W_{95-99m+1}^{00j} \times (P_{01,m+1/00}^{j} - P_{01,m/00}^{j})/P_{01,m/00}^{(m+1)},$$

where $P_{01,m/00}^{(m+1)}$ is the calculation of the aggregate for month m based on the basket for month m+1. However one should note that this measure does generate an increase for total potatoes of 3.8%, like the published FPPI, largely due to the much higher weight attached to the increase in processing potatoes, but also due to the lower weight attached to the decrease in seed potatoes.

Although using the month m basket to measure pure price change has advantages, it also has a substantial shortcoming in the case where there is a dramatic difference between the baskets in months m and m+1. This would seldom be true of livestock series in any given month, but might be, in many months, for crop series. Then neither month is truly representative of the other, and it would be better to calculate some kind of cross of the two series. In this paper, two possible crosses are considered, based on geometric and arithmetic mean formulas.

First, let us look at a geometric mean of indexes based on baskets for months m and m+1. These are Fisher-type comparisons in the sense that they are based on the square root of indexes based on the current and previous month baskets, but they are not Fisher comparisons tout court since the indexes involved do not have the Laspeyres and Paasche formulas.

As noted, if one calculates an index for both months m and m+1 based on the basket for month m+1, the index for m+1 will match the published FPPI but the index for month m will not. The opposite is true for an index based on month m. Thus the geometric mean index will match the FPPI in neither month. As for an index based on month m+1, it would be incorrect to speak of the percent change of the geometric mean index as representing the pure price change component of the FPPI change, since it does not equal the FPPI for month m.

The approximate contribution to change of a component to the geometric mean index would be just the geometric mean of the contributions of components to the indexes based on baskets for months m and m+1, that is:

$$(A.10) \quad [(100 \times W^{00j}_{95-99m} \times (P^{j}_{01,m+1/00} - P^{j}_{01,m/00})/P_{01,m/00})$$

$$\times (100 \times W^{00j}_{95-99m+1} \times (P^{j}_{01,m+1/00} - P^{j}_{01,m/00})/P^{(m+1)}_{01,m/00}]^{1/2}$$

$$= 100 \times [(W^{00j}_{95-99m} \times (P^{j}_{01,m+1/00} - P^{j}_{01,m/00}))$$

$$\times (W^{00j}_{95-99m+1} \times (P^{j}_{01,m+1/00} - P^{j}_{01,m/00})]^{1/2}/P^{GM}_{01,m/00}$$

where $P^{GM}_{01,m/00} = (P_{01,m/00} \times P^{(m+1)}_{01,m/00})^{1/2}$. This would be an approximate, and not an actual contribution, since the sum of the contributions is not generally equal to the percent change of the aggregate. This is in the nature of the calculation; the square root of a sum will not generally equal the sum of the square roots of its components, though the two values should be close.

Table A4 below shows the contributions to change calculated for the previous example of Alberta potatoes. One can see that in the geometric mean calculation the index for total potatoes increases as it does in the published index, but only by 0.9%. This is entirely due to the increase in processing potatoes that would by itself have led to a 4.7% increase in the index. The smaller decrease for seed potatoes has a greater impact on the geometric mean index than the more important decrease for local and table potatoes because the average basket share of seed potatoes in April and May is considerably greater than that of local and table potatoes.

Note that while the sum of the contributions to percent change for all components does not equal the percent change for total potatoes, it very nearly does. In fact, it is only because Table A4 shows these numbers to two decimal places while all other numbers are to a single decimal place that one sees that the percent change for total potatoes (0.93%) differs from the sum of the contributions to percent change (0.94%) by only one hundredth of a percentage point.

Table A4: Approximations to Contributions to Percent Change for an Albertan Price Index for Potatoes. April-May Comparison Based on a Geometric Mean of Indexes for April and May Baskets Respectively (Fisher-Type Indexes). (Neither the April Nor the May Index Number for Total Potatoes Equals the Published FPPI Estimate.)

Commodity	$P_{t/2000}$		%Ch	Cntrbtn to Agg %Ch
	April 2001	May 2001		
Total Potatoes	88.12	88.94	0.93%	0.94%
Local and Table Potatoes	72.54	66.25	-8.7%	-1.5%
Seed Potatoes	81.57	77.50	-5.0%	-2.3%
Processing Potatoes	109.92	124.07	12.9%	4.7%

The geometric mean indexes were calculated following the discussion of the FPPI redesign by the Statistics Canada Price Measurement Advisory Committee on April 24, 2001. The Committee chair, Erwin Diewert, suggested that where there was a big shift in the index basket from one month to another it might be more appropriate to calculate monthly changes based on a Fisher cross rather than a Laspeyres-type estimate. This was good advice and confirmed the doubts that people working on the redesign project had about basing month-to-month comparisons solely on a previous month basket when estimating pure price change.

However, the geometric-mean or Fisher-type indexes have a couple of disadvantages, here listed in declining order of importance:

1.   By their nature, they treat the two months being compared as essentially of equal importance, taking an unweighted geometric mean of indexes based on baskets for each month, even if one of the two months heavily dominates marketings.

2.   Neither Fisher nor geometric mean indexes are consistent in aggregation, so that at each level of aggregation it is necessary to calculate Laspeyres-type and Paasche-type indexes and then take their geometric mean. Essentially one is forced to calculate three sets of analytical indexes even if one is only interested in those of the Fisher type.

The second disadvantage is an operational one rather than an analytical one but may be non-trivial in some production environments. (For the FPPI, given that it is produced on interlocking EXCEL spreadsheets, it is a fairly serious drawback.)

The first disadvantage is the more serious one in general, and is certainly quite serious in our particular example, as the two months are not even remotely of equal importance. At 2000 annual prices, the volume of marketings for Alberta potatoes in April is more than three times as great as in May. These disadvantages can be remedied by calculating a fixed-basket index based on the mean of April and May marketings, that is, an Edgeworth-Marshall-type index. Such an index will appropriately give April more influence on the determination of basket shares than May, and will allow the calculation of weighted averages of component Edgeworth-Marshall-type indexes (i.e. the formula is consistent in aggregation).

The first of these properties is the most important. An Edgeworth-Marshall-type index satisfies the property of transactions equality while the geometric-mean-type index does not.

Table A5 below shows the index generated by an index with an April-May basket, which like the index based on an April basket, shows a price decrease in May, but only a slight decline of -0.4%. It should not be a surprise that both the Laspeyres-type and Edgeworth-Marshall-type indexes show price change in the same direction, since their baskets are quite close to each other, and that the Paasche does not. It is a little more surprising that the geometric mean index also shows price change in a different direction, when both the geometric mean and arithmetic mean indexes are supposed to broker differences between the April and May baskets. However, if one takes the arithmetic mean index's measure as the true measure of monthly price change, the geometric mean index comes closer to it than the Laspeyres-type measure does, if only barely, differing from the preferred measure by 1.35 percentage points while the April-basket measure differs from it by 1.46 percentage points.

**Table A5. Contributions to Percent Change for an Albertan Price Index for Potatoes.
April-May Comparison Based on Arithmetic Mean of the April and May Baskets (Edgeworth-Marshall-Type
Indexes). (Neither the April nor May Index Number for Total Potatoes Equals the Published FPPI Estimate.)**

Commodity	Basket Share	$P_{t/2000}$ April 2001	$P_{t/2000}$ May 2001	%Ch	Cntrbtn to Agg %Ch
Total Potatoes	100.00%	86.40	86.04	-0.4%	-0.42%
Local and Table Potatoes	16.95%	72.54	66.25	-8.7%	-1.23%
Seed Potatoes	60.62%	81.57	77.50	-5.0%	-2.86%
Processing Potatoes	22.43%	109.92	124.07	12.9%	3.67%

An Edgeworth-Marshall index is an asymmetric average of Laspeyres and Paasche ones:

$$\frac{\sum p_1(q_0 + q_1)}{\sum p_0(q_0 + q_1)} = \frac{\sum p_0 q_0}{\sum p_0(q_0 + q_1)} \times \frac{\sum p_1 q_0}{\sum p_0 q_0} + \frac{\sum p_0 q_1}{\sum p_0(q_0 + q_1)} \times \frac{\sum p_1 q_1}{\sum p_0 q_1}.$$

As the base period's share of the total volume of activity evaluated at base period prices becomes very small it will approach a Paasche price index; as the current period's share becomes very small it will approach a Laspeyres price index. It will always lie somewhere between the two measures. Surely this is far more appropriate than to take a symmetric average of the Laspeyres and Paasche indexes, however that symmetric average be defined.

Diewert (2000, p. 206-207) ignores the principle of transactions equality and suggests instead a principle of invariance to proportional changes in quantities test, which makes a virtue of the significant failure of the Fisher formula in this regard. In fact, this principle would eliminate the Edgeworth-Marshall formula from consideration. The rationale comes not from temporal but from spatial price indexes. He postulates that if one is comparing the price levels of a very large country to a small one, the basket of the large country may overwhelm the basket of the small country, and one requires an index formula that is insensitive to these scale differences. In this context this principle makes sense. If one were organizing an exchange of employees between the United States and Canada with the same number of people going in both directions one would want an index of cost-of-living differentials to give about equal importance to the two countries. An Edgeworth-Marshall index based on total consumption in the two countries would be inappropriate. But how does this pertain to measuring price change over time?

Diewert (2000, p.207) notes that "this is unlikely to be a severe problem in the time series context where the change in quantity vectors going from one period to the next is small". It would be much closer to the truth to say: "This is not at all a problem in the time series context; in fact, the opposite is true. Any index that satisfies the invariance to proportional changes in quantities test by definition does not even come close to satisfying the transactions equality principle, and so is more or less unsatisfactory in a time series context, most especially if the change in quantity vectors going from one period to the next is substantial." In the case of our specific problem, getting monthly price comparisons for farm prices that are measures of pure price change, it means that we would rule out Fisher-type measures in favour of Edgeworth-Marshall-type measures. A corollary of this observation (i.e. that a symmetric mean of Laspeyres and Paasche indexes is not generally an appropriate measure) is that it is not true that one can generally be indifferent between Laspeyres and Paasche price measures for two-period comparisons. This is only true if the relative volumes in the two periods are comparable. If the volume of activity in the earlier period is much larger than in the later period the Laspeyres measure is more appropriate; if the opposite is true, then the Paasche measure is superior. But either way, an average of the two would be more appropriate than either measure taken by itself.

For this April-May comparison, where there is such an extraordinary difference between April and May baskets, the numbers shown in Table A5 probably provide the best single analysis of monthly price change. However, for other monthly comparisons, where there is not such a dramatic shift in basket shares from one month to another, it would be easier to base the monthly analysis strictly on a measure of pure price change derived using the basket of the earlier month in the comparison (in this case, April), and the results would not be very different from those both on an April-May basket. Only such a measure of pure price change can truly be said to represent the pure price change component of the monthly change of the official FPPI. It would certainly be appropriate to have both types of monthly analysis, i.e. both Laspeyres-type and Edgeworth-Marshall-type measures. However, if this were beyond the realm of the reasonable in terms of analysis for the FPPI given current resource allocations and only one measure were to be calculated, it would be best to opt for the Edgeworth-Marshall-type indexes.

Whether the Edgeworth-Marshall-type measures are produced in tandem with the Laspeyres-type measures or by themselves, it should be recognized that they do not represent the pure price change component of the monthly change of the official FPPI (this is what the Laspeyres-type measures show). Rather they constitute the best measure of pure price change between consecutive months that can be generated from the inputs used to create the FPPI.

References

Baldwin, Andrew (1990), "A seasonal-basket price index for fresh vegetables", *Consumer prices and price indexes* (Cat. 62-010-XPB), Statistics Canada: April-June 1987, 105-124

Baldwin, Andrew (1990), "Seasonal baskets in consumer price indices", *Journal of Official Statistics*.6 (3), 251-273.

Balk, Bert M. (1980a), *Seasonal Products in Agriculture and Horticulture and Methods for Computing Price Indices*, Statistical Studies no. 24 (CBS/Staatsuitgeverij, The Hague).

Balk, Bert M. (1980b) "Seasonal Commodities and the Construction of Annual and Monthly Price Indexes", *Statistiche Hefte* 21, 110-116.

Balk, Bert M. and W. Erwin Diewert (2011), "The Lowe Consumer Price Index and Its Substitution Bias," in W.E. Diewert, B.M. Balk, D. Fixler, K.J. Fox, and A.O. Nakamura (eds.), *Price and Productivity Measurement: Volume 6 -- Index Number Theory*, Trafford Press.

Bean, L.H. and O.C. Stine (1924), "Four Types of Index Numbers of Farm Prices", *Journal of the American Statistical Association*, XIX, 30-35

Berger, Jacques, *La mesure des mouvements des prix agricoles: Indice des produits agricoles à la production (IPPAP) présentation de la base 1990*, l'Institut national de la statistique et des études économiques, INSÉÉ Résultats no. 429, novembre 1995

Carter, R.G. and E.T. Richards (1975), "An Additional Series of Agricultural Price Indices", *Economic Trends*, No. 259, May, 95-101

Diewert, W.E (1983), "The Treatment of Seasonality in the Cost-of-Living Index", in Diewert and Montmarquette (eds.) *Price Level Measurement: Proceedings from a Conference Sponsored by Statistics Canada*, Ottawa, pp. 1019-1045. An excerpt of this original paper is published as chapter 8 in W.E. Diewert, B.M. Balk, D. Fixler, K.J. Fox, and A.O. Nakamura (eds.), (2011), *Price and Productivity Measurement, Volume 2: Seasonality*, Trafford Press..

Diewert, W.E (2001), "The Consumer Price Index and Index Number Purpose," *Journal of Economic and Social Measurement* 27, 167-248. http://www.econ.ubc.ca/diewert/purpose.pdf

Dikhanov, Yuri (1999), "Sensitivity of PPP-Based Income Estimates to Choice of Aggregation Procedures," Washington, D.C.: The World Bank

Dominion Bureau of Statistics (1985), *Index Numbers of Farm Prices of Agricultural Products (Revised Using the New Time Base, 1961=100)*, Cat.62-529, Ottawa.

Eurostat (1985), *Methodology of EC Agricultural Price Indices (Output and Input)*, Luxemburg: Office for Official Publications of the European Union.

Hill, T.P. (2011), "Lowe Indices," in W.E. Diewert, B.M. Balk, D. Fixler, K.J. Fox, and A.O. Nakamura (eds.), *Price and Productivity Measurement, Volume 6: Index Number Theory*, Trafford Press.

Krabicka, Vaclav and others (1989), "Farm Input Price Index (1981=100) (Reference Paper)" (draft), Statistics Canada, Prices Division.

Milton, Bob, Doug Kleweno and Herb Vanderberry (1995), *Reweighting and Reconstructing USDA's Indexes of Prices Received and Paid by Farmers*, U.S. Department of Agriculture, Economics Statistics Branch, ESB Staff Report No. ESB-95-01.

Rothwell, Doris P. (1958), "Use of Varying Seasonal Weights in Price Index Construction", *JASA*, XLIII, 66-77

Shepherd, G. (1961), "Appraisal of Alternative Concepts and Measures of Agricultural Parity Prices and Incomes", Staff Paper 10 in Price Statistics Review Committee of the National Bureau of Economic Research (ed.), *The Price Statistics of the Federal Government*, National Bureau of Economic Research, 459-502

Statistics Canada (2001 and after), *Farm Product Price Index*, Cat.21-007-XIB, monthly.

Swanson, Earl R. (1961), "Unit Value Pricing of Prices Received by Farmers", Staff Paper 11 in *The Price Statistics of the Federal Government*, 503-525

Szulc, Bohdan (1983), "Linking Price Index Numbers" in W.E. Diewert and C. Montmarquette (eds.), *Price Level Measurement: Proceedings from a conference sponsored by Statistics Canada*, Statistics Canada, 537-566.

Chapter 6

THE RECEIPTS APPROACH TO THE COLLECTION OF HOUSEHOLD EXPENDITURE DATA

Rósmundur Guðnason[1]

1.   Introduction

The receipts approach to the collection of household expenditure data involves allowing Household Expenditure Survey (HES) participants to turn in bar code receipts. This paper describes the innovative introduction of this approach in the Icelandic HES and some of the realized and potential benefits. For the Icelandic HES, each participating household keeps a diary for two weeks and hands in receipts obtained at the point of sale. The use of data from receipts has enabled more accurate estimates of private household consumption than previous traditional surveys. This approach provides comprehensive information on the types of goods purchased as well as on the outlets where the purchases were made. The fact that receipts provide details not only about the goods bought but also about where the transactions took place has enabled improvements in weighting procedures, and has enhanced the value of scanner data collected from outlets. In addition, the receipts approach has proved helpful for addressing questions of broader public interest. For example, HES data were used for analysing the sudden increase in shopping substitution bias when inflation rose in Iceland during the second quarter of 2001.

This paper describes the elements and some of the advantages of the receipts approach. The agenda for future research opened up by the receipts approach is also briefly discussed.

2.   The Receipts Approach

2.1   Detailed data from shopping receipts

The receipts approach involves gathering information from the detailed receipts handed over to consumers when they shop. This method was first described and applied in 1995 in

[1] The author is with Statistics Iceland. He can be contacted at Borgartún 21a, IS - Reykjavík 150, Iceland, e-mail: rosmundur.gudnason@statice.is. The author would like to thank David Fenwick, Guðrún Ragnheiður Jónsdóttir, Alice Nakamura and Philip Vogler for helpful comments.

Citation for this chapter:
Rósmundur Guðnason (2011), "The Receipts Approach to the Collection Of Household Expenditure Data," chapter 6, pp. 105-110 in
W.E. Diewert, B.M. Balk, D. Fixler, K.J. Fox and A.O. Nakamura,
PRICE AND PRODUCTIVITY MEASUREMENT: Volume 2 -- Seasonality. Trafford Press.

© Alice Nakamura, 2011. Permission to link to, or copy or reprint, these materials is granted without restriction, including for use in commercial textbooks, with due credit to the authors and editors.

Iceland.[2] In 2000, the receipts approach was built in as a standard aspect of the continuous HES started that year. The survey cycle for the continuous HES is three years.[3]

During the two weeks of keeping a diary, survey participants record the total amount of each transaction, and then place the receipt into a special pocket in the diary book. In the beginning, the main idea was to make participation in the HES easier for households by allowing them to record their purchases with less writing. However, the receipts turned out to be a valuable source of additional information. As Guðnason (1997, p. 129) explains: "This method allows much more accurate estimates of the composition and quantity of household goods than otherwise would be the case. The utilisation of this method also enables precise information to be gathered about consumer activities at much lower effort and cost than previous methods and show[s] a link between the goods purchased and the buyer."

The following information can usually be found on a receipt:

1. *The total amount, and a breakdown by the items purchased.* The fact that the item components always add up to the purchase total is handy.[4] The results in the survey database can be compared with the total amounts on the receipts. Also, the total expenditures and transactions can be estimated immediately.

2. *The name of the outlet where the purchases were made,* clarifying the point of sale. Hence, the exact share in household expenditures can be measured for each shop. That information is useful for the creation of chain weights for the CPI.

3. *The date and time of the purchase.* This opens up the possibility of mapping consumption behaviour by day of the week and even the time of day.

4. *A detailed description of each item purchased* including the brand and package size, the unit price, and the total dollar cost. Fruits and vegetables are often weighed at the cash register, and this information appears on the receipt as well.

5. *How the items were paid for;* whether by cash, by debit or credit card, or by check.

The household address is known for HES participants. When this information is combined with the receipt information, regional and demographic group shopping patterns can be observed.

Three groups of chain stores dominate the retail market for groceries: Hagar, Kaupás and Samkaup. In calculating the index, the retailers are divided into four groups: Hagar, Kaupás, Samkaup, and "Other". Each group is then divided into its various chains, which now total eleven altogether. Prices at outlets within each chain are similar, regardless of the locality. Hence only chain-specific weights are now used; regional weights are no longer applied.[5] The use of chain-specific weights since 2002 renders calculation of the index simpler, and makes dealing with changes in shopping habits easier, especially when one store replaces another.

---

[2] See Guðnason (1995, p. 173).

[3] The number of households in the sample for each year is about one-third of what it was prior to the start of the continuous HES. In the 1995 survey, 1375 households participated, while in 2000, 2001 and 2002 the participating households numbered 657, 611, and 639, respectively. Data coverage can be analysed by adding up transactions from the receipts and the diaries, and can be viewed by either the number of transactions or by the expenditures.

[4] In an international context, the Icelandic HES was the first household survey to exploit this possibility, balancing one-third of expenditures in this way in each year of the continuous survey.

[5] From March 1997 to March 2002, regional indices for groceries were calculated in the CPI, and the CPI total index was weighted regionally.

Data from the continuous HES is incorporated in April of each year. The weight of individual groceries is based on three-year, price-updated average expenditures.

2.2 Scanner data and receipts: two records of the same information

The majority of retail sales are now scanned at the point of sale. The scanner data on each sale are captured in the outlet database, the buyer obtains a detailed receipt for the transaction. The consumer receipts mirror the information recorded in the outlet database. If all the receipts, whether from private customers or firms, were collected together, they would provide the same result as the sales information available from the retailers.

However, receipts collected in the HES are linked to household information collected by interviews with individuals in the participating households. This information on the consumer side lends a special value to the receipts data. HES data also include receipts for goods bought from shops that do not collect scanner data. Even though electronic data records have become very prevalent, some retail establishments still gather no scanner data.[6]

On the other hand, transactions with other sectors are recorded in the outlet database. HES data are for a sample of households whereas scanner data reflect an outlet's total sales.

Scanner data have been used intensively for research in recent years. For example, data of this kind have been used to evaluate the influence of varying sampling methods on price measurement.[7] There is potential for considerable further development.[8] The next steps in its utilisation can be described as follows (Guðnason and Snorrason 1999, p. 337):

> "Further, shopping habits of households as mapped in the HES could be used as a source for weights. This would be done by utilising information on the detailed expenditure of typical customers at each type of outlet. Calculations of the average price change would then be based on the expenditures of different households at the outlets, so that for each outlet there would be varying indices calculated for the different types of households".

---

[6] In the 1995 survey, 41 % of all transactions were gathered from receipts. This number climbed to about 69 % in 2000 and reached 74 % in 2001 and 77 % in 2002. For food and beverages, 53 % of the records were of this type in 1995, 84 % in 2000, and around 89 % in 2001 and 2002. The prevalence of receipts can also be judged on an expenditures basis. Receipts covered more than 12 % of total household expenditures in the 1995 survey, 26 % in the 2000 survey, some 31 % in the 2001 survey, and 36 % in 2002.

[7] See Haan (2001), Haan et al. (1997), Silver (1995), Reinsdorf (1996), and Dalén (1997).

[8] See Guðnason (1998, p. 209).

3.   Utilising Receipts Data

In the Icelandic CPI, each type of substitution bias is accounted for separately. The geometric mean is used to calculate elementary indices. Outlet substitution is allowed for when an item is not available at a particular store. [9]

The prices of the same or similar goods can vary widely among shops. Consumer price indices measure price changes concerning private consumption at the outlets whereas ideally the prices should be measured for households. The reason that this is not usually done is that sufficient information about the shopping habits of households is normally lacking. Index prices are calculated with prices measured in the shops, and the average prices are weighted by sales information. However, if households change their shopping habits, the average prices of the goods they buy change even if the prices of the goods in each store remain the same. In the Icelandic CPI, shopping substitution is accounted for by measuring it through household weights made possible by the receipts HES data[10].

In April 2001, inflation climbed steeply in Iceland. In 2002, on the other hand, the price level increases slowed.[11] Rising inflation brought changes in shopping habits, especially for groceries, as consumers transferred their trade to shops where prices were lower. These changes can better be analysed by separating the stores into two sets: low-price stores[12] and other. In 2000, the total amount of groceries bought in the low-price stores amounted to 25 %. This share rose to 31.5 % for 2001. Moreover, the low-price share increased further still during 2002 and 2003, from not quite 38 % of the total sales volume in 2002 to over 41 % in 2003. Thus the total market share of low-price stores increased by nearly 64 % during the overall period.

Five types of households are defined in the HES. Separate household-type indices would shed light on cost of living differences by household type and could be used to correct more precisely for biases arising from changes in shopping patterns. The effect of shopping pattern trends on different types of households can be analysed by examining the following categories:

• *One-person households.* The share of their purchases taking place at low-price stores increased in the period of 2000-2002 from over 21 % to over 26 %. This increase is less than the rise for other household types.

• *Couples without children.* About one-fourth of their shopping was carried out at the low-price end in 2000. Two years later, such couples bought nearly 37 % of their groceries at the low-price stores.

---

[9] Substitution bias in household shopping has been called outlet substitution bias, though it in fact has more to do with household shopping behaviour than outlet prices. See Guðnason (2003, pp. 304-308 and 2004, pp. 13-17). See also Reinsdorf (1993). On the construction of the elementary indices and the theory behind these, see Balk (1997), and Diewert (1998, 1999, 2004, 2011).

[10] From December 2001 to May 2003, the total change due to adjustments in household shopping substitution for groceries amounted to an almost 0.44% drop in the consumer price index. See Guðnason (2004, pp. 16-17).

[11] The way households behaved in reaction to the abrupt changes in inflation is shown by twelve tables available from the author.

[12] The Bónus, Krónan and Nettó chains are identified as low-price stores.

- *Couples with children.* While low-price shopping comprised 25 % of their food and beverage purchases in 2000, this portion had risen to nearly 43 % in 2002.

- *Single-parent households.* Just under 23 % of their shopping was conducted at low-price stores in 2000, but this went up to 37 % in the year 2002.

- *Other households.* Low-price shopping initially exceeded 28 % of their purchases (highest among the households of that time) and passed 40 % in 2002.

This assembly of facts makes clear that shopping behaviour changes during the period of 2000-2002 were substantial. Thanks to the receipts approach, these changes could be closely observed.

4. Future Possibilities for Development of the Receipts Approach

The receipts approach is still in its embryonic stage of development. The volume of accessible receipts is the same as that of scanner data. The gigantic amount of data collected at all the points of sale has its counterpart in customer receipts. Collecting HES data from receipts is a more convenient and probably cheaper approach than the traditional HES one.

It is obvious that the receipts approach presents a very powerful method for gathering detailed information about household behaviour. These data sets are available everywhere. It is my belief that every statistical office ought to consider the receipts approach for their future statistical work, as it could improve their household statistics significantly.

References

Balk, B.M. (1997), "On the Use of Unit-Value Indices as Consumer Price Subindices," *Proceedings of the Fourth Meeting of the International Working Group on Price Indices,* W. Lane (ed.), U.S. Bureau of Labour Statistics, Washington DC.

Dalén, J. (1997), "Experiments with Swedish Scanner Data," *Proceedings of the Third Meeting of the International Working Group on Price Indices,* B.M. Balk (ed.), Research Paper No. 9806, Statistics Netherlands.

Diewert, W.E. (1998), "Index Number Issues in the Consumer Price Index, *Journal of Economic Perspectives* 12, 47-58.

Diewert, W.E. (1999), "The Consumer Price Index and Index Number Purpose," *Proceedings of the Ottawa Group Fifth Meeting*, R. Guðnason and Þ. Gylfadóttir (eds.), Statistics Iceland.

Diewert, W.E. (2004), "Elementary Indices," Chapter 20 of the *Consumer Price Index Manual: Theory and Practice,* ILO, Geneva.

Diewert, W.E. (2011), "Axiomatic and Economic Approaches to Elementary Price Indexes," in W.E. Diewert, B.M. Balk, D. Fixler, K.J. Fox, and A.O. Nakamura (eds.), *Price and Productivity Measurement, Volume 6: Index Number Theory*, Trafford Press.

Guðnason, R. (1995), "Note on the Practices in the Field of Insurance, Financial Services and Public Price Policies in the Icelandic CPI," *Proceedings of the Second Meeting of the International Working Group on Price Indices,* Statistics Sweden.

Guðnason, R. (1997), "Improved Methods for the Evaluation of the Composition and Quantity of Household Goods," *Proceedings of the Third Meeting of the International Working Group on Price Indices*, Bert M. Balk (ed.), Research Paper No. 9806, Statistics Netherlands.

Guðnason, R. (1998), "Comparison of Different Sources for Weights of Selected Groups in the Icelandic CPI: Consumers Bar-code Receipts vs. Scanner Data from Supermarkets," *Proceedings of the Fourth Meeting of the International Working Group on Price Indices*, W. Lane (ed.), U. S. Bureau of Labour Statistics.

Guðnason, R. (2003), "How Do We Measure Inflation? Some Measurement Problems," *Proceedings of the Seventh Meeting of the International Working Group on Price Indices,* T. Lacroix (ed.), INSEE, Paris.

Guðnason, R. (2004), "How do we measure inflation?" English translation of an article, Hvernig mælum við verðbólgu? *Fjármálatíðindi* (*The Economic Journal of the Icelandic Centralbank)*, 1, 2004.

Guðnason, R. and H. Snorrason (1999), "The Use of Cash Register Data," *Proceedings from the 52nd session of the International Statistical Institute*, Bulletin of the International Statistical Institute, Book 1.

Haan, J. de, (2001), "Generalized Fischer Price Indexes and the Use of Scanner Data in the CPI," *Papers and Proceedings of the Sixth Meeting of the International Working Group on Price Indices,* K. Woolford (ed.), Australian Bureau of Statistics.

Haan, J. de, E. Opperdoes, and C. Schut (1997), "Item Sampling in the Consumer Price Index: A Case Study Using Scanner Data. Statistics," Mimeo, Statistics Netherlands.

Reinsdorf, M.B. (1993), "The Effect of Outlet Price Differentials in the U.S. Consumer Price Index," in *Price Measurements and Their Uses*, M. E. Manser and A. H. Young (eds.), Studies in Income and Wealth, Volume 57, University of Chicago Press.

Reinsdorf, M.B. (1996), "Constructing Basic Component Indexes for the U.S. CPI from Scanner Data: A Test Using Data on Coffee," *Working Paper No. 277*, U. S. Bureau of Labour Statistics, Washington DC.

Silver, M. (1995), "Elementary Aggregates, Micro Indices and Scanner Data: Some Issues in the Compilation of Consumer Price Indices," *Review of Income and Wealth* 41, 427-438.

Chapter 7

THE POSSIBLE USE OF SCANNER DATA IN DEALING WITH SEASONALITY IN THE CPI

Peter Hein van Mulligen and May Hua Oei[1]

1.   Introduction

Based on intensive study, Statistics Netherlands decided to use scanner data from several supermarket chains in the production of the official CPI beginning in June 2002.[2]

This paper addresses two questions. First, how can we use scanner data to incorporate seasonal products? Currently, such products are excluded from the scanner data that are used for the Dutch CPI. Second, what are the possible effects of products for which there are frequent promotional sales? Scanner data may provide a solution for dealing with such products.

Section 2 gives a summary of the way in which scanner data are currently employed in the Dutch CPI. Section 3 explores different index number formulas first of all for use with fruit products that exhibit both strong and weak seasonal behaviour, and also for children's napkins (i.e., disposable diapers), a product that exhibits seasonal-like fluctuations in prices and quantities because of frequent promotional sales. Section 4 concludes.

2.   The Use of Scanner Data in the Dutch CPI

Following traditional CPI practice, a statistical agency specifies an index basket of products selected from all possible goods and services, and sends interviewers to collect prices for the basket items. The weights used for the CPI are usually for product categories rather than the individual basket products, and are based on household expenditure survey (HES) data supplemented by national accounts data. These weights are not generally associated with actual transactions, and are often held fixed for a year or more at a time.

Statistics Netherlands obtains scanner data from supermarket chains on a weekly basis and uses this data for the official CPI.[3] The scanner data include quantity information corresponding to the product price information, making possible improvements in CPI practice.

---

[1] The authors are with Statistics Netherlands. The first author can be reached at PMUN@cbs.nl

[2] See Schut (2003) for a review.

Citation for this chapter:
Peter Hein van Mulligen and May Hua Oei (2011), "The Possible Use of Scanner Data in Dealing with Seasonality in the CPI," chapter 7, pp. 111-120 in
W.E. Diewert, B.M. Balk, D. Fixler, K.J. Fox and A.O. Nakamura (eds.),
PRICE AND PRODUCTIVITY MEASUREMENT: Volume 2 -- Seasonality, Trafford Press.

© Alice Nakamura, 2011. Permission to link to, or copy or reprint, these materials is granted without restriction, including for use in commercial textbooks, with due credit to the authors and editors.

The scanner data are coded according to the European Article Number (EAN) system. Each product has an EAN. For the scanner data part of the CPI, the EANs are used to match sales information by product for each retailer. EANs are grouped according to the COICOP (Classification of Individual Consumption by Purpose) categories. For each COICOP group containing products sold in supermarkets, several index numbers are calculated: one for each supermarket chain providing scanner data, and one for data collected at other points of sale.[4]

For the scanner data indices, fixed baskets of several thousand EANs are determined each year for each of the retailers providing scanner data. Each EAN in this basket gets a weight based on its expenditure share in that year. The price of an EAN in the current month is matched with its price in the previous month. EAN specific price ratios are chained with the corresponding preceding price ratios, yielding the relatives of the current and the base year prices.[5] The scanner data indices are annually chained Lowe indices.[6] Specifically, the following formula is used for the scanner data price index, P_{Ak}^{rt}, for product group A sold by retailer k, where r is the base year and t is the current month and where i denotes an EAN and w_{ik}^r is the weight of EAN i for retailer k in base year r (Schut, 2003):

$$(1) \qquad P_{Ak}^{rt} = \sum_{i \in A} w_{ik}^r \left(\frac{\bar{p}_{ik}^t}{\bar{p}_{ik}^r} \right) = \sum_{i \in A} w_{ik}^r \prod_{\tau=r+1}^{t} \left(\frac{\bar{p}_{ik}^\tau}{\bar{p}_{ik}^{\tau-1}} \right),$$

The price $\bar{p}_{ik}$ is the average price for EAN i across all stores of retailer k in the stated period.

3. Using Scanner Data to Deal with Two Problems: Frequent Sales and Seasonality

Triplett (2003) points out that scanner data measure acquisition rather than consumption behaviour. The search, shopping and inventory behaviour of consumers are embodied in the

---

[3] For CPI production timeliness reasons, only data from the first two weeks of each month can be used for the compilation of the monthly CPI. Therefore, the assumption is made that prices and sales in the first two weeks properly represent the entire month.

[4] These indices are weighted with the number of price quotes that were collected at each retailer before the implementation of scanner data. Starting from next year, they will be based on actual expenditure shares.

[5] The base year of the CPI is shifted every five years, both for scanner data and non-scanner data. Currently, the base year is 2000. Note that for scanner data, the base year which determines the selection of EANs and their weights in the scanner data index is shifted every year, so that at this moment the base year is 2003.

[6] It appears from the scanner data that the turnover rate of all EANs is very high. Even small changes in the package design or the fact that an article is on sale may lead to a different EAN for this article. EANs constantly enter and exit the market. Only EANs with positive sales figures in at least 48 of the 52 weeks of the base year were considered for basket inclusion. Most seasonal products are therefore excluded. Each year, it occurs fairly often that an EAN disappears, which would result in a missing observation. This problem is solved in a fairly conventional way: when the turnover share of this EAN in its CBL-group (the level of aggregation below a COICOP group) is small, the class mean method is used. In other cases, a replacement EAN is found. When the old EAN and the replacement EAN are deemed too different, a quality adjustment factor is applied. The part of the Dutch CPI that is based on scanner data is therefore a hybrid of traditional matching procedures combined with a new way of collecting data and determining expenditure shares at the lowest level of aggregation.

observed data. Some sorts of consumers tend to hoard some sorts of products, buying these products only when they are on offer (i.e., when they are offered at promotional sale prices), and consuming from household inventories in the periods between promotional sales. With a chained index formula, frequent sales can lead to bias problems.[7] However, scanner data provide statisticians with actual transaction prices, rather than list prices relatively few shoppers may actually pay. Moreover, scanner data allow expenditure weights to be directly based on actual purchases corresponding to the measured prices.

3.1   Seasonal effects in scanner data: the case of fruit

Chapter 22 in the CPI manual (Hill, 2004) deals with the treatment of seasonal products in a CPI. That chapter on seasonal products is referred to hereafter as the manual chapter. Throughout the manual chapter, a modified Turvey artificial data set is used to investigate the effectiveness of alternative methods for dealing with seasonality problems.[8]

In the modified Turvey data (like the original Turvey data), the seasonal patterns for all products are very regular. The strongly seasonal commodities are available in the same months every year. However, actual data on the purchase of fruits and vegetables rarely exhibit these sorts of strictly regular patterns.[9] For example, the scanner data used in this paper show that in 2000, strawberries were available from May through September, but in 2003 they were available from March through June.

Most seasonal products, like fresh fruit, are excluded from the scanner data that were used for the Dutch CPI. One reason for this decision is that many fresh fruits are not sold to customers in fixed quantity lots the way that packaged cereals, for example, come in standard sized boxes. With goods that are not sold in standard lots, individual stores attach product EANs: the so-called in-store EANs. Unfortunately, the in-store EANs are not the same between stores or even in different months. However, articles with a set quantity lot, such as a 500 grams box of strawberries, have their own regular EANs, and could be matched without difficulties.

For this study, five kinds of fresh fruit are used: strawberries, white grapes, red grapefruits, mangos and golden delicious apples. All these products have regular EANs. To simplify calculations, only scanner data from one retailer were used. We have weekly observations over the period of 2000 to 2003. The price and quantity data used for this study are shown in appendix table A1. In that data set, strawberries and grapes are strongly seasonal goods; the other fruits are weakly seasonal.

The CPI manual discusses several price indices, of which three types are considered here: monthly year over year indices, monthly rolling indices, and the Rothwell index.

Year over year indices compare prices in the current month with prices in the same month in the base year. The base year can either be a fixed reference year, yielding a fixed base index, or the previous year, yielding a chained index. Hence, each month only prices are compared of goods that are present in both the current month and the same month in the

[7] See Feenstra and Shapiro (2003) on the bias problems that can result, and their example for canned tuna sales data.

[8] This data set is also tabled in Diewert, Armknecht and Nakamura (2007).

[9] Price collectors have been traditionally instructed to only collect prices of strongly seasonal products in pre-defined periods. Some of these products have been available in some periods when their prices were not collected.

designated base year. For the n products, the monthly year-to-year Laspeyres ($P_L^{t,m}$) and Paasche ($P_P^{t,m}$) indices for month m of year t and base year t_0 can be written as:

$$(2) \qquad P_L^{t,m} = \sum_{i=1}^{n} p_i^{t,m} q_i^{t_0,m} / \sum_{i=1}^{n} p_i^{t_0,m} q_i^{t_0,m} \text{ , and}$$

$$(3) \qquad P_P^{t,m} = \sum_{i=1}^{n} p_i^{t,m} q_i^{t,m} / \sum_{i=1}^{n} p_i^{t_0,m} q_i^{t,m} \text{ .}$$

Seasonal effects will be eliminated in a monthly year-to-year index only if the monthly seasonal patterns in the data for both prices and quantities are the same in both years for the price index comparison. However, the actual Dutch data do not exhibit year-to-year monthly regularity. Hence the resulting indexes for these data show strong fluctuations. This is illustrated in figure 1, which shows two monthly Fisher year-to-year indices based on our scanner data: a fixed base index with 2000 as the base year, and a chained base index.[10] Clearly, such year-to-year indices cannot tell us anything about aggregate price changes on a month to month basis.

Two types of aggregate index number formulas designed for dealing with seasonal products are considered here: rolling year indices and the Rothwell index. In a rolling year index, the prices in a period of twelve months are compared with the prices in the same months of the reference twelve-month period. With a chained rolling index, the reference period is the same twelve-month period one year earlier.

The Laspeyres ($P_{L,R,\text{fixed}}^{t,m}$) and Paasche ($P_{P,R,\text{fixed}}^{t,m}$) fixed base rolling year indices for month m of year t (with base year t_0)[11] can then be written as:

$$(4) \qquad P_{L,R,\text{fixed}}^{t,m} = \frac{\displaystyle\sum_{j=m+1}^{12}\sum_{i=1}^{n} p_i^{t-1,j} q_i^{t_0,j} + \sum_{j=1}^{m}\sum_{i=1}^{n} p_i^{t,j} q_i^{t_0,j}}{\displaystyle\sum_{j=1}^{12}\sum_{i=1}^{n} p_i^{t_0,j} q_i^{t_0,j}} \text{ , and}$$

$$(5) \qquad P_{P,R,\text{fixed}}^{t,m} = \frac{\displaystyle\sum_{j=m+1}^{12}\sum_{i=1}^{n} p_i^{t-1,j} q_i^{t-1,j} + \sum_{j=1}^{m}\sum_{i=1}^{n} p_i^{t,j} q_i^{t,j}}{\displaystyle\sum_{j=m+1}^{12}\sum_{i=1}^{n} p_i^{t_0,j} q_i^{t-1,j} + \sum_{j=1}^{m}\sum_{i=1}^{n} p_i^{t_0,j} q_i^{t,j}} \text{ .}$$

---

[10] These indices and all indices shown in subsequent graphs and tables use weekly data aggregated over months. Since the Dutch CPI only uses the first two weeks of every month all (monthly) indices presented here also refer to the first two weeks each month.

[11] Note that when $t=1$, then $t-1$ and t_0 coincide.

Figure 1. Fixed and chained monthly year-to-year Fisher indices, fruit

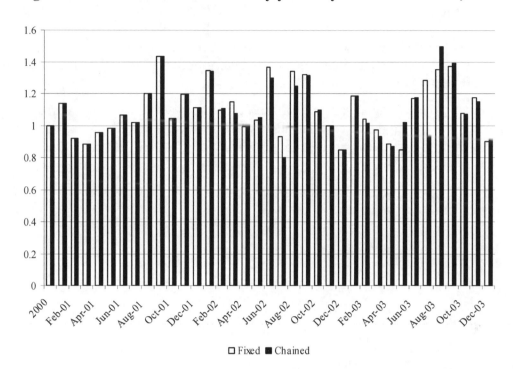

☐ Fixed ■ Chained

Chained rolling year Laspeyres ($P^{t,m}_{L,R,\text{chained}}$) and Paasche ($P^{t,m}_{P,R,\text{chained}}$) indices in month m of year t are defined as:[12]

$$(6) \quad P^{t,m}_{L,R,\text{chained}} = \prod_{\tau=t_0}^{t} \left[\frac{\displaystyle\sum_{j=m+1}^{12} \sum_{i=1}^{n} p_i^{\tau-1,j} q_i^{\tau-2,j} + \sum_{j=1}^{m} \sum_{i=1}^{n} p_i^{\tau,j} q_i^{\tau-1,j}}{\displaystyle\sum_{j=m+1}^{12} \sum_{i=1}^{n} p_i^{\tau-2,j} q_i^{\tau-2,j} + \sum_{j=1}^{m} \sum_{i=1}^{n} p_i^{\tau-1,j} q_i^{\tau-1,j}} \right], \text{ and}$$

$$(7) \quad P^{t,m}_{P,R,\text{chained}} = \prod_{\tau=t_0}^{t} \left[\frac{\displaystyle\sum_{j=m+1}^{12} \sum_{i=1}^{n} p_i^{\tau-1,j} q_i^{\tau-1,j} + \sum_{j=1}^{m} \sum_{i=1}^{n} p_i^{\tau,j} q_i^{\tau,j}}{\displaystyle\sum_{j=m+1}^{12} \sum_{i=1}^{n} p_i^{\tau-2,j} q_i^{\tau-1,j} + \sum_{j=1}^{m} \sum_{i=1}^{n} p_i^{\tau-1,j} q_i^{\tau,j}} \right].$$

Unfortunately, the rolling year type of index has two drawbacks that may be significant for statistical agencies. CPI indexes have traditionally been viewed (and, for some purposes used) as short-term statistics for measuring month to month measure of inflation, whereas a rolling year index measures annual inflation as of a given month. In a rolling index, price

---

[12] Note that, when $t = 1$, then $t-1$ and $t-2$ equal t_0, and when $t = 2$, then $t-2$ equals t_0.

changes in general are smoothed out; not only seasonal effects. These are therefore different concepts of inflation which cannot easily be aligned. For central banks and other parties interested primarily in annual inflation, a rolling year index may be an adequate measure of price change, but for some other users, seems less suitable. Second, because a rolling year index is the average measure of price change over the past twelve months, it actually measures the average annual price change of six months ago.

Different statistical agencies use different methods to seasonally correct their price indices. One popular method of seasonal adjustment is the Rothwell index, of which several variants are in use.[13] In its basic form, the Rothwell index in month m of the current year t compares prices in this month with the annual average prices of the base year, t_0. We refer to this index as the <u>fixed base Rothwell index</u>, because the quantities used are those in the corresponding month m in the base year t_0:

$$(8) \qquad P_{R,fixed}^{t,m} = \sum_{i=1}^{n} p_i^{t,m} q_i^{t_0,m} \Big/ \sum_{i=1}^{n} p_i^{t_0} q_i^{t_0,m} \text{ , with}$$

$$(9) \qquad p_i^{t_0} = \sum_{m=1}^{12} p_i^{t_0,m} q_i^{t_0,m} \Big/ \sum_{m=1}^{12} q_i^{t_0,m} .$$

The Rothwell is a short-term price index, showing monthly price change including seasonal fluctuations. However, the Rothwell index still misses price changes when the seasonal pattern *changes over the years*, as in our data. A changing pattern for strongly seasonal products results in a situation where for some months, $p_i^{t,m}$ is not observed when $q_i^{t_0,m} > 0$, and vice versa. To prevent this from happening, an alternative specification of the Rothwell index could include current quantities in (8) rather than quantities for the base year, yielding what we will refer to as a <u>current base Rothwell index</u>:

$$(8') \qquad P_{R,current}^{t,m} = \sum_{i=1}^{n} p_i^{t,m} q_i^{t,m} \Big/ \sum_{i=1}^{n} p_i^{t_0} q_i^{t,m} ,$$

together with (9) above in unchanged form.

For our data, there are several months when the differences between the two Rothwell indices are quite substantial. This is especially the case in July and August of 2003. Inspection of the scanner data reveals that in July and August of 2003, strawberries had been no longer available whereas they were available in these months in each of the preceding years. This change in the seasonal pattern caused a large difference between the indexes.

We prefer the current base Rothwell index. It seems to give the best reflection of current seasonal patterns. In our view, Baldwin's (1990) recommendation of the Rothwell index should be modified to stipulate that the quantities in the index are the current quantities rather than the base year ones. Of course, in conventional statistical practice, current quantities are generally not available. Scanner data, however, do contain current quantities sold: a distinct advantage of using scanner data for the treatment of seasonal products. Thus, although the conventional Rothwell

---

[13] Statistics Netherlands also uses a variant of the Rothwell index.

index suffers from the fact that a change in the seasonal pattern over the years can create a serious mismatch between current prices and base year quantities, with scanner data and an alternative specification of the Rothwell index that makes use of the current quantity data, this mismatch problem can be eliminated.

If the goal is to smooth out seasonal patterns altogether, a different approach is necessary. An annual index like the rolling year index succeeds well in eliminating seasonal fluctuations in an aggregate price index. However, for CPI purposes, we feel that the current base Rothwell index is the most suitable way to deal with seasonal fluctuations in prices and quantities.

3.2   Promotional sales effects: the case of children's napkins

Children's napkins is a product group where promotional sales are fairly frequent. Many consumers only buy napkins when they are on promotional sale, drawing on household inventories for current consumption in between the promotional sale periods. This pattern of acquisitions is illustrated in figure 2 which shows the quantities purchased of all brands of napkins included in our data set. The promotional sale periods can easily be distinguished.

In the measurement of price changes, acquisition is generally assumed to equal consumption. However, as shown in figure 2, this assumption does not hold for the non-durable (but storable) product of children's napkins.

Feenstra and Shapiro (2003) point out that chained indices of articles with frequent promotional sales can suffer from severe biases. For example, for the Laspeyres index, they report this bias is upward because the price decline in the period when it is on offer gets a much smaller quantity weight than the price increase when the price returns to its pre-sale level.

When Statistics Netherlands first acquired scanner data from two major retailers, the first aim was to construct chained Fisher indices (Schut, 2001). However, the chained indices were found to contain substantial biases. One of the causes of these biases seems to be that some articles are frequently on promotional sale. Hence, the decision was made to use a fixed base Laspeyres index, with the base year shifted every year. The formula is shown in (1).

Because we have no information on the way products on sale are promoted and when they are promoted during the promotional sale period, we cannot form a priori expectations about the likely direction of bias the way that Feenstra and Shapiro (2003) do. The chained Törnqvist index (which compares prices in each month with those in the previous month) is given by:

$$(10) \quad P_T = \exp\left[\sum_{i=1}^{n}\frac{1}{2}\left(w_i^{m-1} + w_i^m\right)\ln\left(\frac{p_i^m}{p_i^{m-1}}\right)\right].$$

We chose 2000 as our base period. This means that for January 2001, p_i^{m-1} is the average price of product i in month m in 2000, and w_i^{m-1} is the corresponding expenditure weight.

Figure 2 Quantity Sold of Baby's Napkins, 2000-2003

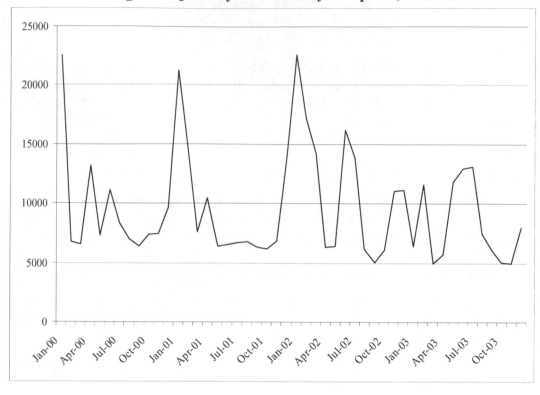

The resulting chained Törnqvist index is rather volatile: in some months the index value change versus the previous month is more than ten percent. As expected, the chained Laspeyres was found to have a strong upward bias.

All the indices turned out to have more or less the same volatile pattern, caused by periodic promotional sales. Rather than an upward bias, the chained Törnqvist was found to have a downward trend vis-à-vis the fixed base indices. Based on taking a closer look at the data, it appears that after a period of sale, in most cases the quantity sold of an article that was on promotional sale dips below the pre-promotional sale period quantity. When this is the case, the price increase after a sale has a larger weight than the price decrease during a sale.

However, the pattern of purchases of napkins that are regularly on sale tells another story as well. While the quantity purchased of napkins that are on sale may be somewhat smaller just after compared with just before the promotional sale, both the before and after quantities are dwarfed by the quantity sold during the promotional sale period. This suggests that there are many consumers who only buy napkins when they are on sale: what Triplett (2003) termed the inventory shoppers. For such consumers, only price changes from one period of sale to the next are relevant, rather than the monthly price changes measured with traditional indices.

Clearly, consumption and acquisition of napkins do not coincide. A solution for this problem is to expand the unit time interval for the index. In the case of napkins, a horizon of one year rather than one month seems reasonable. Within a given year, consumption and acquisition of napkins are more likely to coincide. Choosing such a long price level measurement period, however, implies that the price index for napkins can only be computed over annual time spans; not monthly ones.

A rolling annual index can be updated monthly. As described in the previous section, a rolling index compares the prices in a period of twelve months (the 'rolling year') with those in the same months in the base twelve-month period.

The periodicity of promotional sales is quite regular in the case of napkins. This is actually quite common for both durable and non-durable consumer goods. A rolling year Fisher index seems ideally equipped to deal with 'inventory shoppers' and with the discrepancy between acquisition and consumption, which is a problem area when traditional monthly indices are used with scanner data.

4. Summary and Conclusions

This paper uses scanner data to evaluate and compare alternative methods that can be used for dealing with two problem areas in price index measurement: seasonal products and articles with frequent sales.

We argue that if the goal is to smooth out seasonal fluctuations, rolling year indices offer a way of doing this. Rolling year indices also appear to provide a way to deal with the discrepancies between the periods of acquisition and consumption for storable non-durable goods like children's napkins.

However, rolling year provide a measure of annual price change, rather than a short-term monthly index. Also, rolling indices have a lag of six months; i.e., they provide the average price change over the past 12 months, which equals the average annual price change of six months ago. Thus we conclude that a Rothwell index using current quantities is the best method to use for seasonal commodities in a CPI.

References

Armknecht, P.A., ed. (2004), *Producer Price Index Manual: Theory and Practice* (*PPI Manual*), published by the International Labour Office, International Monetary Fund, Organisation for Economic Co-operation and Development, Eurostat, United Nations, and The World Bank. Chapters and whole can be downloaded for free at http://www.imf.org/external/np/sta/tegppi/index.htm

Baldwin, A. (1990), "Seasonal baskets in consumer price indexes", *Journal of Official Statistics*, vol. 6, no. 3, pp. 251-273.

Feenstra, R.C. and M.D. Shapiro (2003), "High Frequency Substitution and the Measurement of Price Indexes," chapter 5 in R.C. Feenstra and M.D. Shapiro (eds.), *Scanner Data and Price Indexes*, Studies of Income and Wealth, volume 64, University of Chicago Press.

Fisher, I. (1922), *The Making of Index Numbers*, Houghton Mifflin.

Schut, C. (2001), "Using Scanner Data to Compile Price Indices: Experiences and Practical Problems," presented at the Joint ECE/ILO meeting on Consumer Price Indices, Geneva, November 1-2, 2001.

Triplett, J.E. (2003), "Using Scanner Data in Consumer Price Indexes, Some Neglected Conceptual Considerations," chapter 5 in R.C. Feenstra and M.D. Shapiro (eds.), *Scanner Data and Price Indexes*, Studies of Income and Wealth, volume 64, University of Chicago Press.

Turvey, R. (1979), "The treatment of seasonal items in consumer price indices", *Bulletin of Labour Statistics*, Fourth quarter, International Labour Office, Geneva, pp. 13-33

Appendix

Table A.1 Monthly prices and quantities sold of five kinds of fruit, 2000-2003

	Strawberries		White grapes		Red grapefruits		Mangos		Golden del. apples	
	price	quantity	price	quantity	price	quantity	price	quantity	price	quantity
Jan-00	0.00	0	0.00	0	1.81	10339	0.90	8909	1.56	5000
Feb-00	0.00	0	2.26	2535	1.81	10631	0.96	20388	1.59	4512
Mar-00	0.00	0	2.26	3125	1.81	10947	1.36	6145	1.59	4186
Apr-00	0.00	0	1.81	3026	1.81	11912	1.59	4928	1.59	3794
May-00	2.97	34836	1.81	3598	1.81	11865	1.01	17994	1.59	4610
Jun-00	1.95	66445	1.81	1	1.81	11706	0.96	21541	1.93	4439
Jul-00	1.91	43799	0.00	0	1.36	15571	1.23	5242	2.26	4138
Aug-00	1.99	40965	0.00	0	1.36	9779	0.81	17594	2.26	3760
Sep-00	2.72	346	0.00	0	1.44	10180	1.03	11764	1.70	4213
Oct-00	0.00	0	0.00	0	1.81	10965	1.36	5931	1.58	6004
Nov-00	0.00	0	0.00	0	1.81	10995	1.36	5946	1.69	4865
Dec-00	0.00	0	0.00	0	2.03	9400	1.36	5338	1.80	3593
Jan-01	2.72	1	0.00	0	2.04	10493	1.03	9881	1.80	3650
Feb-01	0.00	0	1.81	3091	1.55	19727	0.98	19786	1.58	3591
Mar-01	0.00	0	1.42	24572	2.04	12403	1.19	10906	1.58	3538
Apr-01	0.00	0	1.44	27452	2.04	13137	1.36	7570	1.58	4185
May-01	2.70	11478	1.49	9239	2.04	14537	1.24	8299	1.58	4050
Jun-01	1.97	83228	1.80	1611	2.23	12206	1.35	8055	2.01	4335
Jul-01	1.74	88415	1.81	2	2.26	10450	1.36	7153	2.25	3877
Aug-01	2.19	49337	0.00	0	2.26	9004	1.36	7538	2.26	4559
Sep-01	3.17	5	0.00	0	2.26	9216	1.36	6711	2.25	4102
Oct-01	0.00	0	0.00	0	2.26	9888	0.96	28565	2.25	3840
Nov-01	0.00	0	0.00	0	2.25	8760	1.36	8397	2.25	3839
Dec-01	0.00	0	0.00	0	2.26	9078	1.36	6604	2.25	3569
Jan-02	0.00	0	1.81	40	2.26	10767	1.36	6629	2.26	4166
Feb-02	0.00	0	1.99	3240	2.26	12192	0.87	24542	2.25	4006
Mar-02	0.00	0	1.98	4056	2.26	13386	1.29	7456	2.26	4612
Apr-02	1.99	3	1.98	4199	1.69	23761	1.29	7676	2.26	4754
May-02	2.49	2514	1.98	11211	2.26	13182	1.03	22790	2.26	4043
Jun-02	2.79	3184	0.00	0	2.26	12266	1.51	7866	2.32	4542
Jul-02	1.12	3458	0.00	0	1.80	10855	1.49	6730	2.38	4291
Aug-02	2.85	1188	0.00	0	1.59	11424	1.46	6694	2.49	5638
Sep-02	0.00	0	0.00	0	1.89	10959	1.37	7458	2.25	5596
Oct-02	0.00	0	0.00	0	1.89	9747	1.40	8315	1.99	4092
Nov-02	0.00	0	0.00	0	1.99	8180	0.99	10803	1.98	3675
Dec-02	0.00	0	0.00	0	1.67	11400	0.99	9723	1.99	3477
Jan-03	0.00	0	0.00	0	1.99	11149	1.22	7876	1.97	3857
Feb-03	0.00	0	1.95	2536	1.66	15150	1.11	6065	2.28	3495
Mar-03	0.00	0	1.75	2704	1.99	12206	0.99	24170	2.28	3776
Apr-03	1.87	24691	1.51	20987	1.42	19400	1.13	8063	2.28	4164
May-03	1.99	44375	1.95	5017	1.99	12777	1.59	7381	2.28	3642
Jun-03	2.49	21	1.77	21059	2.29	11635	1.05	28978	2.28	4372
Jul-03	0.00	0	2.29	6	2.48	9921	1.49	6464	2.28	3991
Aug-03	0.00	0	0.00	0	2.48	10674	1.49	8501	2.28	5483
Sep-03	0.00	0	0.00	0	2.48	9473	1.08	16481	2.28	4365
Oct-03	0.00	0	0.00	0	2.03	12748	1.04	13279	2.28	3355
Nov-03	0.00	0	0.00	0	2.48	8875	0.99	9271	2.27	3201
Dec-03	0.00	0	0.00	0	1.78	14151	0.99	10389	2.28	2801

Chapter 8

THE TREATMENT OF SEASONALITY IN THE COST-OF-LIVING INDEX: AN INTRODUCTION

W. Erwin Diewert[1]

1. Introduction

This paper addresses the problem of constructing a monthly (or annual) consumer price or cost of living index given that there are seasonal fluctuations for important product groups. Strongly seasonal products are available only at certain times of year. Weakly seasonal products are available all year, but have substantial fluctuations in prices or quantities synchronized with the time of year. Strongly seasonal products are usually excluded from official price indexes. The included seasonal products are usually just the weakly seasonal ones. In conventional practice, component indexes are compiled using observed data and then are seasonally adjusted.[2]

The approach suggested here is a radical departure from conventional practice. Basically, each seasonal commodity is treated as a separate commodity in each of the designated within-year time periods (e.g., months) that the commodity is available, and then normal index number techniques are applied. This removes the need to seasonally adjust the indexes compiled using the observed data; these series are already seasonally adjusted by virtue of their construction. The proposed approach is easier to understand than most seasonal adjustment methods. The results are also replicable in the sense that different individuals who independently and correctly apply the proposed approach to the same data will produce similar results.

The methods are illustrated using the Turvey artificial seasonal dataset. Turvey (1979) invented four years of monthly price and quantity data for five seasonal products: apples, peaches, grapes, strawberries and oranges. His data are shown in table 1. Turvey sent his artificial data to statistical agencies around the world. He asked them to apply their usual techniques to construct monthly, and annual average, price indexes. About 20 countries did as asked, and Turvey tabled their estimated indexes. Turvey (1979, p. 13) finds that: "[T]he monthly indices display very large differences, e.g., a range of 129.12-169.5 in June...."

---

[1] Diewert is with the Department of Economics at the University of British Columbia, and can be reached at diewert@econ.ubc.ca. This paper is based on sections 1-3 of Diewert (1983).

[2] See Dagum (1983) regarding the seasonal adjustment procedures of Statistics Canada using X-11-ARIMA. While the CPI component (and variant) indexes are often seasonally adjusted, in official practice the CPI itself is not.

Citation for this chapter:
W.E. Diewert (2011), "The Treatment of Seasonality in the Cost-Of-Living Index: An Introduction," chapter 8, pp. 121-126 in
W.E. Diewert, B.M. Balk, D. Fixler, K.J. Fox and A.O. Nakamura,
PRICE AND PRODUCTIVITY MEASUREMENT: Volume 2 -- Seasonality. Trafford Press.

© Alice Nakamura, 2011. Permission to link to, or copy or reprint, these materials is granted without restriction, including for use in commercial textbooks, with due credit to the authors and editors.

Table 1. The Turvey Artificial Data Set: Prices (p) and Quantities (x) of Fruits Sold

		Months (m)											
		1	2	3	4	5	6	7	8	9	10	11	12
							1970 (t=0)							
Apples	p	1.14	1.17	1.17	1.40	1.64	1.75	1.83	1.92	1.38	1.10	1.09	1.10
	x	3.086	3,765	4,363	4,842	4,439	5,323	4,165	3,224	4,025	5,784	6,949	3,924
Peaches	p	--	--	--	--	--	3.15	2.53	1.76	1.73	1.94	--	--
	x						91	498	6,504	4,923	865		
Grapes	p	2.48	2.75	5.07	5.00	4.98	4.78	3.48	2.01	1.42	1.39	1.75	2.02
	x	82	35	98	26	75	82	1,490	2,937	2,826	1,290	338	
Strawberries	p	--	--	--	--	5.13	3.48	3.27	--	--	--	--	--
	x					700	2,709	1,970					
Oranges	p	1.3	1.25	1.21	1.22	1.28	1.33	1.45	1.54	1.57	1.61	1.59	1.31
	x	10,266	9,656	7,940	5,110	4,089	3,362	3,396	2,406	2,486	3,222	6,958	9,762
							1971 (t=1)							
Apples	p	1.25	1.36	1.38	1.57	1.77	1.86	1.94	2.02	1.55	1.34	1.33	1.30
	x	3,415	4,127	4,771	5,290	4,986	5,869	4,671	3,534	4,509	6,299	7,753	4,285
Peaches	p	--	--	--	--	--	3.77	2.85	1.98	1.80	1.95	--	--
	x						98	548	6,964	5,370	932		
Grapes	p	2.80	3.32	5.48	5.67	5.44	5.30	3.93	2.33	1.66	1.64	2.10	2.35
	x	85	32	10	8	53	80	94	1,583	3,021	2,984	1,308	354
Strawberries	p	--	--	--	--	5.68	3.72	3.78	--	--	--	--	--
	x					806	3,166	2,153					
Oranges	p	1.35	1.36	1.37	1.44	1.51	1.56	1.66	1.74	1.76	1.77	1.76	1.50
	x	10,888	10,314	8,797	5,590	4,377	3,681	3,748	2,649	2,726	3,477	3,548	10,727
							1972 (t=2)							
Apples	p	1.43	1.53	1.59	1.73	1.89	1.98	2.07	2.12	1.73	1.56	1.56	1.49
	x	3,742	4,518	5,134	5,738	5,498	6,420	5,157	3,881	4,917	6,872	8,490	5,211
Peaches	p	--	--	--	--	--	4.69	3.32	2.29	1.90	1.97	--	--
	x						1.04	604	7,378	5,839	1,006		
Grapes	p	3.20	4.03	6.06	6.59	6.01	5.94	4.61	2.79	1.94	1.95	2.46	2.92
	x	88	34	11	8	70	87	103	1,668	3,118	3,043	1,441	373
Strawberries	p	--	--	--	--	6.21	3.98	4.30	--	--	--	--	--
	x					931	3,642	2,533					
Oranges	p	1.56	1.53	1.55	1.62	1.70	1.78	1.89	1.91	1.92	1.95	1.94	1.64
	x	11,569	10,993	9,621	6,063	4,625	3,970	4,078	2,883	2,957	3,759	8,238	11,827
							1973 (t=3)							
Apples	p	1.67	1.79	1.85	1.94	2.06	2.13	2.22	2.25	1.95	1.87	1.88	1.73
	x	4,051	4,909	5,567	6,253	6,101	7,023	5,671	4,187	5,446	7,377	9,283	4,955
Peaches	p	--	--	--	--	--	6.10	4.08	2.80	2.06	2.01	--	--
	x						111	653	7,856	6,291	1,073		
Grapes	p	3.52	4.67	6.48	7.34	6.51	6.43	5.00	3.07	2.20	2.19	2.74	3.13
	x	91	37	11	9	80	92	97	1,754	3,208	3,199	1,646	391
Strawberries	p	--	--	--	--	6.89	4.32	4.91	--	--	--	--	--
	x					1,033	4,085	2,877					
Oranges	p	1.68	1.66	1.70	1.85	1.95	2.03	2.10	2.12	2.07	2.13	2.14	1.79
	x	12,206	11,698	10,438	6,593	4,926	4,307	4,418	3,165	3,211	4,007	8,833	12,558

Source: From Turvey (1979). See text for further details.

2.   Background and a Proposed Solution to the Problem of Seasonality

Several approaches to seasonal adjustment have been suggested in the literature. One is to drop seasonal items altogether. A second, and widely used, approach is to use a statistical time series method to smooth the series compiled from observed data.[3] A third approach is to estimate shadow prices for seasonal commodities for the periods when they are out of season.[4] A fourth approach is to directly compare each of the seasons this year with the corresponding seasons the year before (or in a base year),[5] but this approach does not provide price trend estimates.[6]

For the seasonal fruits covered by the Turvey data set, the apples, grapes and oranges are seasonal in a weak way; that is, these products are available in all months. In contrast, peaches are only sold in June through October, and strawberries are only sold in May, June and July. Hence, for this example, peaches and strawberries are strongly seasonal products. We propose to treat each of the five fruits listed in table 1 as a separate commodity in each month it is sold.[7] Hence, viewing our data month by month, we have 3 fruit products in the months of January through April, and in November and December; 4 fruit products in May when strawberries become available, and in August through October when peaches are still available; and 5 fruit products in June and July when both strawberries and peaches are in season.

For the period of a year, there are 12 apple, 12 grape, 12 orange, 5 peach, and 3 strawberry products. Thus, January through April each have 12 products, May has 13, June through July have 14, and the months of August through December each have 13. In contrast, viewed year by year, we have the same 44 products (=12+12+12+5+3) each year.

Let p_i^t and x_i^t be the price and quantity of product i ($i = 1, \ldots, n_t$) in year t, with the number of products each year denoted by n_t. The annual price and quantity vectors for the Turvey data are represented here as $p^t \equiv (p_1^t, \ldots, p_{44}^t)$ and $x^t \equiv (x_1^t, \ldots, x_{44}^t)$ for $t = 1, \ldots, 4$.[8] The Laspeyres price index $P_L(p^b, p^t, x^b, x^t) \equiv p^t \cdot x^b / p^b \cdot x^b = P_L^{b,t}$, the Paasche price index, $P_P(p^b, p^t, x^b, x^t) \equiv p^t \cdot x^t / p^b \cdot x^t = P_P^{b,t}$, and the Fisher price index, [9] $P_F(p^b, p^t, x^b, x^t) \equiv (P_L^{b,t} P_P^{b,t})^{1/2} = P_F^{b,t}$ are the fixed base price index formulae are used in this study with $b = 0$. The resulting fixed based annual index numbers are shown in panel 1, table 2.

---

[3] See Stone (1956, pp. 77-88) and Allen (1975, pp. 169-176). Kuiper (1978) provides a survey of these methods.

[4] Diewert (1980, pp. 501-503) outlines an econometric procedure in the context of the new goods problem that could work well in the seasonal commodities context too.

[5] Allen (1975, pp. 88-191) and Diewert (1980, p. 507) advocate this principle.

[6] See Balk (1980, 1981) for additional approaches.

[7] Stone (1956, p. 75) and Diewert (1980, p. 508) suggested constructing annual indexes with seasonal data this way.

[8] In the original 1983 paper, a "dummy year" of 1969 is inserted and used at various points. That is a non essential detail of how to begin calculating an index from the first year data were collected. Hence the dummy year and all table entries involving the dummy year are dropped in this condensed version of the paper.

[9] In the full Diewert (1983) paper, results are shown too for the translog formula.

Table 2. Annual Price Levels Using Alternative Index Number Formulae

Year	t	P_L	P_P	P_F	P_{CL}	P_{CP}	P_{CF}
			panel 1			panel 2	
1971	1	1.11945	1.11956	1.11950	1.11945	1.11956	1.11950
1972	2	1.25263	1.25238	1.25200	1.25253	1.25174	1.25214
1973	3	1.40296	1.40050	1.40173	1.40259	1.40154	1.40207

Source: Based on tables 2 and 3 in Diewert (1983).

The chain index counterparts to the fixed base indexes are given by $P_C^{0,1} = P^{0,1}$, $P_C^{0,2} = P^{0,1} \times P^{1,2}$ and $P_C^{0,3} = P^{0,1} \times P^{1,2} \times P^{2,3}$, where P denotes any one of the index formulae.[10] The chain index values are shown in panel 2 of table 2. Comparing the panel 1 and panel 2 values in the last two rows of table 2, we see that the Turvey data yield essentially the same annual indexes using the fixed base and chained methods.

Where seasonal products are concerned, price (and quantity) indexes that are for a yearly period can potentially include every seasonal product traded in at least one month. Indeed, for any of the consecutive 12 month periods, it will be possible to include any product traded in at least one month. There is no reason why we must always make January-to-December yearly comparisons. Why not compare the year of, say, February 1971 through January 1972 with February 1970 through January 1971, or the year of December 1972 through November 1973 with December 1970 through November 1971? Why not make rolling year instead of fixed calendar year comparisons?

To represent the rolling year price vectors, we need notation for the monthly price vectors. Let $p_i^{t:m}$ and $x_i^{t:m}$ denote the price and quantity vectors for product i ($i = 1, ..., n_{t,m}$) in sub period m (a month here) in unit time period t (a year here). As noted above, for the Turvey data, $n_{t:1} = ... = n_{t:4} = 3$, $n_{t:5} = 4$, $n_{t:6} = n_{t:7} = 5$, $n_{t:8} = n_{t:9} = n_{t:10} = 4$, and $n_{t:11} = n_{t:12} = 3$. The fixed base conventional calendar year indexes (for which values are shown in panel 1, table 2) can be represented using this new notation as:

$$
\text{(2)} \quad P^{0,1} = P(p^{0:1}, p^{0:2}, ..., p^{0:11}, p^{0:12}; p^{1:1}, p^{1:2}, ..., p^{1:11}, p^{1:12};
$$
$$
x^{0:1}, x^{0:2}, ..., x^{0:11}, x^{0:12}; x^{1:1}, x^{1:2}, ..., x^{1:11}, x^{1:12})
$$
$$
P^{0,2} = P(p^{0:1}, p^{0:2}, ..., p^{0:11}, p^{0:12}; p^{2:1}, p^{2:2}, ..., p^{2:11}, p^{2:12};
$$
$$
x^{0:1}, x^{0:2}, ..., x^{0:11}, x^{0:12}; x^{2:1}, x^{2:2}, ..., x^{2:11}, x^{2:12})
$$
$$
P^{0,3} = P(p^{0:1}, p^{0:2}, ..., p^{0:11}, p^{0:12}; p^{3:1}, p^{3:2}, ..., p^{3:11}, p^{3:12};
$$
$$
x^{0:1}, x^{0:2}, ..., x^{0:11}, x^{0:12}; x^{3:1}, x^{3:2}, ..., x^{3:11}, x^{3:12}),
$$

---

[10] For example, the chained Laspeyres index for 1973 ($t=3$) versus 1970 ($t = 0$) is:

$$
P_{CL}^{0,3} = P_L(p^0, p^1, x^0, x^1)P_L(p^1, p^2, x^1, x^2)P_L(p^2, p^3, x^2, x^3) = P_L^{0,1} \times P_L^{1,2} \times P_L^{2,3}.
$$

The full set of fixed base rolling year index comparisons for the Turvey data, using 1970 as the base year, can be represented as follows:

(3)

$$P^{1:1-1:12,2:1-2:12} = P(p^{1:1},p^{1:2},...,p^{1:11},p^{1:12}; p^{2:1},p^{2:2},...,p^{2:11},p^{2:12};$$
$$x^{1:1},x^{1:2},...,x^{1:11},x^{1:12};x^{2:1},x^{2:2},...,x^{2:11},x^{2:12})$$

$$P^{1:2-2:1,2:2-3:1} = P(p^{1:2},p^{1:3},...,p^{1:12},p^{2:1}; p^{2:2},p^{2:3},...,p^{2:12},p^{3:1};$$
$$x^{1:2},x^{1:3},...,x^{1:12},x^{2:1};x^{2:2},x^{2:3},...,x^{2:12},x^{3:1})$$

$$\vdots$$

$$P^{1:12-2:11,3:12-4:11} = P(p^{1:12},p^{2:1},...,p^{2:10},p^{2:11}; p^{3:12},p^{4:1},...,p^{4:10},p^{4:11};$$
$$x^{1:12},x^{2:1},...,x^{2:10},x^{2:11};x^{3:12},x^{4:1},...,x^{4:10},x^{4:11})$$

$$P^{2:1-2:12,4:1-4:12} = P(p^{2:1},p^{2:2},...,p^{2:11},p^{2:12}; p^{4:1},p^{4:2},...,p^{4:11},p^{4:12};$$
$$x^{2:1},x^{2:2},...,x^{2:11},x^{2:12};x^{4:1},x^{4:2},...,x^{4:11},x^{4:12})$$

Alternatively, we could compute index values using the chain principle. The chained index numbers are tabled in panel 2 of table 3.

The values of the annual inflation rates from panel 1 and panel 2 of table 2 can be found in panel 1 and panel 2 of table 3 in rows 1, 13 and 25: the cases where the specified 12 months for the rolling index comprise a calendar year. Hence, it seems that our suggested method does, in fact, remove the seasonal fluctuations in the original Turvey data set.[11]

When implemented on the Turvey data, the Laspeyres, Paasche and Fisher formulae all yield very similar figures, and this is true for both the fixed base and the chain principle methods. However, for longer periods than the four years covered by the Turvey data and for real data that may differ in other important ways from the Turvey artificial data, we would expect the differences among the different types of index numbers to be more substantial.

Our proposed method of seasonal adjustment should be useful in the producer context too.

---

[11] Treating each seasonal product as a separate product in each sub-annual seasonal period (e.g., in each month here) when it is sold will greatly increase the dimensionality of the product space. Thus, in the original paper, Diewert suggests a two-stage procedure based on the two-stage aggregation theorem in Diewert (1978, pp. 889-890) that could be used to obtain an approximation to the results for his full new method.

Table 3. Year-to-Year Price Levels by Month

Row	Base period	Current period	P_L	P_P	P_F	P_{CL}	P_{CP}	P_{CF}
					panel 1		panel 2	
1	0:1-0:12	1:1-1:12	1.11945	1.11956	1.11950	1.11945	1.11956	1.11950
2	0:2-1:1	1:2-2:1	1.13164	1.13228	1.13196	1.13179	1.13224	1.13201
3	0:3-1:2	1:3-2:2	1.14193	1.14319	1.14256	1.14204	1.14304	1.14254
4	0:4-1:3	1:4-2:3	1.15240	1.15479	1.15360	1.15260	1.15439	1.15349
5	0:5-1:4	1:5-2:4	1.15999	1.16302	1.16150	1.16015	1.16242	1.16128
6	0:6-1:5	1:6-2:5	1.16755	1.17100	1.16927	1.16743	1.17008	1.16875
7	0:7-1:6	1:7-2:6	1.17742	1.18090	1.17916	1.17674	1.17951	1.17812
8	0:8-1:7	1:8-2:7	1.18917	1.19326	1.19121	1.18839	1.19123	1.18981
9	0:9-1:8	1:9-2:8	1.20447	1.20806	1.20627	1.20355	1.20594	1.20474
10	0:10-1:9	1:10-2:9	1.21534	1.21830	1.21677	1.21414	1.21596	1.21505
11	0:11-1:10	1:11-2:10	1.22757	1.23011	1.22884	1.22653	1.22776	1.22714
12	0:12-1:11	1:12-2:11	1.24235	1.24148	1.24191	1.24215	1.24172	1.24193
13	0:1-0:12	2:1-2:12	1.25263	1.25138	1.25200	1.25253	1.25174	1.25214
14	0:2-1:1	2:2-3:1	1.26151	1.26039	1.26095	1.26155	1.26141	1.26148
15	0:3-1:2	2:3-3:2	1.27157	1.27077	1.27117	1.27163	1.27220	1.27191
16	0:4-1:3	2:4-3:3	1.28195	1.28206	1.28201	1.28210	1.28359	1.28284
17	0:5-1:4	2:5-3:4	1.29175	1.29242	1.29208	1.29198	1.29397	1.29297
18	0:6-1:5	2:6-3:5	1.30185	1.30272	1.30229	1.30171	1.30409	1.30290
19	0:7-1:6	2:7-3:6	1.31400	1.31462	1.31431	1.31292	1.31550	1.31421
20	0:8-1:7	2:8-3:7	1.32715	1.32845	1.32780	1.32601	1.32867	1.32734
21	0:9-1:8	2:9-3:8	1.34791	1.34794	1.34793	1.34664	1.34872	1.34768
22	0:10-1:9	2:10-3:9	1.36044	1.35919	1.35981	1.35873	1.36022	1.35947
23	0:11-1:10	2:11-3:10	1.37419	1.37230	1.37325	1.37286	1.27272	1.37329
24	0:12-1:11	2:12-3:11	1.39192	1.39002	1.39097	1.39136	1.39084	1.39110
25	0:1-0:12	3:1-3:12	1.40296	1.40050	1.40173	1.40259	1.40154	1.40207

Source: Based on tables 4 and 5 in Diewert (1983).

References

Allen, R.G.D. (1975), *Index Numbers in Theory and Practice*, MacMillan.

Balk, B.M. (1980), "A Method for Constructing Price Indices for Seasonal Commodities," *Journal of the Royal Statistical Society Series A* 143, 68-75.

Balk, B.M. (1981), "A Simple Method for Constructing Price Indices for Seasonal Commodities," *Statistische Hefte* 22, 72-78.

Dagum, E.B. (1983), "The X-11 ARIMA Seasonal Adjustment Method," Statistics Canada Catalogue No. 12-564E.

Diewert, W.E. (1978), "Superlative Index Numbers and Consistency in Aggregation," *Econometrica* 46, 883-900. and reprinted as Chapter 9 in Diewert and Nakamura (1993, pp. 223-252).

Diewert, W.E. (1980), "Aggregation Problems in the Measurement of Capital," in *The Measurement of Capital*, ed. by Dan Usher, NBER Studies in Income and Wealth, Vol. 45, University of Chicago Press, 433–528. http://www.econ.ubc.ca/diewert/1capital.pdf and http://www.econ.ubc.ca/diewert/2capital.pdf

Diewert, W.E. (1983), "The Treatment of Seasonality in a Cost of Living Index", in W.E. Diewert and C. Montmarquette (eds.), *Price Level Measurement*, Statistics Canada, 1019-1045. http://www.econ.ubc.ca/diewert/living.pdf

Kuiper, J. (1978), "A Survey and Comparative Analysis of Various Methods of Seasonal Adjustment," in A. Zellner (ed.), *Seasonal Analysis of Economic Time Series, Proceedings of the Conference on the Seasonal Analysis of Economic Time Series*, Washington, D.C., September 9-10, U.S. Government Printing Office, 59-76.

Stone, R. (1956), *Quantity and Price Indexes in the National Accounts*, Paris: OECD.

Turvey, R. (1979), "The Treatment of Seasonal Items in Consumer Price Indices," *Bulletin of Labour Statistics, Fourth Quarter*, Geneva: ILO, 13-33.